BRAND NEW MAN

MY WEIGHT LOSS JOURNEY

Don McNay

CHFC, MSFS, CLU, CSSC

INTERNATIONAL
RRP
PUBLISHING & DIGITAL MEDIA

RRP International Publishing LLC
Lexington, Ky.

RRP International LLC, DBA Eugenia Ruth LLC
838 E. High St.
Box #285
Lexington, Ky. 40502

www.rrpinternational.org

ISBN-13: 978-0-9971536-0-6

DEDICATION

"I will remember that there is art to medicine as well as science, and that warmth, sympathy, and understanding may outweigh the surgeon's knife or the chemist's drug."
-Hippocrates[1]

"Doctor, my eyes have seen the years
And the slow parade of fears without crying
Now I want to understand"
-Jackson Browne[2]

I dedicate this book to Dr. Phillip Hoffman, Dr. Jim Roach and Dr. Derek Weiss, three talented doctors who care about me as a friend and a patient. Also to Cindy Jester Caywood, Director of Bariatrics at Georgetown Kentucky Hospital, and my daughter Angela Luhys, whose practical understanding of healing was honed years ago while working in the medical tent at Rainbow Gatherings.

You will get to know them throughout the course of this book, and it has been a blessing to have them in my life.

This "Son of a Son of a Gambler" hit the jackpot when it came to assembling a team that truly made a difference.

-Don McNay
December 2015

TABLE OF CONTENTS

INTRODUCTION

"I've been baptized
By the fire in your touch
And the flame in your eyes
I'm born to love again
I'm a brand new man"
-Brooks and Dunn[1]

"The real glory is being knocked to your knees and then coming
back. That's real glory. That's the essence of it."
-Vince Lombardi[2]

Exactly one year ago, I started a journey that would allow me to lose more than 100 pounds and cure physical ailments like diabetes. It was more than just fixing my body. It was about fixing my outlook on life. What weight loss success did for my confidence and courage is what made me a Brand New Man.

Fighting a lifelong battle against obesity made me feel like Sisyphus, the character from Greek mythology who was doomed to push a rock up near the top of a hill, only to have it go back down the hill.[3] Through a process of education, good systems, great advisors and focusing on the positive, optimism has replaced a lifelong feeling of impending doom. As Vince Lombardi said, there is real glory in being knocked to your knees and coming back. Especially if you wind up in a place where you have never been before.

"You cannot swim for new horizons until you have courage to lose
sight of the shore."
-William Faulkner[4]

My struggle with obesity has been a negative out of kilter with the rest of my life. I have a wonderful family, great friends and deep relationships. I'm respected in my community, well-educated, quasi-famous and professionally accomplished. I've never been indicted or convicted of a crime. I don't have any other addictions. I've lived a life of reasonable moderation, but wound up being morbidly obese. I was a streetwise consumer, but before last year, I was a sucker for numerous quick and easy weight loss gimmicks. Then, I would be overwhelmed with "failure syndrome" the first time anything would go wrong. If I gained a pound, I would give myself permission to gain 10 more. It was the opposite of how I reacted to anything else in life. It was like I had been taken over by a body snatcher. A body snatcher that was determined to keep my health in a state of chaos.

It was time to kick the body snatcher out.

> *"Life's gonna suck when you grow up*
> *And then you're gonna die"*
> -Denis Leary[5]

A year ago, I had reached a point where I weighed 377 pounds and far past the point where they consider you morbidly obese. I was 55 years old and my health issues were starting to impact my relationships, business and the rest of my life. I was on my way to a miserable and reasonably quick death, but still buried inside was that part of my personality that truly believes that anyone can achieve anything if they put their mind to it.

That "can-do" mindset is back on the front burner. I made a plan and implemented it.

I would love to define a burning bush moment when I decided that it was time to stop being fat. The closest thing I have is a 4 a.m. email to Dr. Jim Roach, which I include in the book. There were wake up calls. One of the most coveted items in Lexington, Kentucky is tickets in the front of the stands at a University of Kentucky basketball game. When that happened for me, I was too fat to fit in the seat.

I was becoming diabetic and would have blood sugar spikes when my temper would rage out of control. Vince Lombardi is one of my heroes, and the Green Bay Packers players lived on "Lombardi time" when they showed up for all meetings at least 15 minutes early. I spent decades living that philosophy, but when I got so heavy, I started showing up late and cancelling things. I didn't even realize I was doing it. My income and enthusiasm were slipping, and my health issues were taking away the characteristics that made me proud of who I am.

My father was a professional gambler and I have a secondary career helping lottery winners with their finances. I picked up a few things from a lifetime of watching gamblers. One is that I am always looking for a business "edge" that will help my side of a calculation. I do research, study and weigh the odds. When I see an opportunity, I immediately go "all in," devoting all my resources, like a poker player would. If I have done my homework, it ought to work out.

It turns out that one of my biggest edges was deciding to write this book. I've written seven other books, but all have been about topics that I already knew a lot about.

I committed to writing the book before I made the bigger decision to have weight loss surgery. The surgery was literally a life or death decision and I researched the topic to the extreme, asked lots of questions and set up my world to give me the best chance at success.

Writing forced me to be honest. Before I committed to the book, I would never tell anyone, including my wife and family, my exact weight (377.7 pounds). Now I post my current weight on my Facebook page.

I wrote *Huffington Post* articles about my weight loss journey, including an article on the day before my gastric sleeve surgery on Dec. 1, 2014.[6] The support of a vast throng of people, many that I had never met, was a big edge. A sense of accountability was another edge. If I had gained 100 pounds, I still would have written about it. I was determined to tell the story: win, lose or draw.

I committed to writing the book because I was afraid of big

medicine. I know that the medical business can swallow up, injure and kill people just because no one notices that the people are there. Being well-known is a huge edge and I made sure that I let people in the process know that I planned on writing a book.

When they wheeled me into the operating room at Georgetown Hospital one year ago, I looked at Dr. Derek Weiss and told him, "If you kill me during surgery, it won't do much for your career." Derek responded confidently saying, "I have not killed anyone yet and you won't be the first." I was out of surgery and walking around the hospital a few hours later. I was back home the next day. A first class team did everything possible to ensure a good outcome.

In a world full of unique people, I am more unique than most. Each person has their own set of goals, character traits and values and needs to find an individual plan that works for them. People can learn from my story, but I don't offer many hard and fast rules. Rules need to have consequences when they are broken. The Ten Commandments are a wonderful guideline for society, but I am much stronger in following "thou shalt not kill" (where I have a perfect score) than "thou shalt not covet thy neighbor's goods" (not so perfect). Violating the commandment about coveting my neighbor's wife would be a good way for both my wife and my neighbor to decide that "thou shalt not kill" is no longer operable. A viable enforcement action is important in making sure edicts and laws work.

The enthusiasm and courage that I draw from the weight loss experience has made me better at what I do and happier about who I am than any other time in my life. I keep pushing the envelope of what I can be. At age 56, a point in life when many people are looking at slowing down, I'm kicking into a new and faster gear.

I include chapters about the economics of weight loss. I have chapters about some of the people who helped me make weight loss happen and some of the heroes who inspired me. I write about how I have embraced exercise concepts like CrossFit and competing in 5K races.

The last half of the book is Don's Reality Show. Like some of the better television reality shows, it gives the good, bad and the ugly. It's an accurate picture of life immediately after weight loss surgery, in stark and ironic detail.

> *"Ain't singin' for Pepsi*
> *Ain't singin' for Coke*
> *I don't sing for nobody*
> *Makes me look like a joke"*
> -Neil Young[7]

I've inspired several friends and family members to take on their own battle with obesity. By getting my story to a wide audience, I will move many more.

I've read more than 100 weight loss books. Many of those books do not include documentation and some are trying to sell a concept, service or product. Thus, this researched and footnoted book has a detailed bibliography and the book is not sponsored by anyone but me. Although part of me would enjoy the irony (and the big dollars) of the *Brand New Man* book having an advertising tie to Coke, Pepsi or Budweiser (none of which I have touched in the past year), this journalist wants to tell the story, exactly the way it came down.

In describing how I got to this point in my life, I start by drawing literary inspiration from the great philosopher of Margaritaville, Jimmy Buffett.

How I Got Fat (In Four Hundred Words)

> *"I wanna talk about me*
> *I wanna talk about I"*
> -Toby Keith[8]

> *"In three words, I can sum up everything I've learned about life: it*
> *goes on."*
> -Robert Frost[9]

"We are the people there isn't any doubt
We are the people they still can't figure out
We are the people who love to sing 'Twist and Shout'
We are the people our parents warned us about"
-Jimmy Buffett[10]

Jimmy Buffett's book *A Pirate Looks at Fifty*[11] is well worth owning just to read his chapter "My Life (In Four Hundred Words or Less)."

He gets most of his biographical highlights into a witty and insightful 400-word essay.

I could write an entire book tracing my early life and how I got past the point of morbid obesity, but Jimmy Buffett wrote two other lyrics that are appropriate to remember:

"Yesterday's over my shoulder, so I can't look back for too long."[12]
And *"but I know it's nobody's fault."*[13]

Thus, here is the story of how I got fat in exactly 400 words:

My dad was a bookie and my mom worked in a potato chip factory. Everyone in my family was overweight and died at a young age. I was fit in first grade, but we moved to the suburbs and my parents got divorced. I got chunky, picked on and someone tried to cram cottage cheese down my throat. Then I had an early growth spurt and became a decent athlete. I did well academically my last year of high school and became semi-popular.

My skewed childhood gave me a sense of ambition, self-confidence and determination tempered with feelings of exclusion, irony and empathy with the underdog.

None of that has changed.

College at Eastern Kentucky University was wonderful, and my nonstop activity balanced my diet of fast food, Coke and frozen pizzas. I stayed at a good weight for five years. I started gaining 10 pounds a year in graduate school at Vanderbilt. I was at 270 pounds in 1989 when I went on a liquid weight loss program. I lost 90 pounds and eventually gained it back. I did the program several times, never lost less than 50 pounds and gained more every time. That went on for about 25 years.

I've slept with a CPAP for 20 years, been on blood pressure medicine for 30 years and stalled the move to insulin by staying on a low carb diet. I rarely drink, don't smoke and don't do illegal drugs.

I traveled frequently and have been to zillions of nice restaurants, but kept the stockholders of McDonalds happy along the way. I was married, divorced and married again. I started my own "fat guys" group. We stayed together for several years, but no one really lost weight. A hypnotist got me to stop eating potato chips. A shrink helped me deal with my childhood traumas, sudden family deaths and anything else that bugged me. A personal trainer helped my 377-pound body exercise, and I read more than 100 books on nutrients and diet. I became friends with some of the best doctors in Kentucky and occasionally listened to them.

I led a productive, high-profile life, but at age 55 my body was falling apart.

Then I did the weight loss surgery. I lost more than 110 pounds. I started eating correctly and taking lots of vitamins and supplements. I exercised daily. I embraced CrossFit. I even tried cottage cheese.

Now it is on to the post-obesity era.

WEIGHT LOSS HEROINES

SHEILA HIESTAND:
MOM, WIFE, TRIATHLETE, LAWYER, IN THAT ORDER

"Play the game, you know you can't quit until it's won
Soldier on, only you can do what must be done
You know in some way you're a lot like me
You're just a prisoner and you're trying to break free"
-John Parr (*St. Elmo's Fire* theme song)[1]

"Mom, wife, triathlete, lawyer, in that order"
-Sheila Hiestand's "About Me" on her Facebook page

Louisville trial lawyer Sheila Lloyd Hiestand is six-foot-tall, outgoing and vivacious. She has the total inner confidence that made her a Hall of Fame college basketball player and now one of Kentucky's top trial attorneys. Even with her big dollar verdicts, you learn quickly that her priorities have the balance and precise order noted on her Facebook page.

During our two-hour meeting, we spent more than an hour talking about her children, her husband and faith. How she went from weighing more than 300 pounds to competing in Ironman races took most of the next hour. I'm able to expand upon the five minutes we spent talking about her legal career as she has worked with my structured settlement firm and is a cherished friend.

Her "secret" as to how she "does it all" is a small tattoo on her wrist. It's a turtle. Slow and steady wins the race. That is the true philosophy of Sheila Hiestand.

Early success in athletics and growing up taller and stronger than your classmates can give you a deep rooted self-confidence that you are ultimately going to succeed, even when you find yourself at a low point. Like many who grew up competing at a high level, Sheila does not do anything halfway.

Outrageous goals are a key motivator to success. Amazon wanted to be the largest retailer in the world before they ever launched their website. Google's initial goal was to digitize every piece of information in the world. People laughed at them then, but no one laughs now.

In 2007, When Sheila Hiestand found herself at the weight of 315 pounds, she decided she was going to complete an Ironman competition. In 2012, she did.

Award-winning journalist John Boel told Sheila's Ironman story in an Aug. 22, 2012 story for WAVE 3 television news in Louisville.[2] It took Sheila three times. After losing 125 pounds, she entered the Ironman Louisville in 2010 and blew out her knee four miles from the finish line. The second year, she ran in 102-degree heat and had to stop.

Boel interviewed Hiestand as she was preparing in 2012 and noted her "never say die" attitude: "I don't want to fail, but if it happens, I'll sign up the next day."

She made it on try number three. Her slow and steady focus made it to the goal line.

The Magic of Centre College to an Adult High Achiever

"Summer has come and passed
The innocent can never last
Wake me up when September ends"
-Green Day[3]

"Yeah, do you believe in magic?
Believe in the magic of rock and roll

Believe in the magic that can set you free
Oh, talking 'bout magic"
-John Sebastian and the Loving Spoonful[4]

Centre College in Danville, Kentucky was a magical place at a magical time for Sheila Lloyd Hiestand. She came to the highly regarded liberal arts college on an academic scholarship and was a starter on college basketball teams that made two final four appearances and four NCAA appearances during her college career.

Sheila is in the Centre College Athletic Hall of Fame twice. Once as an individual basketball player and once as a member of the 1988-1989 women's basketball team, which was Centre's first team to ever make it to the NCAA Division III Final Four. Sheila holds the Centre career record for most games and most blocked shots. She also has the single-season record for rebounds and the single-game record for blocked shots (11), which she did three different times.

Sheila could really play some hoops.

She credits her basketball coach, Lea Wise Prewitt, a former University of Kentucky basketball star, who helped Sheila hone her capacities for hard work, drive and playing to win.

Centre was more than basketball. She received a degree with a double major in English and Spanish. She played the viola, violin, cello and piano. Centre has a strong history of fraternities and sororities, and it was at a Greek function where she met the love of her life, Dr. David Hiestand. Although they recently celebrated their 23rd wedding anniversary, Sheila describes their relationship with the smitten excitement of a brand new romance.

I know David and he is a great guy. Also an incredibly smart guy. Not only is he a medical doctor, he has a doctorate and a number of high-powered certifications in the medical field.

"The gypsy swore our future was bright
But come the wee wee hours

Well maybe baby the gypsy lied"
-Bruce Springsteen[5]

Sheila seemed to be living the fairy tale life. She graduated from the University of Kentucky Law School and became a partner in the Lexington office of Landrum & Shouse, one of the top insurance defense law firms in Kentucky. Then she had an opportunity to be a partner in a firm that represented injured people. She and David eventually moved to Louisville. Along the way, they had the first of their three children.

Life got very hectic and complicated. Sheila was a huge success as an attorney, and her magnetic personality was a hit with juries and her peers. She won a boatload of awards. She is the kind of person who is elected President of everything, and she has been President of the Kentucky Association for Justice and the Kentucky Bar Association's Young Lawyers Section. She served in a plethora of activities, raised her three children, practiced law at the highest level and was a devoted wife.

And she started gaining weight. And drinking more than she should. The pressure of a nonstop life, with little or no exercise was starting to get to Sheila. In 2007, Sheila weighed 315 pounds and was unhappy.

It was time to make some bold moves.

The Journey from Weight Loss Surgery to Finishing the Ironman Race

"In my religion, they say, 'Act as if ye had faith...and faith will be given to you.' If we are to have faith in justice, we need only to believe in ourselves."
-Frank Galvin (Paul Newman's character) in the movie *The Verdict*[6]

In 2007, Sheila was going to do whatever it took to get healthy. She was not interested in just getting to an average size or average weight. She had never done anything ordinary in her life and was not going to start now.

She went to Georgetown Community Hospital in Georgetown, Kentucky (which happens to be the place where I had my weight loss surgery) and had the Adjustable Gastric Banding Surgery (better known as Lap Band). The surgery was a major tool in allowing Sheila to control her food portions and bring alcohol consumption to a minimum level. Like many of us who lose weight, as the pounds came off, Sheila got interested in exercising again.

A year after the surgery, she had lost 125 pounds and was near basketball playing weight. Then the Hall of Famer set her eyes on bigger targets. First to run a marathon, and then to finish an Ironman competition.

She was not interested in actually winning an Ironman race. She just wanted to make it to the finish line in the allotted amount of time. In 2012, she did it.

Now she plans on doing it again.

"I thought that dreams belonged to other men
Cause each time I got close
They'd fall apart again"
-Eric Carmen (from the soundtrack to the movie *Footloose*)[7]

There were several questions that I personally needed answered by Sheila. Since I have had a lifetime of losing weight and gaining it back, I can't always totally get that fear of failure out of my head. Talking to Sheila gave me a tremendous amount of reassurance. It's been nearly eight years and she kept the weight off and is doing athletic things that few humans can do. She gave me the confidence that I am on the right course and will continue to have tremendous success.

My next question was very personal: Is the devotion to Ironman and exercise impacting her law practice?

I came into the interview with a very negative bias against Ironman races. I had a former employee whose productivity fell dramatically when the employee got in Ironman competitions. Any focus on work shifted to a near obsession with Ironman. Although we had been close, we did not part on good terms and have not spoken in the years since the employee left.

I suspect that Ironman was a symptom of our problems and not the problem, but it has been hard to get the bias against Ironman out of my mind. I also suspect a person that devoted to Ironman training might have passively but aggressively resented a boss who weighed 377 pounds. Even so, my mind equated Ironman with obsessive training until Hiestand set me straight.

Sheila wrote the phrase "Mom, wife, triathlete, lawyer, in that order" on her Facebook page in 2009, and it accurately reflected her values. Sheila goes at everything with a sense of excellence and full abandon. Her legal practice and mastery of the courtroom continues to get better as she maintains the benefits of a balanced life.

A Hall of Fame basketball player is never going to lose that quest for competition and community. Sheila talked about the close bond she has developed with others who are training for the Ironman. Going into an extreme competition is just a part of who she is.

Many employers and clients may intellectually give lip service to a balanced lifestyle, but really want people and themselves devoted to their work 24 hours a day. (I have been a sinner in sometimes embracing this management mindset.) Obsessive work habits aren't a long-term business strategy unless you treat your body like it has disposable parts, but many people do it anyway.

Sheila gave me a new way to look at life. I love that she has a turtle tattooed on her arm. Slow and steady wins the race. She understood the lesson that Aesop taught us thousands of years ago.

In a race between the Tortoise and the Hare, always bet on the Tortoise.

The Economics Of Obesity

"Every great cause begins as a movement, becomes a business and eventually degenerates into a racket."
-Eric Hoffer[1]

"Lesson number one: Don't underestimate the other guy's greed."
–Frank Lopez (from the movie *Scarface*)[2]

"If you got the money, honey
I've got the time"
-Lefty Frizzell[3]

Weight loss is a multibillion dollar business where desire and emotion can overtake reason. Which means it is a fertile ground for rip-off artists.

Americans spend more than $60 billion a year trying to lose weight.[4] And only five percent of those people keep the weight off for five years or longer. The best predictors of life expectancy are nutrition, access to quality health care, income and education.

Increased life expectancy is a valid reason to seek better health and body shape. Unless you have a true desire to die at an early age.

Society puts a premium on looks, and "fat shaming" is a form of bigotry that is acceptable by many in the mass media. Television news stories on obesity are normally accompanied by a film clip of some overweight (and usually poorly dressed) person's rear end. Fat people are often stereotyped as lazy and stupid. Through the lens of popular media, an overweight man often has the intellect, manners and physical makeup of Chris Farley or the guy who played Flounder in the movie *Animal House*.[5] Fat, drunk and stupid.

Billions of dollars of advertising convince us that we need to be thinner and the health risks of obesity are very real. As Michael Pollan, Gary Taubes and others have articulately written, we need to wage a full blown battle against fructose and its addictive properties. I reached a point where I was drinking at least six diet soft drinks a day and dropped them cold turkey. I felt like a junkie kicking heroin. It took a couple of months before the physical cravings went away.

"Down here it's just winners and losers
And don't get caught on the wrong side of that line"
-Bruce Springsteen[6]

Many overweight people start to get pushed into the "loser" category in childhood. Some stay emotionally defeated. Some grow up and overcome emotionally, physically or both. Some buy into every quick fix and fad diet coming down the pike.

For decades, I fell into the last category.

When I made the decision to get weight loss surgery, they had me fill out a form that listed a plethora of well-known and obscure weight loss programs and asked how many I tried. All of them. I also had tried 20 other programs that were not listed.

On top of all the programs, special foods, gym memberships, personal trainers, diet coaches, exercise equipment, books and computer programs I had spent money on, I had also taken the diet drug Redux, which killed several of my friends during its short run on the market, and hardcore prescription amphetamines, which would cause me to gain and lose weight rapidly and snap into violent rage for no particular reason.

People die of amphetamine abuse, but if I had stayed on amphetamines, I would have been killed in a road rage incident or beaten to death. I have not been in a fist fight since high school, but had about 20 near misses during the six months I took amphetamines. Not to mention losing friends and clients along the way.

I kept gaining weight and I kept spending time and money in a vain attempt to fight back. I am cool and rational in a business setting, but emotions would take over when the issue turned to weight loss. I wanted to believe. I wanted to find the quick and ultimate answer.

Finally, I realized that I had to do what I understood how to do in business: Take emotion out of the decision making and develop a plan based on facts.

I had to consider every option that would lead to a long-term solution. Just like I would in a business setting. For the first time in my life, weight loss surgery made it to my list of options.

My Long, Strange Trip to Bariatric Surgery

"Good and bad, I define these terms
Quite clear, no doubt, somehow
Ah, but I was so much older then
I'm younger than that now"
-Bob Dylan[7]

"Lately it occurs to me
What a long, strange trip it's been"
-The Grateful Dead[8]

"Only Nixon could go to China."
-Vulcan proverb quoted by Mr. Spock in
Star Trek VI: The Undiscovered Country[9]

It's hard to believe I am a living example of the advantages of weight loss surgery.

In my work as a structured settlement and litigation-related consultant, I've seen several situations where people died from gastric bypass surgery. I've gotten to know the intimate details of how they died and know their families. If your primary experience with skydiving is dealing with the families of people who died during jumps, you are less inclined to embrace the idea of parachuting yourself. That's exactly how I felt about weight loss surgery. Not only was I opposed to it, I tried to talk anyone and everyone out of doing it. All I knew were the horror stories.

Ten years ago, statistics backed up my inferential conclusions. *CBS News* did a story in 2005 saying that one in 50 people died within a month of gastric bypass surgery and the figure jumped fivefold if the surgeon was inexperienced.[10] Rather than betting on a 50-to-one chance of coming home in a body bag (or a 10-to-one chance of dying at the hands of an inexperienced surgeon), it was a simple decision to sign up for weight loss programs again and again and again.

I've never had a client die during a Weight Watchers meeting. But if morbid obesity knocks 10 years off your life, you are dying slowly and painfully as opposed to dying quickly. There is a point where radical measures are needed.

I was at that point.

I saw a lot of stories like the one on CBS. I missed the move of the medical community towards fixing the problem. The story quoted Dr. Harvey Sugerman, then President of the American Society for Metabolic and Bariatric Surgery, who noted the development of the "Center of Excellence" programs. Being a Center of Excellence is like the "Good Housekeeping Seal of Approval" for weight loss facilities. It is an excellent idea to weed out surgeons who "dabble" in weight loss surgery, but the focus is on the hospital and not on the surgeon. The federal government pays for weight loss surgeries through Medicare, Medicaid and Centers for Medicare and Medicaid Services (CMS) and their rules revolve around facilities. Any hospital receiving Medicare and Medicaid money has to be a Level 1 Bariatric Surgery Center or a Center of Excellence. Being a Center of Excellence was definitely a consideration for me. There was no way I would be at a facility that did not have that standard, but that was a first step and not a final step. Being a Center of Excellence is an incredible marketing opportunity for the hospital. On the other hand, hospitals can make their reputation with one set of surgeons, replace them with a lesser group, and still maintain their Center of Excellence standing in the short run. An outside seal of approval is great, but I needed to get inside and talk to the people before I made a life or death decision.

A few years ago, one of my trial lawyer friends was discussing weight loss surgery and noted, "They don't seem to be killing as many people as they used to." I followed up privately with several star medical malpractice attorneys and found that his statement was correct. When you look at the numbers, weight loss surgery had gotten safer.

A study published in the March 2014 Journal of the American Medical Association concluded that "death rates are, in general, very low."[11] The study showed that the death rate was between 0.08 percent and 0.31 percent. A dramatic improvement from 2005. The team went through 150 studies of weight loss surgery, involving 162,000 patients. The average BMI of the group was 46. A BMI of 46 on a person six-foot-tall (like I am) would mean a weight of 339 pounds. The study showed that their BMI dropped between 12 and 17 points in the five years following surgery.

Translating BMI to layman's terms, that means if a person had weighed in at 330 pounds before weight loss surgery, five years later, he or she would weigh between 250 and 214 pounds. A weight loss between 80 and 116 pounds.

The weight loss dramatically increases the chance to live to a normal age. A huge motivator for me was the possibility of reversing diabetes. I had inched into the diabetic category and knew that not only is it a killer, it is a horrible and painful killer. The jury is out as to whether the actual surgery will reverse diabetes on everyone. It worked for me. A March 31 *NPR* story said that more than one-third of people who had gastric bypass surgery met their targets three years later.[12]

I'd been incredibly lucky. I made it to age 55 without heart disease or permanent injuries. I've been on blood pressure medicine since age

25 and used a CPAP for sleep apnea for more than 20 years. I was just starting to inch across the border from pre-diabetic to diabetic. My cholesterol level is low. I'd been in the hospital twice for short stays unrelated to obesity. Once when I was five years old and once when I was 50. Yet, I was 140 pounds overweight.

The odds of me living a longer life after weight loss surgery were better than my dying during the surgery. My decision was strictly based on health and longevity. To focus on looks and sex appeal diminishes the basic message of weight loss: this is all about health. I have places to go, people to see and things to do. The surgery was a tool to make that happen.

The Illogical World of Bariatric Surgery and Health Insurance

"It's a fact - I'm a quack
The disgrace of the A.M.A.
'Cause my patients die, yah my patients die
Before they can pay"
-"Like a Surgeon" by Weird Al Yankovic[13]

"A new car built by my company leaves somewhere travelling at 60 mph. The rear differential locks up. The car crashes and burns with everyone trapped inside. Now, should we initiate a recall? Take the number of vehicles in the field, A, multiply by the probable rate of failure, B, multiply by the average out-of-court settlement, C. A times B times C equals X. If X is less than the cost of a recall, we don't do one."
-Ed Norton's character in the movie *Fight Club*[14]

"America's health care system is neither healthy, caring, nor a system."
-Walter Cronkite[15]

I went into the process of weight loss surgery backwards. My first goal was to get a hospital that would allow me to have it.

When I decided to make a move, I found that I could not purchase a plan for my small business or an individual health insurance policy that would even cover the COMPLICATIONS of weight loss surgery. I purchased Anthem group insurance for my Kentucky-based businesses and pay 100 percent of the premium for my employees and their families. I had insurance brokers search high and low for a policy that would cover weight loss surgery. No luck. My employees were willing to switch to a different plan if it could help me get weight loss surgery, but we had nowhere to go.

I wound up paying for my own weight loss surgery, but complications remained an overwhelming concern. If I had a heart attack during surgery or the day after, my health insurance wouldn't cover it. If I didn't get the surgery and had a heart attack induced by my obesity, the insurer would pay for that. They would also pay for all my blood pressure medicines, CPAPs, diabetes medicines, walkers, amputations, hospital stays and doctor visits if I did not get surgery.

The insurance company attitude doesn't make sense long-term, but the companies are not thinking long-term. One of the big arguments in favor of a single-payer system for health insurance is that insurance companies are not interested in solutions to long-term problems. Like most publicly traded companies, health insurance companies are focused on the next fiscal quarter, not the next decade. What is best for the patient may not be best for the immediate profit margin.

From a cash flow basis, many health insurance carriers find it more profitable to pay for medicines, sleep apnea equipment, doctor and hospital visits and things associated with obesity than to write a large, one-time check for weight loss surgery. People can change insurance carriers on a regular basis, and an insurer can write a check to make a person healthy only to have them jump to another company. According to the Obesity Action Coalition, the cost of surgery is paid for in 3.5 years, but most health insurance carriers choose the immediate over the long-term.[16]

Anthem Insurance hit the jackpot with me. I paid for my own surgery and dramatically decreased my risk factors. They did not have to pay a dime for that result.

Risk management can be like the decisions that Ed Norton's character made in the movie *Fight Club*. He decided it was cheaper to let people die than to fix a small automobile problem. Many real life car manufacturers make the same decision.

What is logical in health care is not always most immediately profitable for the insurance company.

I've spent years and hundreds of hours looking for bariatric coverage. There are 974 pages in the Affordable Care Act.[17] I've read them all, looking for a provision that would help me. No luck. No insurance carrier in Kentucky offers small businesses, or individuals not receiving Medicaid, a chance to buy a plan that will cover bariatric surgery or its complications.

If I lost all my money and went on Medicaid, I could get the surgery for free. If I managed to stay healthy until age 65 and go on Medicare, I could get the surgery for free. If I was in Congress, my insurance would pay for the surgery and its complications. Most government entities offer insurance that covers the surgery and its complications. If I worked for a large company, most of them offer weight loss surgery, or at least cover the complications of weight loss surgery.

Bariatric surgery is an example of where Main Street loses to Wall Street. Small businesses can't buy the same kind of coverage as people who are richer, poorer or work for a large organization. Some individuals and small businesses can get coverage for obesity surgery through a health insurance exchange. It all depends on where you live. Kentucky joined roughly two dozen other states in not offering obesity surgery as part of their health insurance exchange. A story on *NPR* from Kaiser Health News noted the almost direct correlation between the states with highest obesity problems and the states that are not offering obesity surgery through their exchanges.[18]

The worse the obesity problem, the less the politicians want to do anything about it.

I thought about moving to another state. My wife is employed in Louisiana and I could have easily moved there, but Louisiana doesn't offer obesity coverage either and Louisiana's implementation of the Affordable Care Act was light years behind Kentucky. None of the states bordering Kentucky offered the coverage and moving to a state like New York or Maryland took me too far away from my family and where I do business.

I decided to pay for my own surgery, but then I had to find a hospital that would take me. A few years ago, I went to a seminar (every bariatric program makes you sit through a seminar like you are signing up to participate in a multi-level marketing program) for a hospital based in Central Kentucky, and they made me leave the seminar when they found out what kind of health insurance I had.

This time around, I was determined to keep looking. This got me to Dr. Derek Weiss, Georgetown Community Hospital and a blissful solution to my insurance problem.

How I Found BLIS in the Health Insurance World

"Don't you know things can change
Things'll go your way
If you hold on for one more day"
-Wilson Phillips[19]

"Help me if you can, I'm feeling down
And I do appreciate you being 'round
Help me get my feet back on the ground
Won't you please, please help me?"
-The Beatles[20]

"High risk insurance
The time is right"
-The Ramones[21]

BLIS is a fascinating specialty insurance program run by Regi Schindler in Oregon.[22] His customers are people paying for their own weight loss surgery. Schindler uses the analogy that BLIS is similar to a warranty on a new car. It allow patients the comfort of knowing that if something goes wrong, they won't be hit with additional medical expenses.

Because of BLIS, I was able to have weight loss surgery on Dec. 1, 2014.

Schindler has skin in the game. If a surgery goes wrong, his company is on the hook. Following the car warranty analogy, it could be the cost of some new wheel covers, but in today's expensive health care world, it might be the cost of a new Mercedes or maybe a fleet of Mercedes with a Cadillac thrown in. Schindler is very choosy about who he insures. His data and loss ratio calculations come to the same conclusion: it is not about the patient. It's not about the facility where you do your bariatric surgery. What makes the difference to BLIS is the surgeon who does the work.

It was luck or divine providence when I found my way to Dr. Derek Weiss, one of only three surgeons in Kentucky that BLIS had chosen to insure. At the time, Georgetown Community Hospital was one of the hospitals where Weiss performed surgery.

Schindler has an extensive background in medical risk management, including several years at the Mayo Clinic, but in 2005 he left the safety net of a corporate career to develop an insurance concept he is passionate about.

Regi helped to create a terrific idea in offering insurance coverage for specialty types of surgery, such as bariatric surgery, plastic surgery and orthopedics that many insurance carriers don't cover. Schindler calls his program "surgeon-centric" and in a 2012 article in *Bariatric Times*, he explains his business model in intricate details.[23] I assumed that BLIS would base their pricing on the health of the individual patient. Instead, it is based on the type of procedure and the experience BLIS has had with the surgeon doing the procedure.

When I asked Schindler to sum up by saying, "the better the surgeon, the lower the patient's premium," he tended to agree. Regi has built the company with a laser focus on getting excellent surgeons to participate.

Like any insurance provider, BLIS wants to keep their claims low and track the individual results and outcomes to make sure that the surgeons in their program are doing their best to stop minor complications from becoming major complications. BLIS and I had parallel goals. They wanted to increase access to surgery for as many people as possible. I wanted to increase access to surgery for me. Schindler is passionate in his commitment to offering a way for people to have surgery that could not previously and is focused on improving the patient experience.

Surgeons in the BLIS program have a number of incentives to look at the bigger picture and focus on minimizing and avoiding complications. I was thankful that BLIS is not a traditional health insurance carrier and has a model that seems to put patients over profits. On the other hand, I was a profitable client for BLIS. I purchased coverage which cost me $1,697.23 and I never had a complication or claim. I came away a happy customer. BLIS came away with $1,697.23. A win-win.

My frustration is that I did not find BLIS five years ago. In my hundreds of hours of searching, I kept looking at traditional health insurance carriers, rather than looking for a company like BLIS. None of my physicians, or physician friends, had ever heard of BLIS. BLIS is well thought of by the surgeons who use their services. Since that universe is extremely small and focused, the name recognition for BLIS amongst people outside that world is low. But people are finding their way to BLIS. According to their website, which Regi confirmed, the company has offered protection on 14,000 cases since 2006.

BLIS brought a degree of sanity to the illogical world of health insurance for weight loss surgery.

Any Member of Your Staff Will NOT Be Able to Assist Me

"Courteous treatment will make a customer a walking advertisement."
-J.C. Penney[24]

"I'll reach out my hand to you"
-Jackson 5[25]

The fastest way to irritate me is to say (usually via a voice mail recording), "Any of our fine professionals will be able to assist you." Big corporations like that concept as it allows them to treat employees like throwaway parts. Customers don't develop a personal relationship with staff members, and the corporation is able to promote their brand more than the people who make up that brand.

A lifetime of experience has taught me to connect with the very best experts I can find. In every form of endeavour, there are always a handful of experts whose results dwarf others in the same category. I've worked with at least 2,000 different attorneys. I can see the difference between a good lawyer, a great lawyer, a mediocre lawyer and a bad one. A good lawyer will get you a good settlement or jury verdict. A great one will usually get a great settlement. A mediocre one earns an OK result and a bad lawyer may get you zero. Or get you thrown in jail.

I had a stretch several years ago when I worked on nine different death cases involving trucks slamming into a car at the exact same intersection. The road was poorly designed and eventually corrected, but each of the nine people that were killed had similar demographics. Each lived in the same neighborhood and made about the same amount of money. Each was hit by a truck running a stop light. Each death was an individual driver without passengers, and each accident happened in the early morning when the sun was in the truck driver's eyes and the passenger was on their way to work. I don't remember any of the drivers drinking or taking drugs. All of settlements were confidential, but I was there for the mediations and settlement conferences. Most of the families of the victims had mediocre lawyers and received about $400,000. One had a good lawyer who got about $600,000, and the one who had a superstar attorney received a settlement in the millions. The family with the superstar had a true expert. The rest were operating on a system of "any attorney will do" and never knew they could have received 500 percent more.

I can't imagine a more important expert than a doctor. They literally have your life in their hands and their decisions can have an overwhelming impact on the quality of your life. I've made it a point to really get to know any medical professional in my life, from the receptionist in my physician's office to every nurse, assistant and other person in the process. An expert can solve a problem that another cannot. Usually they attract good people around them, too.

Let's not forget that many aspects of the medical profession are run by big corporations. Thus, many medical providers are pushing the "any of our staff members will do" approach. If doctors become interchangeable parts, it's easier to pay them less and replace them without losing customers or market share.

Having a "Go-To" Person

"Whenever you call me, I'll be there
Whenever you want me, I'll be there
Whenever you need me, I'll be there
I'll be around"
-The Spinners[26]

"No matter how busy you are, you must take the time to make the other person feel important."
-Mary Kay Ash[27]

Anyone who does business with me understands that I want a "go-to" person in an organization that I deal with. Sometimes it will be the president of a company, sometimes it is someone buried deep in the bureaucracy. My method is to find a main contact at places where I do business and cultivate a relationship. No matter what my problem is, I want to deal with just one person and let them guide me to the finish line.

My philosophy drives many big companies crazy, but those who "get it" get lots of business from me. Companies that let me choose my contact person do well. Companies that try to make me fit into their bureaucratic structures do not. I have been known to drop companies because they moved a contact person away from me and start doing business with a corporation because I have a contact person I trust. I followed one actuary to three different companies. I had never done business with any of the companies before she worked there.

One of the reasons that the weight loss process has gone so well is that I have "go-to" people in every aspect of the journey. I have my doctors and people that work for the doctors. I have one in the hospital and "go-to" coaches at my CrossFit box. I have a "go-to" pharmacist. I throw medical questions out on social media sites and develop connections.

In a world where the medical establishment is working to develop cookie-cutter responses, I am determined to find individuals who are truly interested in my wellbeing.

WEIGHT LOSS HEROINES

LORI SOBKOWSKI-RODRIGUEZ:
LIVED LIFE LIKE SHE WAS DYING

"And I loved deeper and I spoke sweeter
And gave forgiveness I'd been denying
And he said someday I hope you get the chance
To live like you were dying"
-Tim McGraw[1]

It was Dec. 2, 2014, the day after I had gastric sleeve weight loss surgery. A cardiologist stopped in my hospital room and asked me if I had ever had a heart echocardiogram done before. I told him I had four.

He said, "Do you have a history of heart problems?" and I said no, but I had taken Redux.

He looked at me strangely and said, "What is Redux?"

I nearly fell out of my bed. The doctor was younger and did his medical training in another country. He was in grade school when the drug was on the market in 1996 and 1997. Still, I couldn't believe that a cardiologist had never heard of the diet drug, taken by thousands of Americans, that wound up killing several of my friends.

One of those friends was Lori Sobkowski-Rodriguez. She died at age 43 on Dec. 27, 2014.

Lori had been living under a death sentence for more than a decade, because the Redux drug triggered a terrible disease called pulmonary hypertension. Even though she had her illness to deal with, it didn't surprise me that she had been checking on me daily via Facebook to see how my recovery from weight loss surgery was coming. Lori had a warmth, humor and empathy that radiated through her. I was lulled into a false sense of security about Lori. She seemed to be doing great. As we stayed in regular touch on social media, I would see her and her husband Noel having fun and enjoying life. She would occasionally pop up in a hospital, but a few days later, she would be out and about. They traveled and were getting ready to go on a cruise.

It was like getting hit with a baseball bat when Noel contacted me about her death.

I met Lori in 2004, a period when I traveled around the country helping people with their finances who had pulmonary hypertension triggered by Redux. The life expectancy of people who had pulmonary hypertension was roughly 4.3 years. I had taken the medicine myself and even now, I sometimes think a cough or cold is one that will signal pulmonary hypertension knocking on my door. The medical data says I should be "in the clear," but the medical data has been wrong about that diet drug since the day the Food and Drug Administration allowed it to be on the market.

In 1999, I started a journey that would introduce me to more than 50 people who had taken Redux. They were in every part of the United States and nearly every demographic. Lori was my last survivor. In fact, she had been the only one still alive for the past four years.

On first meeting, I would not have picked Lori to have lived another decade. I met her in her apartment, along with her roommate and fiancée, as she could not get out to meet in an office. She had some kind of breathing equipment nearby, and it was obvious after 90 minutes that she was completely worn out.

Part of the process of setting up a structured settlement annuity is to look into an option called a "rated age annuity." Someone buying life insurance has to pay more for it because of things like smoking or diabetes that reduce life expectancy. It works the opposite with a lifetime annuity. Someone with a reduced life expectancy gets a better monthly payment than someone healthy.

Lori's long-term did not look good, but I guess someone forgot to tell Lori. She went on with life. She married her fiancée. She was dedicated to the cause of finding a cure for pulmonary hypertension and seemed to have excellent health care. She definitely had an incredible support system with her husband and friends. She always seemed to be having fun.

She dealt with her illness with a sense of irony. One of her friends noted on Facebook that when Lori collapsed at work and was being taken in an ambulance going 20 miles an hour, Lori sat up and told the ambulance driver, "Miss Daisy wants to go faster." When she told me about her wedding plans, I told her she should go by the hyphenated name of Lori Sobkowski-Rodriguez as it would be the longest name in the universe. It became a running joke between us for the rest of her life.

Most of all, Lori went at life with the gusto of someone who truly lived like they were dying.

Making Plans for Death at a Young Age

"Holding you, I held everything
For a moment, wasn't I a king?
But if I'd only known how the king would fall
Hey, who's to say? You know I might have changed it all"
-Garth Brooks[2]

The work that I did with the Redux victims was the most rewarding thing that I've done in my 33 years in the structured settlement business. I had taken the medicine myself and I felt the victims were walking in shoes that could have been mine. I normally keep a professional distance between myself and my clients, but that was not the case with the people who took Redux. I hugged them and loved on them. I knew their families, their friends and the names of their pets. They knew how much I cared about them. I had one that I talked to literally every day, including the day she died. Lori is one of the rare situations where I did not get to help plan the funeral.

They were dealt a bad hand by a greedy pharmaceutical company, wanting to cash in on America's obsession with weight loss, and the lobbyists and government bureaucrats who let them get away with it. Because it happened so long ago, you have an entire generation, like the doctor I met, who never heard of the drug or the horrible consequences.

Each time I met a former Redux patient, I also felt a sense of awe. I never met a person who seemed bitter. All of them fought as hard as they could, and all of them are now dead, but they had a chance to make some plans for themselves and their families and they allowed me to help them.

I was fascinated by the television series *Breaking Bad* when the main character, Walter White, went from good to evil when he found out that he had a terminal illness.[3] The people who took Redux were the opposite. They went from good to tapping into their highest values. All of them asked me some form of the question, "How can you help my family go on without me?"

I'm not a social worker and I'm well-compensated for my financial insights, but working with people with pulmonary hypertension was personal, not business.

It could have been me.

Alicia Mundy wrote a terrific book called *Dispensing with the Truth: The Victims, the Drug Companies and the Dramatic Story Behind the Battle over Fen-Phen.*[4] In an investigative journalism style, Mundy disclosed what most of us had guessed all along: American Home Products (now Wyeth) lied to us and misled us, and the Food and Drug Administration let them get away with it. Innocent people lost their lives.

People went to their doctors to get this "magic pill" that would help them lose weight. The medicine showed immediate results in the short-term. I lost about 60 pounds, which came back on when I stopped taking the medicine.

My doctor was a former medical school professor and he read every piece of literature concerning Redux. He gave me a boatload of reading material, and we studied the decision carefully. We thought I was making an informed decision. I only took it for a few months because I suddenly got pneumonia. I've never had pneumonia before (or since), so maybe that was my body's version of a canary in a coal mine. I stopped the drug. It took me a few months to recover from the pneumonia and by then, the news about pulmonary hypertension was breaking. The drug was only on the market for about a year, but enough time to do plenty of damage.

And kill people, at age 43, like Lori.

As a financial consultant, I was dealing with a very unique dynamic. All of the people I worked with were under 50 years old and the overwhelming majority were women with young children and husbands. Several were about Lori's age, in their late 20s or early 30s. Most were well-educated and all received confidential settlements.

All of them understood that they were going to die too soon, but all had a great desire to live. There was also that chance that someone would come up with a cure. Pulmonary hypertension is not a common disease and I'm not sure many people had it before drug companies started peddling diet pills. It seemed logical that if they invented a pill to cause it, there might invent another pill to cure it.

Every time I look at the PH literature, it seems like they are closer and closer to finding ways to stop it and control its symptoms. It's a situation where some intense focus and research dollars can make a cure actually happen.

I met with young people planning for life after their deaths. I hit the subject dead on. We discussed how things like remarriage of their spouses and stepparents for their children were almost certain to happen. We made sure their money would go to the right people, in the right format, when they died and walked through all possible scenarios.

No one wants to die before their time. What they really don't want is to have their estate wind up in the hands of someone they never met or cared about. Steps were taken to keep that from happening.

It was a tough time for the families. Many people around the victims had a sense of doom. I did not. I had a true belief that a cure, or maybe a miracle, could be found. My father died of prostate cancer at a young age, and he lived his last year motivated by a sense of hope and a search for a cure. His death was slow and painful, but he did a lot of great things because he did not sit around and wait to die.

My friends who had pulmonary hypertension were the same way. I never had one that gave up without an intense fight.

One of the reasons that I included a lifetime annuity part of every victim's financial package was that it was an inexpensive way to make sure if a cure came along and they lived a long life, they would never run out of money.

I am a realist and most decisions were made with impending death in mind. The fact that I insisted on adding the lifetime annuity portion meant that I truly believed in the possibility of a cure. I would get in disagreements with attorneys and family members who did not understand why I wanted to add a lifetime annuity component. All of the actual victims understood. I was telling them to have hope for a cure.

Trusting a Stranger with Your Money

> *"You may never understand*
> *How the stranger is inspired*
> *But he isn't always evil*
> *And he is not always wrong"*
> -Billy Joel[5]

The settlement of the Redux claims normally came via a process called a mass tort settlement, and there were deadlines and quick decisions to be made. Clay Bigler, who is now the President of McNay Settlement Group (www.mcnay.com[6]), and I flew all around the country meeting with Redux victims, and we did all of our meetings face-to-face. (Thus, we would do things like wake up in Philadelphia and think we were in Boston.) Her attorney had arranged for us to come to Florida and meet Lori at her apartment. Her finance Noel Rodriguez and her roommate Jennifer Bowman were there. We all hit it off immediately.

A lifetime of working with injured people and lottery winners has always made me skeptical about family and friends at meetings about money. I normally won't allow it to happen. I just want the person getting the money and maybe their legally married spouse or domestic partner. I explain why in my book *Life Lessons from the Lottery*.[7] Family and friends are the primary reason that a person with a large sum of money runs through it all quickly. In at least 70 percent of the cases I've seen, family and friends with their own agenda try to steer the victim away from professional advice.

I let the other two stay. It was just a gut instinct, based on thousands of other meetings, but I could tell that Lori had a true and loving support team, and I am glad they were there. Clay Bigler happened to be facing Noel and watched him carefully. He was blown away by Noel's obvious dedication and devotion. We see a lot of guys hanging around settlements with dollar signs in their eyes. Noel only had love in his.

Noel had planned on marrying a healthy young woman and spending a long life together. Instead, he was marrying a woman living under a death sentence who was going to need a lot of support and care. Noel was up to the task. Noel and Lori seemed to be having more fun than most people I know. Noel was there for her, every step of the way.

Lori trusted our recommendations and agreed to them on the spot. We stayed in touch over the years and when she showed up on my

Facebook page (with her complete name Lori Sobkowski-Rodriguez), ours became a regular interaction.

Noel got in touch late on Dec. 29 and told me about Lori's death. I was devastated. I wrote a long post on Facebook and then a *Huffington Post* piece about how heartbroken I was.[8] I've heard from tons of her family and friends since then.

I felt a true sense of gratitude that I got to make a difference in her life. It certainly made me proud that I chose setting up structured settlements and working with the finances of injured people as a career.

I've spent 33 years in the structured settlement business, but this note from Lori's friend Tina Workman Harris was one that made me cry and not be able to stop:

> "Hello Don, my name is Tina and I am Lori's friend and have been since high school. Your post was beautiful and I just wanted to say thank you for everything you did for her. Because of you, she was able to spend the last part of her life not having to worry about finances...she was able to live a quality life (as much as anyone with PH can), and she and Noel were able to go and do and experience things together without worrying about money and medical bills. Because of you, Noel was able to be with her where she wanted him and where she needed him...he took such great care of my friend. Thank you so much for fighting for her...I also took that damn pill right along with her, I don't know why I was the lucky one...anyway...thank you."

I took the damn pills, too. One of my great frustrations is that parts of society treat obesity as a moral weakness instead of the disease that it truly is.

Lori sought a medical solution to help her lose weight, and the solution caused her body to die. I've been fortunate that my weight loss surgery has been successful and that the medical world has found a solution that works for people like me. The attempt with diet pills was definitely not the answer.

Lori lived like she was dying for the past decade. There are famous people like Jesus, Martin Luther King, Alexander the Great, Janis Joplin, Buddy Holly, Abraham Lincoln and Amy Winehouse who made a huge impact in a short period of time. Then there are people who aren't well known, like Lori, who make the same kind of lasting impact in their universe. It's not the hours you clock in on earth that count; it's what you do with them. As the poet Vachel Lindsay said, "to live in mankind is far more than to live in a name."[9]

Lori made that kind of lasting impression on those who were lucky enough to know her.

QUESTIONS TO ASK BEFORE YOU START YOUR WEIGHT LOSS JOURNEY

"Step by step
Ooh baby
Gonna get to you girl
Step by step"
-New Kids On the Block[1]

"A, I'll always want you
B, because my heart is true
C, come, come, come closer
And I'll tell you of the ABC's"
-Frankie Lymon and the Teenagers[2]

"It does not matter how slowly you go so long as you do not stop."
-Confucius[3]

Your first and most important conversation should be with yourself. Before you go on any kind of weight loss journey, find the answers to the following questions:

1. What is your Body Mass Index (BMI)?

Body Mass Index (BMI) is a way to measure obesity calculating height and weight. There are numerous calculators on the internet such as at nih.gov.[4]

According to the tables, a BMI of 30 or more is obese and less than 30 is not. On a person who is six-foot-tall, the 30 mark is about 220 pounds. On someone five-foot six-inches, it is about 185 pounds.

If your BMI is 35 or over, you may want to look at weight loss surgery. That is especially true if you are diabetic or near diabetic and have other life-shortening factors such as heart disease, sleep apnea or high blood pressure.

2. Do you drink, smoke or use medicines to cope with life?

I was fortunate that I did not smoke or use drugs and rarely drank. That made it easier to focus on the primary issue of obesity. For those who have other addictions, those habits have the chance of killing you as quickly, if not more quickly, than obesity. If you are going to focus on developing positive, long-term behaviors, it will be worth your while to get negative habits under control before taking on the obesity war. You can't win a war by fighting a battle on too many fronts. If you can limit the fight to obesity, you will be far more successful.

3. How long do you think you will live?

Few people consciously articulate this number, but you will find that almost all people unconsciously have a number in their minds. They can usually state a number once they think about it for a minute.

The number is often based on how long their family member or friends have lived and how well their health is holding up. You will find that the number is a primary driver in decision making. People who don't expect to live a long time have a different game plan than those who plan on living to be 100.

Much of my business career has been connected to the life insurance industry, and they have actuaries and underwriters who are extremely good at figuring out who will live a long time and who may not. The companies allocate billions of dollars based on those decisions.

If you smoke or skydive, you will pay more for life insurance than those who don't. It works the other way with a "rated age" lifetime annuity. If someone has an injury or occupation that will reduce their life expectancy, the annuity will pay them more per month than a healthy person of the same age.

The insurance companies have a good idea of how long they think you will live and in the back of your mind, you do too.

I bought an annuity when I was morbidly obese. Now that I am getting healthier, I feel like a gambler in Vegas who has figured out a way to "beat the dealer." When I get monthly checks into my very old age, I'll pat myself on the back for outsmarting the actuaries. It is not an easy thing to do.

People who think they are not going to make it much longer may not be willing to make changes in their diet. Then there are people who recognize that if they change their habits, they have a good chance of being around a lot longer.

Thus, it's important to get "the number" out on the table and in the front of your mind.

4. What can you afford and what are you willing to allocate?

I paid for my weight loss surgery and a variety of services out of my own pocket. My health insurance did not pay for anything. Organic and healthy foods cost far more than the stuff with additives. I took enough time off of work to completely recover and was willing to do what it took, or pay whatever it cost, to get my health in order.

Not everyone has access to money, resources and support people. A lot of people are fighting to stay afloat financially and doing it with little or no outside help. It's economical to buy cheap food or go through the fast food drive-thru. If you are working two jobs, it's hard to find time to exercise. If you are a parent, especially a single parent, getting time to yourself can be tough.

Some people have the time and money to get healthy. Some people have to rob Peter to pay Paul. Income is a primary indicator of obesity and the two go hand-in-hand. Being healthier allows you to open up more income opportunities.

When I was in high school, my mother was working in a potato chip factory and decided she wanted to be a nurse. She was a single mother with two children, working in the factory in the day and studying at night. I didn't fully appreciate until I was older how hard that was. She sacrificed because she could visualize the workplace happiness and economic security that nursing would bring her. It was the hardest decision of her life, but also the best one. She loved every day that she was a nurse.

Giving up health for wealth was a tradeoff I made for most of my life. I'm lucky that medical science is allowing me to atone for my past mistakes. Actually, my weight loss has helped my business. I'm more productive, active and alert than ever. Getting in shape can help make you money. And feel better. And live longer. Overall, that is a pretty good investment.

MAKING YOUR WEIGHT LOSS DREAMS COME TRUE

"Give us any chance, we'll take it
Read us any rule, we'll break it
We're gonna make our dreams come true
Doing it our way"
-Theme song from *Laverne and Shirley*[1]

"Sweet dreams are made of this
Who am I to disagree?"
-Eurythmics[2]

"Deep into that darkness peering, long I stood there, wondering,
fearing, doubting, dreaming dreams no mortal ever dared to dream
before."
-Edgar Allan Poe[3]

There are five steps to follow to make your weight loss dreams a reality.

1. Visualize a goal and make a plan on how to get there.

The late football legend James Street has been recently featured in the motion picture *My All-American*.[4] After football, Street made a career shift into the structured settlement business, and he was as successful off the field as he was on it. He and I developed a close friendship and business relationship. We were once working together against a company with far larger resources when he said, "I decided when I was a junior in high school that I was never going to be the quarterback in a losing football game. We are not losing this either."

We didn't.

Street never lost a football game in college and led the University of Texas to the national championship. James had an infectious sense of enthusiasm and self-confidence, and it rubbed off on the people around him. Street had a simple, but complicated mission: he never wanted to lose a football game. A lot of outside factors play into never losing a football game, but James had the focus and will to overcome them. He knew what he wanted his end result to look like: undefeated champion.

Like Street, I knew exactly what I wanted, too.

I didn't want to die during surgery. Or have complications that would hurt me for the rest of my life. I wanted to lose more than 100 pounds. I wanted to find the best weight loss surgeon I could find in my region. Some of my friends go to high-powered specialists in other cities or countries for surgery. I wanted to recover in Kentucky, where my family and doctors who cared about me were nearby.

All of that happened because I was very specific in my vision and had definite goals.

2. Find the best advisors you can get.

I had a "dream team" of doctors and health-related experts to help me. Weight loss is a business that can morph into a racket. It's a place where a lot of people are offering quick fixes and trying to make a quick buck.

So how do you find people who can truly help you and not rip you off?

President Ronald Reagan said, "Trust, but verify."[5] It is a good philosophy for dealing with any aspect of life. Businesses have outside auditor systems to make sure that people are doing what they are supposed to be doing.

The best way to find an advisor is a referral from a person who has had a successful experience. When I decided to get weight loss surgery, I knew some of my advisors well, but totally checked out the others. I did digging and research using public records and the internet. I found previous clients and interviewed them. I interviewed the potential advisors and asked lots of detailed questions.

It's the same thing people should do with any important decision. Do your homework and don't be afraid to ask for more information.

3. Your family and friends can help or hurt you.

If you follow the saga of any lottery winner, injury victim, movie star, pro athlete or someone who gets a lot of money and then blows it all, the primary source of their downfall seems to always be family and "friends." Family and friends can be the forces that make or break you in weight loss.

Sometimes it is blatant, but more often it's subtle. People don't want to lose their lunch or drinking buddy or have them change their routines. Family members don't want to adapt their food and lifestyle around another person trying to lose weight.

The best strategy with family and friends is to hit the issue dead on. I met with each of my family members individually before I had weight loss surgery and had specific projects that I asked them to do.

All of them were eager to help and came through for me. Each member of my immediate family lost at least 20 pounds in the past year. The fact that I included them, and they knew I needed them, made my journey a lot easier. Family and friends can be a true support team if you ask them to be part of your life.

4. Think long-term. Changing habits is more important than short-term results.

Before I started my weight loss journey, I drank at least six Diet Cokes a day, starting first thing in the morning. Now I don't have any and have not for more than a year. Rolling through the drive-thru of a fast food place every day, like I used to, is a habit. Now it may happen once a month, but the daily habit is broken and I am careful when I do go.

Walking and exercising is a habit, just like sitting on the couch and watching football can be. I get antsy if I can't get out and exercise now. From a guy who used to drive the car down from the back of his driveway to the mailbox (maybe 30 yards), this is a huge step forward.

I take the steps instead of taking the elevator. I park in the far reaches of shopping malls. I walk between terminals in an airport instead of taking the train.

Pick one habit and focus on making it better.

Radio personality Dave Ramsey teaches a concept called the "snowball" to help people get rid of credit card debt.[6] You pick the credit card with the smallest balance and focus your attention on getting that one paid off and eliminated. Once you pay off one credit card, you are likely to take the same system and pay off another.

Eventually, you are out of debt.

Use the "snowball" analogy with your weight. With the help of a hypnotist, I was able to give up my daily potato chip habit 12 years ago. Even though I was still 100 pounds overweight, I took great pride in knowing that I had knocked a 150 calories-an-ounce habit out of my life. It gave me a sense of confidence that I could do bigger and better things.

5. Think of Yourself as a Role Model

"Everybody dies famous in a small town"
-Miranda Lambert[7]

People who have lost weight or gotten their health together should be a role model. If you are doing things to improve your health, you are making a statement. One that your family, friends, coworkers and neighbors will pick up on. You don't have to go marching in the streets. You just need to be the kind of person that other people want to be like.

I see people who have had weight loss surgery go to great lengths to hide it. Celebrity Star Jones had gastric bypass surgery in 2003 and lost 160 pounds, but denied for years that she had surgery.[8] Compare that to Carnie Wilson, who was exceptionally open about her weight loss surgery, then her weight gain, then her second surgery and her ongoing struggle.[8] Carnie has inspired thousands of others to look at weight loss surgery as an option. The fans of Star Jones turned on her for being dishonest, and Jones' high profile career went into a spiral. Nine years after the surgery, Jones noted on *The Today Show* that lying about the surgery damaged her credibility and says that she did not want to go public about her surgery as she was afraid to fail. Jones' delayed disclosure was a lose-lose. Her career took a huge hit and her lack of candor denied her the empathy of people who would otherwise support her battle against obesity.

You don't have to be a celebrity to make an impact. Someone is noticing what you are doing. Getting yourself healthy is a tremendous accomplishment. Inspiring others to do the same is even greater.

"It is not the critic who counts; not the man who points out how the strong man stumbles, or where the doer of deeds could have done them better. The credit belongs to the man who is actually in the arena, whose face is marred by dust and sweat and blood; who strives valiantly; who errs, who comes short again and again, because there is no effort without error and shortcoming; but who

does actually strive to do the deeds; who knows great enthusiasms, the great devotions; who spends himself in a worthy cause; who at the best knows in the end the triumph of high achievement, and who at the worst, if he fails, at least fails while daring greatly, so that his place shall never be with those cold and timid souls who neither know victory nor defeat."
-Theodore Roosevelt[9]

I'm writing on a day when Sheila Hiestand competed in the Louisville Ironman. She finished the 2.4-mile swim in the Ohio River, but ran into medical problems near the end of the 100-mile bike ride and had to drop out.

Some people would consider that a defeat. It's the opposite. It was an amazing feat to be a part of an ultimate test of human endurance. Ironman has swimming and biking and ends with the participants running a marathon, which is 26 miles, 285 yards. Marathons are named in honor of the Greek soldier Pheidippides, who ran that exact distance from Marathon to Athens to announce that "victory is ours at Marathon."[10]

Then he dropped over dead.

The marathon was a pretty tough race when Pheidippides did it in 490 BC and hasn't gotten any easier since. The fact that Ironman adds swimming and biking to the race that caused Pheidippides to die proves that humans are always pushing forward to find new ways to achieve. And occasionally we stumble, fall or drop over dead along the way.

I used to carry the Teddy Roosevelt quote in my wallet when I was in college. It was a coming of age time in life and it was a reminder that trying and not succeeding is better than not trying at all.

Those of us who want to battle obesity have to keep getting back up when we get knocked down. And encouraging others to follow in our positive footsteps. Only five percent of people in the nation keep their weight off for five years or longer; it's a pretty small subset that makes it to the top of the weight loss world. When people do make it, or even if they are they trying to make it, it helps to let the people around them know what they are doing. All of us in the weight loss struggle need support and encouragement. The winners of life's genetic obesity lottery, who don't understand being obese, have not always been kind to the people on the other side.

My Medical Dream Team

"His success in dealing with the strong egos of the men in his cabinet suggests that in the hands of a truly great politician the qualities we generally associate with decency and morality— kindness, sensitivity, compassion, honesty, and empathy—can also be impressive political resources."
-Doris Kearns Goodwin, *Team of Rivals: The Political Genius of Abraham Lincoln*[1]

"No matter how close to yours another's steps have grown In the end there is one dance you'll do alone"
-Jackson Browne[2]

I had four primary advisors through my weight loss journey.

Dr. Jim Roach, M.D. in Midway, Kentucky is an internationally known expert in the field of integrative medicine and he tends to favor plant-based, organic foods, along with vitamins and supplements. Dr. Phillip Hoffman in Nicholasville, Kentucky has a traditional internal medicine practice and a "balanced diet" approach to food. Cindy Jester Caywood, Director of Bariatric at Georgetown Community Hospital in Kentucky, spent many years working with Dr. James Anderson, the retired University of Kentucky doctor whose book *The Simple Diet* promotes the concept of portion control and meal replacements.[3] Dr. Derek Weiss in Lexington is a highly acclaimed surgeon who favors a high protein diet for the patients he does weight loss surgery on.

So who did I ultimately listen to? All of them.

Doris Kearns Goodwin wrote *Team of Rivals: The Political Genius of Abraham Lincoln*, which focused on the leaders that Lincoln assembled as his presidential cabinet. They had differing viewpoints and many had their own presidential ambitions. The people around

55

Lincoln knew that they could freely express their opinions, but understood that President Lincoln would make the call on the ultimate strategy, even if he did not have a consensus of opinion.

The idea is to get as many smart people thinking about the same problem as you can. I was lucky to have some sharp and honorable people in my life.

Dr. Phil Hoffman, Cindy Caywood and Dr. Jim Roach are longtime friends and Dr. Derek Weiss is a friend now. I dedicated this book to them as I value the relationships and admire their expertise. I have their private contact information and can get a hold of them quickly and easily. They truly care about me as a person. Few people have that kind of direct interaction with their doctors, and I don't have an easy way to replicate that. Having these trusted advisors was the most important part of the process.

Here are the four people who made such a huge impact in my quest to be a Brand New Man.

Meet Dr. Derek Weiss

"I can call you Betty
And Betty, when you call me
You can call me Al"
-Paul Simon[4]

"Yeah, I wanna be well
I wanna be well
I wanna be"
-The Ramones[5]

I've known a lot of doctors. My mother spent 27 years as an operating room nurse and for my first years in the financial business, all of my clients were doctors. I've learned a lesson about doctors that holds true for almost any professional: the less pretentious they are, usually the better doctor they are. People who hide behind titles are not people I want to do business with. Informal people have more self-confidence and the ability to allow others to buy into their self-belief.

Titles do have a purpose and I let you know about all of mine. I put all of my professional initials behind my name as it is a shorthand way to let people see that I have been to the rodeo on almost any kind of financial issue. But I want you to call me Don. My grandchildren are the only people who refer to me by a title: "grandpa." I hate being called "Mr. McNay."

Derek Weiss, M.D., FACS, FASMBS is "Derek," not Dr. Weiss. He introduces himself as Derek and prefers it that way. He is friendly, but oozes with self-confidence. Few medical professionals like to be interviewed by the media, and having a patient who is writing a book about their performance can be nerve-racking. Derek is the opposite. He did three interviews with me and spent three hours on a Sunday afternoon answering a plethora of questions, from hardballs to softballs, including all kinds of stuff about his personal life, business practices and finances. His answers were 100 percent dead on. He never ducked one.

When you are a journalist or work with trial attorneys, you can get skeptical and cynical. You see people's worst sides. It's extremely hard to win me over, but Derek did. I bought into his confidence that things would go smoothly and I would be well on my way to a second chance at life.

He was correct.

Derek is a man of strong opinions and not afraid to clash with those who disagree with him. I've interviewed many of his former patients. The overwhelming majority like him and the ones that don't are usually put off by on his strong personality, not his surgical skills. Hey, he's a surgeon. I have not met one yet that was a shrinking violet. If I do meet one, I am not sure that I want them to cut on me.

I like Derek as a person, but my most important concern was that he be a great surgeon. He is. After doing thousands of procedures, he pushes forward to continuously improve his craft with an intense enthusiasm. He was terrific on helping me keep costs down. He was affordable and highly aware that I was paying for every dime of the medical procedure without the help of my insurance company.

The main thing you get from Derek is his zest for living. Derek Weiss loves being Derek Weiss, and it shows in his infectious zeal for his work. He is a great surgeon and I have done incredible and extensive research to make that statement. Even if I had not done the spadework, I would have guessed on our first meeting that Derek is a master of his craft. Weiss talks about bariatric surgery the way that some people talk about sex, money or their hobbies. It is his passion. He bubbles with enthusiasm and recognizes that his profession gives people a second chance at life.

In the year after surgery, Derek stayed on me to try the CrossFit gym that he belongs to. I've really loved it.

Weiss was born into the surgical business. His father was a surgeon at the military base at Fort Knox and his mother was an operating room nurse. He grew up in Louisville, was Magna Cum Laude in Biochemistry at Dartmouth, was in the top 10 percent of his class at the University of Louisville Medical School and did his surgical training (residency) at Emory University where he worked under Dr. John Hunter, an internationally known leader in laparoscopy. Derek brought his laparoscopy skills back to Louisville and spent eight years as a successful general surgeon when Dr. Tom Lavin, one of the nation's most successful bariatric surgeons, asked Derek to move just outside New Orleans to join his booming weight loss practice. Weiss would have been happy spending his career in New Orleans, but a big opportunity came up for him to come home to Kentucky and partner with another surgeon in the bariatric field. They were together for several years and dominated bariatric surgery in Kentucky. His former partner now practices in Louisville, while Derek focuses on Central Kentucky. Derek fits all my criteria for an expert. He is well-educated, passionate about his craft, continuously learning, connected to other top experts and sees his work as his calling, not an occupation.

Derek was the result of a lot of research and asking a lot of questions, but I found the right surgeon for me.

America's Healer, Dr. Jim Roach

"I don't know if we each have a destiny, or if we're all just floating around accidental-like on a breeze, but I think maybe it's both."
-Forrest Gump (in the movie *Forrest Gump*)[6]

"There is no reason to be suffering from anything right now if you have access to this guy right here...I literally can't talk highly enough about how much I think you are really doing good stuff in the world."
-Jack Canfield, author of *Chicken Soup for the Soul*, talking about Dr. Jim Roach[7]

"Do you believe in Miracles?"
-Al Michaels (when the United States Olympic Hockey Team defeated Russia in 1980)[8]

Dr. Jim Roach was the answer to a prayer that I didn't know I was praying. One of the most important things I ever wrote was an email to Dr. Jim on July 15, 2014 at 4:08 a.m. I had been Dr. Jim's patient a few years prior, but gave my time slot to a friend with stage four cancer and I never got back to seeing him again. I was a desperate man when I wrote this 4 a.m. email:

> "I am writing because I need your help. As of today, my weight is 373 pounds and my BMI is more than 50. I have other diseases that you helped me treat: Sleep Apnea, Diabetes and High Blood Pressure."

Jim responded and then said:

> "I have 23 patients with near death experiences and 100 more that shared spiritual stories. Intend to explore a book sharing those stories later; they have changed my perspective on life."

I said:

> "Do you have a publisher for your book? I am the chairman of a book publishing company, RRP International Publishing. We are extremely selective in whom we add as an author, but your book idea is a winner and one we would be interested in."

As Humphrey Bogart said, that was "the beginning of a beautiful friendship."

It also put the forces in play for Dr. Jim to write a number one best-selling book.[9] On April 1, 2015, the number one bestseller on Amazon in Holistic Medicine was *God's House Calls* by Dr. Jim Roach. The number one best-selling new release in Alternative Medicine was *God's House Calls* by Dr. Jim Roach. The number one best-selling new release in Healing was *God's House Calls* by Dr. Jim Roach.

The book was number one in four categories and on the top Amazon bestseller lists in numerous other categories including Health, Fitness, Dieting, Professional and Technical books. It was barely out of the top 100 in the overall nonfiction category.

The previous night, Dr. Jim had an invitation-only kickoff event for his book that drew more than 400 people and packed every nook and cranny of the historic Holly Hill Inn in Midway, Kentucky. Dr. Jim Roach, a first time author from that tiny city, wrote a book that is an absolute monster success. And he helped me find my way to weight loss surgery.

An improbable story if there ever was one. I got up in the middle of the night and sent an email to a doctor I had not seen in a couple of years. He responded by offering to help me, but also mentioned that he wanted to write a book, even though he had never written one before. I immediately responded that I knew it would be a hit and that I wanted to publish it. I never do that, especially with a first time author.

So to answer the Al Michaels' question, "Do you believe in miracles?" My experience with Dr. Jim shows that they occurred in my life.

The story of how first I hooked up with Dr. Jim to begin with has the feeling of being another of "God's House Calls."

"It must've been wild angels, wild angels
Watching over you and me
Wild angels, wild angels
Baby, what else could it be?"
-Martina McBride[10]

It could have been a wild angel that connected me to Dr. Jim Roach, M.D., but that angel came in the form of a (then) 82-year-old journalist named Al Smith. Al is one of the greatest living Kentuckians, but I thought in November 2009 that he was hitting the finish line. He did not look good at all. Al spends his winters in Sarasota, Florida. When he came back to Lexington in April 2010, he was in high spirits and invited me to lunch at the Bangkok House, which is at the bottom of a steep flight of steps near the University of Kentucky campus. It wasn't until we started to leave that I noticed that Al was basically skipping up the long flight of steps.

When I asked him what caused the turnaround, he credited Dr. Jim and the regimen of supplements, vitamins and diet changes that Dr. Jim recommended. Al turned 88 in January 2015. He is still writing, influencing public issues and maintaining a busy schedule. After I saw what Dr. Jim did for Al, I became one of Dr. Jim's patients and his friend.

As Jack Canfield noted, Dr. Jim is one of the nation's leaders in a concept called Integrative Medicine. Some call Roach "America's Healer." Jim combines his medical school education and decades of daily practice as a family doctor with an approach that combines a variety of concepts. It is all designed to help a person live a longer and healthier life. Dr. Roach and his team at the Midway Center for Integrative Medicine will often spend a couple of hours with a patient. Seeing how many medical corporations are forcing their doctors to practice like they are on a time clock, Dr. Jim is a refreshing change from the medical experience that many people endure.

Dr. Jim and his team get to know their patients on a deep and personal level. Located in genteel horse country, the Midway Center is a glimpse of what the practice of medicine was like in the days of small town doctors and house calls, but Midway has all the latest research and cutting-edge technology at their fingertips. Dr. Jim is all over the United States, doing lectures, going to high-powered conferences and interacting with the biggest experts in the Integrative Medicine field. He is a well-respected physician. He's built a tremendous medical practice and has the sense of grace and manners of someone who grew up in horse country with a family that owned a famous and successful horse farm. His late father Ben and his late brother Tom, along with famed horse breeder William Farish, bred the 1999 Kentucky Derby winner Charismatic at their well-known Parrish Hill Farm. Charismatic won the Preakness and ran third after breaking his leg at his Triple Crown attempt at the Belmont. The farm also bred Princess Rooney, a winner at the Kentucky Oaks and in the inaugural Breeders Cup.

Jim has a strong devotion to his wife and two children. He and Dee Dee were married on July 3, 1976 and work together every day at the Midway Center. To see them, you would think they are still on their honeymoon, and they have a love and devotion to be admired. Both of his children are excellent people and have successful careers. His son James is a meritorious attorney in Ohio and his daughter Liz had been a speechwriter and assistant to Kentucky Governor Steve Beshear before taking a position with the Council of State Governments.

Jim learned about more than horses from his family. He learned the art of giving back. His father, Dr. Ben Roach, was the founder of the Markey Cancer Center at the University of the Kentucky, one of the top cancer centers in the region. Jim also learned from his family to do good deeds quietly. Although there is a building as part of the

Markey Center named for Dr. Ben Roach, the center is not. Jim's mother, a civic activist extraordinaire, was killed in a car crash on New Year's Eve several years ago as she was delivering baskets of food to poor people and drove off an icy and snowy road. Jim was one of the first advocates of a statewide smoking ban in Kentucky and an early leader in Habitat for Humanity in Kentucky.

One of Dr. Jim's great heroes was Millard Fuller, the founder of Habitat for Humanity. He took a simple idea and a focused message and built an organization that made a huge impact on the world. Dr. Jim is a rebel. A quiet, self-effacing rebel who grew up on a horse farm and studied at Duke University, like his father and brother did, but a rebel nonetheless.

It would have been easy for Dr. Jim to keep rolling along, handing out pills and practicing the same kind of medicine that many family care doctors do. See a lot of patients, hand out a lot of prescription drugs. Instead, Dr. Jim created an entirely new medical model. He promotes healthy living, vitamins and supplements over prescription medicines. He focuses on breaking edge information and seems to be doing research and studies on the latest trends 24 hours a day. Not many doctors schedule two and a half hour visits with their patients or test for allergies and ailments that no one has ever heard of or thought about. Jim does. Dr. Jim, spawned from the most conventional of backgrounds, is an unconventional man. He took a lot of cheap shots from the traditional medical community when he changed his practice to one that works exceptionally well. He took on unpopular causes, like trying to implement a statewide smoking ban in a tobacco state like Kentucky, long before anyone dreamed that would be possible.

As the Tom Petty song says, he won't back down.[11]

Dr. Phil Hoffman: Babydaddy's Daddy

"Gonna take your mama out all night
Yeah we'll show her what it's all about"
-Scissor Sisters[12]

"I hear you're feeling down
Well, I can ease your pain
Get you on your feet again"
-Pink Floyd (and the Scissor Sisters)[13]

I thought my friendship with Dr. Phil Hoffman was going to end my writing career before it began.

After a 20-year absence, in 2003 I started writing a weekly newspaper column and the *Richmond Register* in Kentucky was my only outlet. My stuff was pretty edgy and controversial. My first publisher hated it. We went through multiple editors in the first couple of years and then I submitted a column about a musical group called the Scissor Sisters that was just starting to hit it big in England. They had a platinum album, opened concerts for Elton John and were headliners for large arena concerts. They won a number of big awards.

The Sisters musical leader and producer was Scott "Babydaddy" Hoffman of Lexington. Scott's parents, Dr. Phil and Nancy Hoffman, are dear friends of mine. I got to know Scott when I was invited to his Bar Mitzvah. It was the first Bar Mitzvah I was ever invited to. I went to Catholic schools and rarely met anyone from another faith until I got to college. By including me in a precious ritual of their faith, the Hoffman's broke down a barrier in my life. The Bar Mitzvah marked a turning point: I began making friends from diverse backgrounds.

The theme of the column was diversity, but for another reason. Scott, along with several other members of the Scissor Sisters, was openly gay. Supporting them in small town Kentucky is a bold move in 2015. Kim Davis, the county clerk in nearby Rowan County, Kentucky, went to jail rather than issue marriage licenses to sex same couples. (She received national attention and later got to meet the Pope.) Writing the column a decade earlier, when I had no other outlets for my writing, seemed like a sure end of my career. The publisher emailed and wanted to schedule a meeting with me before the column hit the paper. Instead, a brand new editor called and invited me to lunch.

Veteran journalist Jim Todd showed up at lunch, told me he was the new editor and that he loved my columns, especially the one about Babydaddy. He assured me that they would have to fire him before they fired me. It turns out the publisher resigned when Jim came in so I was safe on all fronts. The next publisher, Nick Lewis, took the position that Jim was the king of the editorial kingdom and he would never interfere. Those two guys had my back.

I dedicated one of my previous books to Jim Todd. He took the worst daily newspaper in Kentucky and, one year later, won an award as the best. He was instrumental in helping me get my column syndicated. He was the editor every "cutting-edge" columnist hopes for. Note he was still an editor. He yelled at me, chopped my wording and fired me at least twice. I knew my "firing" was a way to get my attention and I was brought back in after a couple of days. He was devoted to making all his writers better writers and better people.

Jim kept me in the writing business, but I would have given up my column before I gave up Dr. Phil. Phil is the model for what every doctor should be. He is calm, caring and knows his stuff. For years, I never waited more than 30 seconds in his lobby for an appointment. The medical profession would do well to study Phil and operate like he does.

The politics of the time played into the Babydaddy column, but actually Phil came into my life as a result of political action. In 1988, I was a state coordinator for Al Gore's first campaign for President and Phil's wife Nancy was on our campaign team. Nancy is a terrific organizer, tireless fundraiser and a super nice person. We became close friends and worked on many other campaigns and civic causes together. Thus, I met her husband Dr. Phil and her three sons. Babydaddy is known for his musical career. Another son, Ben, is a comedian and the star of *The Ben Show* on Comedy Central where Dr. Phil has made guest appearances.[14] The other son, Dr. Mark Hoffman, is an OBGYN and teaches in medical school.

World events played a part in how Phil became my doctor. I had an excellent relationship with my previous internal medicine doctor, who volunteered for the army after the terrorist attack on Sept. 11, 2001 and wound up doing several tours of duty in Iraq and Afghanistan.

When I came to Phil, he asked if I felt comfortable seeing such a close friend on a professional level. I told him, "If something ever goes wrong, I want a doctor that is going to care if they get a call from me at 3 a.m." Phil does care. He keeps up on the medicine and seems to have a relationship with every specialist in the state, but his ability to truly care is what I admire about Phil. It's not about the money, it's about the healing.

My son-in-law Clay Bigler is from New Orleans and when Hurricane Katrina hit in 2005, his closest childhood friend and his mother came to live with them near Lexington, Kentucky. The mother started having pains in her chest and tried shaking them off. Then she couldn't get admitted to an emergency room as her insurance carrier, Blue Cross of Louisiana, did not have a way to be contacted. I called Phil at home and asked if he would look at her (for free) and the Tulane graduate did so. Within a few minutes of seeing her, he had her admitted to a hospital where they immediately performed multiple bypass surgery. Without Dr. Phil, the woman would have died. From the stress of the hurricane and the bureaucratic screw-up that followed. Ten years later, she is doing fine.

It's pretty neat to have a friend whose sons are celebrities. I've been able to have dinner with the Scissor Sisters and see the concerts from a few feet from the stage. More important than having a celebrity connection, I've had a first-rate doctor for more than a decade. I made it to the point where weight loss surgery could turn my life around because I never had a stroke, heart attack or other game changers before that. Dr. Phil did what it took to keep me going and eventually we found a better, long-term solution.

Thank you Dr. Phil.

Cindy Jester Caywood

"She was a friend to me when I needed one
Wasn't for her I don't know what I'd done"
-Jackson Browne[15]

"Grasshopper, fear is the enemy. Trust is the armor."
-Master Po in the television show *Kung Fu*[16]

I was lucky that Cindy Jester Caywood has been eager to be my "go-to" person throughout my weight loss journey. She is the Director of Bariatrics at Georgetown Community Hospital and was an administrator at the hospital at the time of my surgery.

Cindy is a fellow graduate at Eastern Kentucky University and has her Masters from EKU as well. She was my health educator when I was in a weight loss program founded by Dr. Jim Anderson, her mentor at the University of Kentucky, a decade ago. When I was trying to decide whether to have weight loss surgery, or where to have it at, the fact that Cindy was at the Georgetown hospital was a big factor in selecting that facility. I knew I could trust her and she would shoot straight with me. She is a kind and caring person by nature, and I knew she would have my back whenever I had a question or needed to know the lay of the land. Her knowledge of the weight loss world is tremendous and she has been a great educator.

My fear of any kind of surgery was immense, but especially weight loss surgery. Having a person like Cindy on the inside allowed me to get over my stress.

Trust is the most important component in developing any kind of relationship. That seems obvious, but I constantly run into people who are blinded by a "too good to be true" deal and don't pay attention to who is offering "the deal."

There are some people you do business with and others you don't. Wayne Rogers had a simple way of ferreting them out. Rogers, best known as Trapper John on the television show *M*A*S*H*, had a second career as an investment and business guru.[17] According to Rogers, there are four kinds of business deals: good deals with good people, bad deals with bad people, good deals with bad people and bad deals with good people. The first two are simple: Everyone wants good deals with good people, and no one wants bad deals with bad people. Regarding the other possibilities, Rogers said that good deals with bad people will always fail and that a bad deal with good people could potentially work out someday.

A bad person will always make a good deal go bad, and a good person might make a bad deal right.

I like working with Cindy, as she is encouraging without being overbearing, and I respect her knowledge. A good deal with a good person.

Cindy suggested that I read a book called *The Simple Diet* that Dr. James Anderson wrote. I have a complicated view of Dr. Anderson's work. He was one of my neighbors so I saw him frequently when I was in the HMR program the first time in 1989, and Jim is one of the nicest men I have ever met. He is internationally recognized and sincerely believes in a high carb, low fat diet. He got into medicine for all the right reasons and truly cared about his patients.

Because it was a university program, it tended to draw highly educated participants. Some of the people I bonded with were PhD research scientists, a Supreme Court Justice, a high profile minister, a pro football player, several professors and attorneys. A cool bunch of people to hang with. The focus was on mandatory attendance for the meetings and great educators like Cindy.

I have a love-hate relationship with HMR because I was in the program six times. I never lost less than 50 pounds, but always gained back (within 18 months) more than what I lost and I think it messed with my metabolism. Being the Amy Winehouse of HMR did not really change my personal affinity for Dr. Anderson, but I stopped believing in his systems. I became a believer in high protein and low carb. Then, I read his book and realized that a couple of his ideas could be adapted to what I am doing now.

Dr. Anderson is big on using shakes as meal replacements. HMR sold their own shakes which had to be made in a blender and were incredibly inconvenient. Also extremely expensive. I adapted by using the protein shakes I like in the meal replacement fashion that Dr. Anderson advocates in his book. That helps me to get enough fluid and protein into my day.

The second thing that Dr. Anderson pushes is having a meal replacement every few hours and not letting yourself get hungry. HMR was rigid on only using the meal replacement products that they sold. Those were similar to Lean Cuisine and other packaged meals you find in grocery stores. In the book, Dr. Anderson moves away from the "HMR only" mantra and allows for other meal replacements. I take it a step further. I've gone to a system of using high protein or fresh foods, but keeping to the every three-hour system. I also have some packaged meals available, like Lean Cuisine, so that I don't get hungry or let my energy levels drop. That seems to be working well.

Cindy has a quiet persistence and truly wants me to succeed. Getting me to open up my mind to *The Simple Diet* was a breakthrough and I was lucky to have her as part of my medical dream team.

WEIGHT LOSS HEROINES

ELIZABETH WHITT:
21-YEAR-OLD EASTERN KENTUCKY UNIVERSITY STUDENT LOST 175 POUNDS AFTER GASTRIC SLEEVE

"You're the meaning of my life
You're the inspiration"
-Chicago[1]

Elizabeth Whitt, a communications major at Eastern Kentucky University from Richmond, Kentucky, has the maturity of a 40-year-old in the body of a woman who just turned 21. It's 175 pounds thinner than the same body that she had at age 19, when she made the decision to have gastric sleeve weight loss surgery and focus on her health.

Elizabeth figured out how to get to her goal weight with a business plan that she created herself.

"Did this meeting of our minds together
Happen just today, somewhere"
-Chicago[2]

Outside of our shared love for Eastern Kentucky University, Elizabeth and I came at the decision to do the gastric sleeve surgery from very different perspectives.

She was 19 years old when she did her surgery, and I was age 55. She is a single woman, and I am a married grandfather. I was faced with a number of middle age, life-threatening, weight-related ailments like diabetes and high blood pressure.

Weight loss surgery was my last chance to avoid a very early death.

Elizabeth recently celebrated her 21st birthday. As an Eagle's song notes, no one thinks about death at age 21. At least not enough to undertake major, life-changing surgery.

Our study and research brought us to similar conclusions. We chose different hospitals and different programs, but both of us chose the same surgery and the same surgeon, to operate on us.

Since she is 175 pounds lighter than when she started, and I have lost more than 100 pounds, it's hard to argue with the decision.

> *"Tell me you will stay*
> *Make me smile"*
> -Chicago[3]

Elizabeth's father, public relations guru Marc Whitt, has been a friend of mine since college and I followed Elizabeth's journey on social media as I was contemplating my own surgery.

I thought her 175 weight loss was a great story, but I had a selfish motive to want to interview her.[4] I needed her help.

I have terrific access to medical professionals and experts, but I really needed to talk to someone who had walked the walk. I had a lot of questions that needed answers and gastric sleeve is different from gastric bypass, lap band and other types of weight loss surgeries.

I've talked to nearly 100 people who have done other surgeries. In my career as a wealth transition and structured settlement expert, I've talked to the families of several people who died while having the surgery. (None of the people who died were patients of Dr. Derek Weiss. I checked carefully. It turns out that Elizabeth checked Derek out carefully, too.) I followed the online boards and services enough to talk about weight loss surgery with anyone.

Elizabeth was the first person I had met who actually had the gastric sleeve, like I had.

My guide was less than my half my age, but I could not have picked a better advisor.

You can tell Elizabeth was the daughter of a public relations wizard by the way she prepared for our interview.

The confident, level-headed, but empathetic communications major at Eastern Kentucky University showed up promptly for our meeting armed with tons of data. That included a month-to-month printout of how much weight she lost, an essay she had written about the experience, and before and after pictures. She was dressed appropriately for a photo (I suggested that both of us wear the school colors of our alma mater), and she had a photographer nearby (her father) to make sure we had a professional picture.

She could have been doing the media planning for a presidential news conference. Or running for President herself.

Her excellent interview preparation skills are a byproduct of her education and upbringing, and her goal is a noble one. Fame is not the motivation. Giving back and educating is. She wants to inspire others to follow in her footsteps.

She understands that her achievement is unique, but that the gastric sleeve surgery gave her the tools to make a near miracle happen.

Although we had the same surgeon, Elizabeth and I went to different hospitals and programs for our surgeries. Her hospital recently filmed a video featuring her that is used for education and marketing. Elizabeth also gave me permission to talk to Dr. Weiss about her success.

Weiss told me that doing weight loss surgery on a teenager had been rare before the gastric sleeve became more common. The risk of complications is lower than other surgeries. Derek gives credit to Elizabeth for following the steps for her "exceptional" weight loss and said, "LSG (gastric sleeve surgery) is a tool. It limits the amount you can eat very successfully. But I think all LSG patients who succeed can take most of the credit themselves; they chose what to eat (and drink) and how much to exercise. The average LSG patient can expect to lose about 70 percent of their excess body weight (EBW) in about a year."

Elizabeth is a really unique model for me. She lost the exact amount that I want to lose in roughly the same time frame that I want to lose it in. She started at a lower weight and got to her absolute ideal.

I needed to know how she did it.

I had a bunch of questions. Some for the article and some just for myself. She spent three hours answering them and followed up several times via email to answer more questions and give me advice.

> *"Sometimes I wonder*
> *Where I've been*
> *Who I am, do I fit in?*
> *Make-believing is hard alone*
> *Out here, on my own"*
> -Lesley Gore and Michael Gore (from the movie *Fame*)[5]

Weight loss surgery did not change Elizabeth's character or personality; it allowed her body shape and overall health to be different.

Michael and Debi Benson, the president and first spouse at Eastern Kentucky University, trusted Elizabeth as the babysitter for their three small children.

President Benson said, "Debi and I are very grateful for Elizabeth and have marveled at her physical transformation. This change has allowed her inner beauty, which has always been radiant and contagious, to shine through even more. As a family, we value a great deal the friendship we have with Elizabeth and very much appreciate the bond she has developed with our children."

Elizabeth and I discussed how having the surgery has allowed her to be more energetic and active, but as President Benson said, her inner beauty had been there for a long time.

> *"And knowing that you would have wanted it this way*
> *I do believe I'm feeling stronger every day"*
> -Chicago[6]

There were two questions that I had to ask Elizabeth.

The first was whether she liked the music of the group Chicago. The one college memory of her horn-playing father was that he was an absolute, diehard Chicago fan at a time when genres like punk, new wave and disco were more popular. The band was way off the charts at the time. Chicago made a big comeback in the early 1980s, but Marc took a lot of college grief for his undying affinity for Chicago.

She said that she felt like the member of the band; they were like a part of their family. They frequently go to Chicago concerts together and she gave me "before" and "after" pictures of her weight loss as she posed with the group.

The second question was a lot more personal.

My true area of expertise is not my new passion of weight loss, but how injured people, lottery winners and those who suddenly get a large sum of money deal with life and financial changes.

The biggest problem is always family and friends. Especially newfound "friends."

It's amazing how people are drawn to success. When someone becomes rich or famous, it changes the way others look at them and deal with them. It's the primary reason that I recommend that lottery winners or anyone who receives money keep that information to themselves.

It's hard to say no to people who act like they are admiring you, especially if that person is a potential romantic connection.

My daughter Angela Luhys developed a concept for people going through a wealth transition called the "trailer park test."[7]

Would that person be interested in you if you lived in a trailer park instead of having money? Or it can work the opposite way: Would a new romance be as romantic to you if the person lived in a trailer park?

A weight loss twist on the "trailer park test" is whether a person would have paid attention to you if you were fat.

The idea is not as relevant to a married middle age man. Losing weight will help me stay around longer and develop healthy behaviors, but I won't be attracting groupies. For a female college student, who had been overweight since she was eight years old, it is an entirely different world. I had to wonder how Elizabeth was handling the sudden surge of attention.

The answer was very well.

As I suspected, her stunning looks were now bringing a lot of interest from the opposite sex, many of whom had ignored her over the years. The attitude she articulated is that if they were not interested when she was overweight, it was shallow of them to start getting interested now.

Which is the right attitude to have.

Not many people handle success well. About 70 percent of people who get a lump sum of money run through it all in about five years. You constantly read about people, especially in Elizabeth's age category, who become stars one day and train wrecks the next. Too much change in countries brings on revolutions. Too much change in people can bring on divorce, substance abuse and a loss of self.

I came away thinking that the "inner beauty" that President Benson spoke of allowed her to deal with a dramatic change in life and keep her perspective and core values.

"I am a man who will fight for your honor
I'll be the hero you've been dreaming of"
-Chicago original member Peter Cetera (from the theme song to *The Karate Kid*)[8]

The Whitt's are a super close knit, church-centered family. They seem to do everything together and are the type of family that you want to develop for the next generation. It also seems logical that a young woman with the skills to babysit the president of a university's children is going to want to be married and have children of her own someday.

Elizabeth told me that her parents opposed the idea of surgery until she did the research and data to convince them of its benefits. She had the long-term vision that being healthy and active is part of the process that will someday allow her to have the same kind of family life that she currently enjoys.

She understands that her unique achievement serves as a role model for others. Some people want to keep their weight loss surgery a secret. It deprives the rest of society when people who ought to be role models step to the sidelines.

Elizabeth and I are on the same wavelength. We feel it is our duty and mission to let the world know about a tool that can improve health, lifestyle and lifespan.

It took all of my focus and courage to have the surgery at age 55. There is no way I would have undertaken it at age 19. It's not just that she has had such an incredible result; it is that she had the guts and fortitude to go down that road in the first place

She has been my inspiration. And my hero.

Racing In The Streets And Brand New CrossFit Man

Winning in a Race of Life, Death and Renewal

"Tonight, tonight the strip's just right
I wanna blow 'em all out of their seats
Summer's here and the time is right
For goin' racin' in the street"
-Bruce Springsteen[1]

"She told me 'Baby, when you race today
Just take along my love with you
And if you knew how much I loved you
Baby, nothing could go wrong with you'"
-Brian Wilson[2]

"The miracle isn't that I finished. The miracle is that I had the
courage to start."
-John Bingham, running speaker and writer[3]

June 5, 2015 was a big day for me. The Tuttle Tots 3K in Carrollton, Kentucky was the first time I had been in a running race in 26 years, and I came in second in my age division. The McNay Financial team won two first place plaques, including fastest team, and we supported a cause I believe in.

The day before, I had a medical checkup that confirmed that I had lost more than 90 pounds in the past six months.

Without the weight loss, I would have never attempted the race. At my current weight of 285 pounds, I was one of the heavier people running, but at my previous weight of 377, they would have had an ambulance waiting for me at the finish line.

It was a major life victory just to be there. To come back with plaques and a medal were beyond my wildest dreams.

God gave me the ability to overcome adversity and help others do the same.

Both motivations brought me to the Tuttle Tots race.

"Beyond the door
There's peace I'm sure
And I know there'll be no more
Tears in heaven"
-Eric Clapton[4]

"Carroll County's pointed out as kinda square
The biggest thing that happens is the county fair
I guess that's why it seems like such a big event
What we all call the Carroll County accident"
-Porter Wagoner[5]

Caroline Tuttle was three years old when she (along with another three-year-old) was killed in a school bus crash in Carroll County, Kentucky in 2012. Several other children were injured.

Caroline's parents, Stacy and Chris Tuttle, are friends of mine and I stay in touch on Facebook. Losing a three-year-old is something you never completely come back from. When you see psychological lists that try to quantify stress, the loss of a child is usually at the top of the list. Two psychiatrists, Thomas Holmes and Richard Rahe, developed the Social Readjustment Rating Scale, which is better known as the Holmes and Rahe Stress Scale.[6] It attempted to rank stressful events and how those changes would impact your mental and physical health.

I've hit a number of things on the top of the Holmes and Rahe scale.

My sister, father and mother died at young ages. I've been through divorce, illness, the death of a close friend and many other top stressors. None of those compare to what the Tuttle family went through. They are terrific people and I am not sure how they have stayed so strong. They could have turned bitter and coldhearted after such a terrible loss. Instead, they used Caroline's death as a way to make a positive impact in their community.

The Tuttle Tots race honors the memory of Caroline and the money goes to the Tuttle Tots Educational Scholarship Fund, which awards scholarships to early childhood development teachers who live in Carroll, Gallatin and Trimble Counties in Kentucky.

Running in a race had not been on my wish list. Even after losing 90 pounds. But when Stacy Tuttle sent me a Facebook invite for the Tuttle Tots race, I immediately knew I had to be there.

I had to overcome a lot of internal roadblocks. When I ran in my last race in 1989, it was the only year in my adult life that I weighed less than 200 pounds. Could I make this race at 285 pounds? I organized a team and we needed a 4:30 a.m. wake up call to get to Carrollton for the race. Would someone oversleep? Everybody was in my parking lot 30 minutes early. We were one of the first groups to arrive.

I started the race way too fast and hit a virtual wall in the middle of the race. I wore the wrong shoes and definitely the wrong socks. I could feel large and painful blisters forming on my feet and I realized that my primary goal had to be to finish. But I still remembered I was in a race. I pushed to get my best time and gave it all that I had.

When it was all over, my team took home two first place plaques and one of my teammates was the overall winner. This 56-year-old came in second in his age group and won his first medal in more than 30 years. I could have done cartwheels for the 100 miles home.

We stopped at a truck stop for lunch and I did not take my race number off my shirt or my winner's medal from around my neck. A lot of big tough truckers looked at me strangely. I figured that even if I could not take them in a fight, I could outrun them all. With my severely blistered feet, running anywhere might have been a struggle, but we had an excellent lunch without any violent incidents.

It was a day of true joy. I helped bring attention (and the largest team) to a cause I believe in. I broke through my negative barriers about running and can't wait to enter the next race.

And when we come back to defend our Tuttle Tots championship next year, I am confident that I will not be the heaviest person there. The gastric sleeve surgery gave me the opportunity to change all of my habits and lose 90 pounds in six months. I won't be surprised if I am another 90 pounds lighter by this time next year.

The surgery gave me life. And the chance to honor the life of a young girl who died three years after her life started.

Life, death and renewal seemed to tie together as I ran through that park in Carroll County, Kentucky.

> *"I'll find a place to rest my spirit if I can*
> *Perhaps I may become a highwayman again*
> *Or I may simply be a single drop of rain*
> *But I will remain*
> *And I'll be back again and again and again..."*
> -Jimmy Webb[7]

> *"I've been a puppet, a pauper, a pirate, a poet, a pawn and a king*
> *I've been up and down and over and out and I know one thing*
> *Each time I find myself flat on my face*
> *I pick myself up and get back in the race"*
> -Frank Sinatra[8]

I went to the Tuttle Tots race with the purpose of supporting a good cause and showing myself that I could run in a race and finish it.

Coming home with the awards was a bonus. It told me my plans for a healthy life are working. And that my philosophies on how to live life are solid, too.

I came to the race to honor the life of a little girl who died too young. I came away with a sense of gratitude. And that I have been granted a second chance to do things right.

My First 5K in 27 Years, After Losing 100 Pounds

"Over hill, over dale, thorough bush, thorough brier, over park, over pale, thorough flood, thorough fire, I do wander everywhere."
-William Shakespeare, *A Midsummer Night's Dream*[9]

The August 2015 Midsummer Night's Run in downtown Lexington was the second 5K in my lifetime, and the first was the Midsummer Night's Run in 1989. That was the last year that I weighed less than 200 pounds. My teammate and editor Adam Turner politely pointed out that he was not born in 1989.

Ok, so it's been awhile. I was excited to be in the race.

I had forgotten about the excitement of "race day" until I wrote a story about my friend Sheila Hiestand, who went from weighing more than 300 pounds to competing in Ironman races. Something about her enthusiasm caught on with me. Like a baseball fan going to fantasy camp. I got to act like a big-time runner and be in a competitive situation.

As it turns out, there were roughly 3,800 people in the 2015 race, and I came in absolutely dead last. Like the police were closing down the street behind me. But with blisters on both feet and at an incredibly slow pace, I finished. The picture of me crossing the finish line is one of sheer ecstasy. One of the great nights of my life. Roughly 1,200 Facebook friends liked the picture of me crossing the line, and they also gave me tips on purchasing better socks, better shoes and creams and lotions that prevent blisters. Several running groups and Ironman gatherings invited me to participate. I get nonstop invitations to compete in other races.

All the insights came in handy a month later. I ran in a 3K race at Lexington's Christ the King Elementary, where my wife had been principal when we were first married. I did not come in last, I did not have any blisters on my feet and I don't see myself lining up for the next Olympics, but I don't really care. Each time I get out on the race course, it's another reminder of how far I have come.

Even if I am travelling at a very slow pace.

Brand New CrossFit Man

"We choose to go to the moon in this decade and do the other things, not because they are easy, but because they are hard, because that goal will serve to organize and measure the best of our energies and skills, because that challenge is one that we are willing to accept, one we are unwilling to postpone, and one which we intend to win."
- President John F. Kennedy[10]

"I wonder if you know
I wonder if you think about it
Once upon a time
In your wildest dreams"
-Moody Blues[11]

" 'You have plenty of courage, I am sure,' answered Oz. 'All you need is confidence in yourself. There is no living thing that is not afraid when it faces danger. The true courage is in facing danger when you are afraid.' "
-L. Frank Baum, *The Wonderful Wizard of Oz*[12]

When I finished an intense program and "tested out" of the Maximus CrossFit Academy on Oct. 29, 2015, it was the highlight of a fitness journey that has left me 111.2 pounds lighter in less than a year and a Brand New Man in every sense of the word.

In "testing out," I proved I could perform all the exercises, weight lifting procedures and fitness skills necessary to participate in CrossFit. For the first time in my life, I could jump rope. For the first time in my adult life, I could do things like push-ups, sit-ups and an occasional pull up or two.

One year earlier, I had been morbidly obese and had difficulty tying my own shoes. CrossFit has been the trigger that finally made me recognize, like Dorothy in the *Wizard of Oz*, what I was looking for was in my own back yard.

I grew up with the spirit of President John F. Kennedy. I was born slightly before he was elected president and don't really remember his assassination. Many things that happened immediately afterwards, like the space program and the Beatles coming to America, are some of my most vivid and favorite childhood memories. Kennedy was the ultimate goal setter. He gave us the challenge of doing something impossible, like going to the moon, and set a timeline to do it by the end of the decade.

I wrote about President Kennedy in my book *Wealth Without Wall Street* and how the country had changed by 2008.[13] The concept of asking people to sacrifice and embrace hard work had long fallen out of favor with our business and political leadership. We would have avoided the 2008 economic crisis and government bailouts if Washington had operated in the spirit of Kennedy instead of the spirit of pandering to special interests. Washington lacked courage. Wall Street lacked courage.

I lost 100 pounds in seven months, but my focus and intensity were starting to slow down. I was starting to lack the courage to make sure that my weight loss and fitness journey stayed at a high level. When I stumbled onto CrossFit, the spirit and energy inspired by President John F. Kennedy came back to me.

My Journey to the CrossFit "Box"

"There's something to be said about this man's enthusiasm and willingness to live outside his comfort zone. The reason I love my job

*is men (or women) like Mr. Don. It's a beautiful thing to see
someone do something they've never done, and even more so when
they have a relentless spirit like this man does. It's been a pleasure
to be a part of your journey, Mr. Don. You are truly an inspiration to
us all."*
-Dex Hopkins, Coach at CrossFit Maximus, Lexington, Kentucky

*"I had the honor and privilege of being able to help Don McNay
achieve his first jump rope EVER last night in Academy. It's people
like him and moments like these that remind me of why I absolutely
love what I do. He is such a positive man and his smile is
contagious. You inspire all of us, Don! Blessed to share this journey
with you!"*
-Erica Spitz, Coach at CrossFit Maximus, Lexington, Kentucky

*"The most important thing in the Olympic games is not to win but to
take part, just as the most important thing in life is not the triumph
but the struggle."*
-The Olympic Creed[14]

I should have been a one hit wonder in CrossFit. I made it to the first
session for four reasons:

1) Friends, like David Helmers and Dr. Derek Weiss, were members
and encouraged me to try it.
2) The box is only three blocks from where I live.
3) My daughter found a Groupon where I could try the Academy at a
low price.
4) I had met with manager Kathy Childress and coach Dex Hopkins
the week before. They assured me that I would not die during the
first session.

I needed the spirit of John F. Kennedy to get me to walk into the box
(CrossFit has its own language and gyms are called "boxes"). I
arrived 15 minutes early and the intimidation factor was
overwhelming. There was a gymnastics class finishing up and the
instructor, Erica Spitz, was flying across the bars like a 21st century
version of Mary Lou Retton. There were men and women lifting

heavy barbells and dropping them on the floor like they do in the Olympics.

I saw my Academy classmates gathering and none of them were in my age bracket. Half my age was more like it. No one else in the box had been born when John Kennedy was alive. Only a few of them were born before Bill Clinton. I was the oldest and heaviest member of my Academy class, and there was not a close second. I had seen those kinds of gym dynamics before and usually a form of Darwinism occurs. The young and stronger run off the older and weaker.

Not in CrossFit.

CrossFit operates with a concept called scaling. It turns out that Erica, the woman doing the Mary Lou Retton imitation, was our Academy instructor and recognized immediately that I was not going to be able to do the traditional pull-ups part of the program. She moved me over to rings, like those you see in gymnastics, and taught me a technique to do pull-ups using those. I did pretty well using that technique. Then we went through a series of weight lifting and exercise programs, many that I had done in high school football and track. It had been 38 years since the last time I tried them, but I had a degree of familiarity that led to a degree of confidence. Enough confidence to survive the hour-long session.

When the class ended, Dex Hopkins was waiting for me. Everyone told me that I would like the former Delta State University football star and everyone was right. With his long hair and beard, Dex looks like Jesus if Jesus was tall, tattooed and had zero percent body fat. Both he and Erica were part of a team from CrossFit Maximus that came in seventh in the world in the 2014 CrossFit games. Dex and his wife Marilyn, a surgeon, competed as individuals in the CrossFit games before moving from Richland, Mississippi to Kentucky.

Although Dex was a tight end at Delta State, I knew he had been a quarterback in high school. He is incredibly smart and insightful, but keeps it slightly muted behind an outgoing, country boy persona. He is a world class motivator. He understands how to get the highest level of effort out of the people around him and the highest level of effort out of me in particular. It's a rare leadership trait that produces true championships.

Dex talked to me for more than an hour. He told me that he had been watching closely and that I could move very well for a man of my size. He focused on the positives and made me enthusiastic to take my aching body back for the next class, when he would be teaching the Academy.

When I came in the next day, co-owner Lincoln Brown was waiting for me. Lincoln, a Wharton School graduate, is a successful "serial entrepreneur" who comes to entrepreneurship naturally. His father, John Y. Brown, Jr., was a former Kentucky Governor, and a founder of Kentucky Fried Chicken. His mother is the groundbreaking sports journalist Phyllis George. It was the first time Lincoln and I had met, but we had a mutual friend in Dr. Jim Roach, and I am a friend of Lincoln's half brother, former Kentucky Secretary of State John Y. Brown III. Lincoln and I talked about how he got interested in CrossFit personally and from a business standpoint. I had noticed the quality and education status of everyone working at the box. Most of the coaches had degrees in fields like kinesiology and weightlifting guru Ben Welter was an engineering major. All of the coaches are role models of fitness and had the same kind of enthusiasm that Dex and Erica exhibited. Lincoln articulated how he attracted such a high-powered group and how well they worked as a team.

Then my love affair with CrossFit began.

A couple of things started to happen. One is that I went on a reading binge. I'll never write an extensive book solely on CrossFit as it would be impossible to outdo books like *Learning to Breathe Fire* by J.C. Herz[15] and *Inside the Box* by T.J. Murphy.[16] I liked *Embrace the Suck* by Stephen Madden as I connected with the author's personal journey.[17] I read every article I could find about CrossFit founder Greg Glassman and discovered that almost anything you wanted to know about CrossFit could be found at CrossFit.com.[18]

I understood why CrossFit worked so well for me. As opposed to a large corporately owned gym, the focus in CrossFit is not on equipment, a fancy building or cramming in new memberships. The focus is on "back to the basics" exercise and training in the most Spartan of settings. The routines change daily, and they focus on pushing a person to their maximum potential. The workout of the day (WOD in CrossFit world) is so intense and fast paced that it is impossible for your mind to drift. I burn about 1,200 calories in an hour. The coaches are there to coach and instruct and they teach in a small group, participatory setting. They teach the correct way to lift weights and do exercises to increase success, but also to make sure we don't hurt ourselves. The concept caught on early in the military and law enforcement communities, but I also see why it seems so perfect for a driven, anti-authority, low boredom entrepreneur like myself. It's a place where improvement is constantly measured and attainable no matter what your fitness condition was when you started. Most importantly, there is a true sense of teamwork and community.

One of the great moments was when Erica Spitz (whose husband Nathan Spitz is also a coach and manager) taught me how to jump rope for the very first time in my life. Fit or unfit, I had never been able to do it. Erica was not going to give up until I did. We did it in stages. She had me jump up and down in place. Then she had me move my hands without a rope. Then she had me jump without a rope, but still moving my hands. Then we put a rope in hands. After a few tries, I had it. Each time I get a little bit better as confidence was built on achievement. Erica kept pushing until we got the proper result.

The community became important to me. Very quickly, I started bonding with the people in the box, both inside the gym and through social media. In the Academy setting, my younger and fitter classmates started rooting for me and my relentless work ethic started inspiring them. CrossFit is not a world where you advance by beating the other person. You inspire the rest of the people in your group to keep pushing forward and to keep pushing you forward. A true sense of teamwork really connects with people like myself who grew up on team sports. Fitness has been a lonely journey in my adult life. Now I felt like part of a group. You don't see people on treadmills with headsets at a CrossFit gym. You see people interacting and bonding. It's the first time in my adult life where I walked in a gymnasium and felt like I belonged there.

From the outside, especially if you only know about CrossFit from the ESPN CrossFit games where some of the fittest athletes in the world compete, you would think of CrossFit as a world where only people with perfect fitness need apply. The true, untapped market for CrossFit is middle aged, recovering fat people like me. Putting us in an environment where we can feel like competitive athletes and inspire others is the best way to make everyone better, physically and mentally.

Where I Have Been and Where I Am Going

"I think that he's achieved a success far beyond riches and fame. Look around you. There is not a life in this room that you have not touched, and each of us is a better person because of you. We are your symphony, Mr. Holland. We are the melodies and the notes of your opus. We are the music of your life."
-Mr. Holland's Opus[19]

*"Baby you look at me and tell me what you see
You ain't seen the best of me yet"*
-Irene Cara (from the Oscar-winning song "Fame")[20]

Thanks to my CrossFit participation, at age 56, I get to be a rock star in an athletic setting surrounded by some of the fittest and most motivated people I have ever met. All I have to do is keep showing up and let them watch me go at CrossFit with complete abandon. I have a new set of friends and admirers.

A year ago I made a lot of major life decisions, like weight loss surgery and changing my eating habits, with the simple goal of staying alive to a normal life expectancy. Now, 111 pounds later, I realize that just staying alive is a pretty weak ambition. I want to achieve excellence in whatever I do, and CrossFit is a terrific outlet for allowing me to achieve it with my health. The goal is no longer just to live and grow old, but to operate at peak efficiency and make the most out of life. My role model, the greatest living Kentuckian Al Smith, is going strong at age 88. He has been sober for 52 years, but he once told me that his devotion to public service and being active stems from making up for the early years when he was drunk. I want to get back the decades when I was morbidly obese by getting into peak shape at a time when others are dialing it back.

As I get healthier, good things have happened. Business has improved as my mind is sharper and stamina is longer. Everyone in my world comments on how happy I am and when you feel good, it makes everyone around you feel good. Life is at its high-water mark, and I have the wisdom of experience to appreciate how lucky I am.

I did not realize the impact that fitness and exercise would have on my inner psyche. I've always been situationally fearless. I've been willing to take risks in certain areas of life, like starting new businesses or asking an accomplished woman to marry me, but held back in other areas, especially related to my health.

Starting with the weight loss, then with competing in 3K and 5K races, and now with CrossFit, I keep knocking down the barriers against fear. I was afraid of surgery and then surgery helped to save my life. I was afraid to run foot races and I finished them all, even when my feet were blistered and swollen. CrossFit has forced me to push and keep pushing myself on the exercise front, in front of other people who are universally supportive.

There is a reward in making a full, all out, focused effort. The reward is in waging the battle, not necessarily in winning the war. I'm going all out to improve my health and to inspire, encourage and motivate those around me to do the same. It's a challenging, worthwhile and achievable goal. The kind of goal President Kennedy would be proud of.

MY WEIGHT OVER THE YEARS

1) 1983 - Don and former Kentucky Governor Steve Beshear

2) 1989 - Serving as best man in Lee Gentry's wedding on a day when Don's weight was the lowest in his adult life: 179 pounds

3) 1993 - Don and President Bill Clinton when Clinton met with several Kentucky business leaders in Lexington

4) 2009 - Don, Nancy and Dr. Phil Hoffman at Don's 50th birthday party

5) 2009 - Don and Mike Behler, Don's 50th birthday

6) 2009 - Don, Laura and Bob Babbage, Don's 50th birthday

7) 2010 - Don and Arianna Huffington in Louisville, Ky.

8) 2011 - McNay Settlement Group: Don, Gena Bigler, Angela Luhys and Clay Bigler (Richmond, Ky.)

9) 2011 - *Wealth Without Wall Street* kickoff: Nick McNay, Angela Luhys, Don, Adelaide Bigler, Abijah Luhys, Clay Bigler

10) 2012 – McNay Wedding Party

11) 2012 - Don anchoring election night radio coverage for the Wallingford Broadcasting network

12) 2012 - Don and his grandson Liam Bigler

13) 2013 – Don, Karen and Anthony Davis in New Orleans Pelican's locker room

14) 2013 - Don with Pete Rose and the Music Professor Jim LaBarbara, who is a member of the Broadcasting Hall of Fame

15) 2013 - Don doing a studio interview for the *CBS Morning News* with anchor Rebecca Jarvis

Important Players

My Medical Dream Team:
Dr. Phillip Hoffman, Dr. Derek Weiss, Cindy Jester Caywood and Dr. Jim Roach

My Weight Loss Heroines:
Sheila Hiestand, Lori Sobkowski-Rodriguez and Elizabeth Whitt (before and after)

My Family:
Karen Thomas McNay, Clay Bigler, Gena Bigler and Angela Luhys

Don with some of the greatest journalists in Kentucky history:
Ken Kurtz, Ed Staats and Al Smith at the Capitol in Frankfort

Through the magic of Facebook, Don connected with his younger
brother Joey, whom he had not seen in 25 years

The Don McNay Reality Show

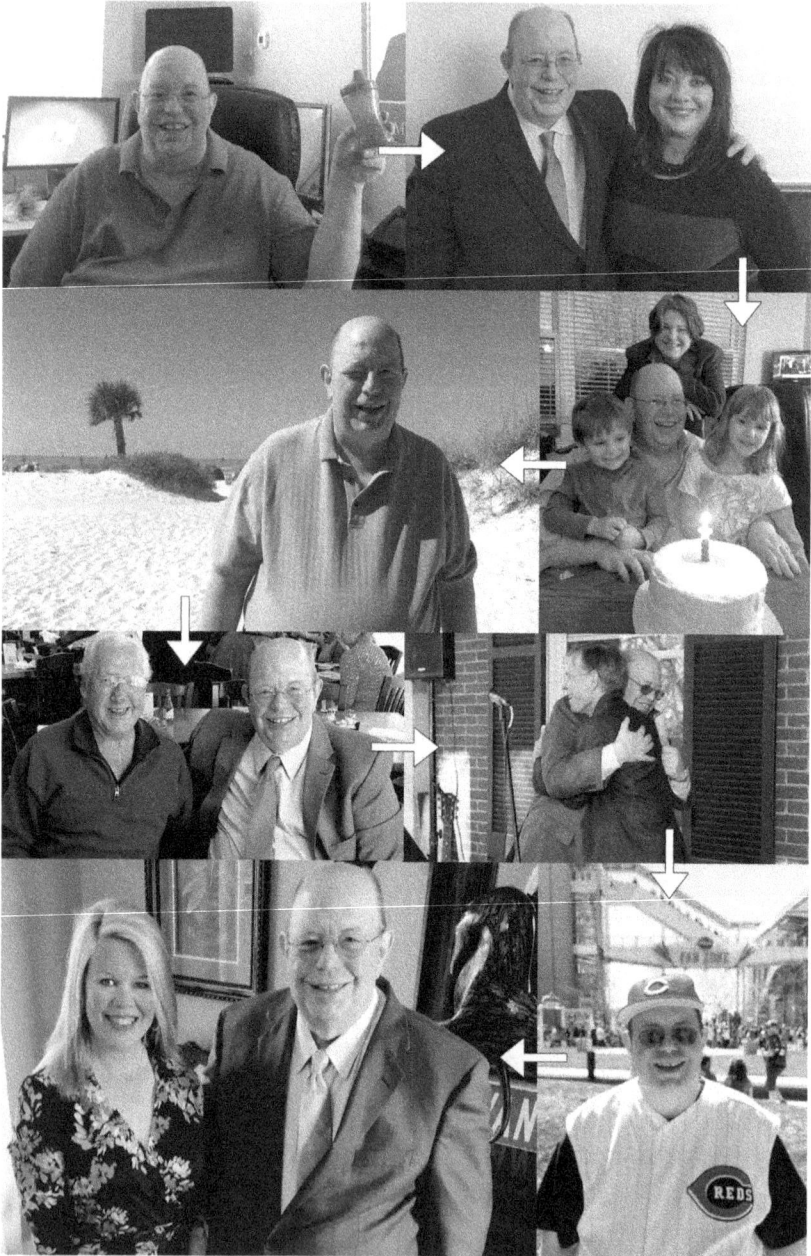

December 2014: Don with his "self-regulating intake device" right after surgery

January 2015: Don's first post-surgery event was the swearing in for Kentucky Court of Appeals Judge Debra Lambert in Somerset, Kentucky. RRP International did the web site and social media for her winning campaign.
(Photo by Adam Turner)

February 2015: The three grandchildren, Liam Bigler, Abijah Luhys and Adelaide Bigler at grandpa's birthday number 56
(Photo by Gena Bigler)

February 2015: Don on the beach in Clearwater, Florida
(Photo by Karen McNay)

March 2015: Lunch at Mandina's in New Orleans with Moon Landrieu, former HUD Secretary and cabinet member for President Jimmy Carter and former Mayor of New Orleans. The lunch became the focus of a highly acclaimed feature that Don did for the *Huffington Post*.

April 2015: Don introducing Dr. Jim Roach and his best-selling book, *God's House Calls*, at Holly Hill Inn in Midway, Ky.
(Photo by Adam Turner)

April 2015: Don at the Cincinnati Reds game, waiting to be called onto the field
(Photo by Adam Turner)

April 2015: Don with Lexington attorney Karen Walker, as they co-author an article on Financial Wellness for Attorneys for the *Kentucky Bench and Bar Magazine*

Settlement Group, I

rvices   uct
          Settlements   curity
          Administration   Future Ind
                                    Inc

| | Jul-14 | Jul-16 | Jul-18 | Jul-20 | 27 |

RECORD TODAY'S WEIGHT

STATUS

277.4lbs   **100.3**   0

Current weight   pounds lost   Days to goal

3974

A MIDSUMMER
NIGHT'S RUN

May 2015: Don golfing with his daughter Gena Bigler on her birthday
(Photo by Clay Bigler)

May 2015: Don with former American Trial Lawyers Association President Peter Perlman and Lana Perlman at the dinner inducting Pete into the University of Kentucky Hall of Distinguished Alumni
(Photo by E. Andre Busald)

June 2015: Don with Lexington Mayor Jim Gray, as both were out exercising on a hot summer day

June 2015: Don at the Kentucky Bar Association with the McNay Settlement Group summer intern, University of Kentucky law student Evan Sloan. Evan's father Craig Sloan was the person who started Don in radio at WKQQ-FM in 1983 before Craig went on to graduate from the University of Kentucky law school himself.
(Photo by Angela Luhys)

June 2015: Clay Bigler, Don and Adam Turner at Tuttle Tots
(Photo by Stacy Tuttle)

July 2015: Don taking in the Chicago White Sox versus the ultimate world champions Kansas City Royals with Chicago's great structured settlement guru Larry Niemi
(Photo by Karen McNay)

July 2015: Hitting the 100-pound weight loss goal

July 2015: Retirement dinner for Don's college friend, highly acclaimed federal prosecutor David Grise, with Lee Gentry, David and Don.
(Photo by Owen Grise)

August 2015: Don preparing for A Midsummer Night's Run 5K

August 2015: Don in New Orleans on the 10th anniversary of Hurricane Katrina with Gary Rivlin, author of *Katrina: After the Flood*, which was honored as one of the 100 most notable books of 2015 by the *New York Times*
(Photo by Karen McNay)

September 2015: Crossing the finish line at the Christ the King 3k
(Photo by Adam Turner)

September 2015: Don with Lexington bank president Whitney Greer Sisson, who finished slightly ahead of Don in the Christ the King 3K
(Photo by Adam Turner)

October 2015: Don at EKU's Homecoming with Karen McNay and President Michael Benson

October 2015: Don graduates CrossFit with coaches Erica Spitz and Dex Hopkins
(Photo by John Sam Steele)

November 2015: A new, thinner professional headshot
(Photo by Carroll Crouch)

November 2015: GE Executive Deborah Elam receiving Outstanding Alumnus award at Ursuline Academy in New Orleans, with Don, Karen Thomas McNay and Cary Grant

November 2015: Don and Karen McNay celebrating Thanksgiving at Thomas Dairy Farm (Karen's mom and dad) in Cecilia, Ky.
(Photo by Byrle Thomas)

December 2015: Don pumping iron at Maximus CrossFit in Lexington, Ky.
(Photo by Jordan Baker)

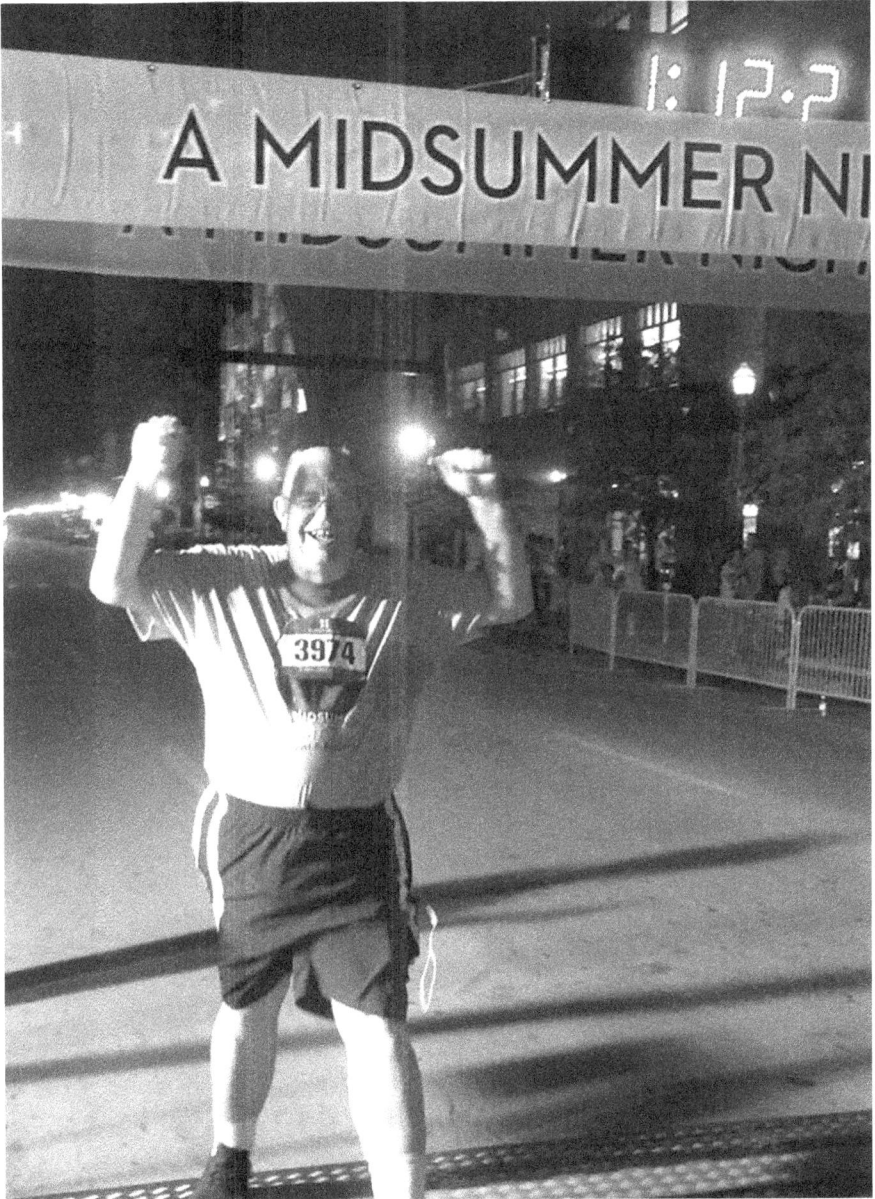
Crossing the finish line at A Midsummer Night's Run 5k
(Photo by Adam Turner)

THE DON MCNAY

REALITY SHOW

(Photos by Steve Bates, Carroll Crouch)

The Don McNay Reality Show is a detailed, day-by-day account of my weight loss surgery and the months that followed it.

THE FIRST MONTH

November 30, 2014

The night before surgery, I posted this on Facebook:

I am touched and greatly appreciative of the outpouring of prayers and support as I go to surgery tomorrow. One of my greatest blessings is my ability to connect with wonderful people. In a world where there are billions of people worse off than me, I wonder if God is tired of hearing about me, but I truly appreciate it.

I'm headed to bed shortly as my 4 a.m. wake up will be one I can't miss, but I have reached a point of Zen-like calm. Several of the attorneys I work with have noticed how my personality changes when the game is on the line. The bigger the stakes, the calmer I get. I don't get nervous on a $100 million settlement, but I might on a $100,000 one. I don't get nervous appearing on national television; I might on a small town interview.

When the stakes are high, I have the ability to take it to another level, and it's giving me serenity at this moment.

I've done everything possible to allow for a good outcome and have contingency plans for every possible bump along the road. This will go smoothly.

Thank you again.

December 1, 2014

The day of surgery I posted this on Facebook:

Up before my 4 a.m. alarm went off. Excited as a child on

Christmas and ready to get this party started.

Later that day I posted:

Sore and very sleepy, but surgery was excellent. Won't be online much today, but feeling fine. Thank you for prayers and concern.

I sent this out to some of my close friends as a summation of the actual surgery:

Most of my friends follow me on Facebook, but famous Kentucky publisher Al Smith told me Tuesday he did not want my medical information filtered by Mark Zuckerberg.

Thus, I am sending this to my dearest friends who want more than a Facebook-style report.

Things have gone incredibly well. Beyond my wildest dreams. It's hard to believe I had major surgery three days ago.

Dr. Derek Weiss had me in for surgery at 8 a.m. and I was out by Tuesday afternoon. My daughter Angela Luhys took charge of being my patient advocate in a style that you would fully expect from her, and my other daughter Gena Bigler, in similar style, took the afternoon shift. My son-in-law Clay Bigler came on Tuesday to find there was little to do, as I was intent on proving that I was well and ready to check out.

I took the Dec. 1 for surgery day knowing that my wife Karen had an important meeting in Washington, and Dr. Derek Weiss insisted that she keep her trip. He predicted I could call her that afternoon and tell her I was doing fine. He was totally correct. If not, Karen would have killed him and come back to kill what was left of me. Now she wants to hug him. She has an excellent chance that her husband will live to an old age.

The nursing staff at Georgetown Hospital was first-rate, and I highly recommend them. They have the bariatric unit attached to ICU, but it's an ICU with large private rooms so I got a ton of attention and the nurses were never more than 30 seconds away. It was quiet when I wanted it quiet, and people were there when I needed them. The exact opposite of my experience in a "big city" Lexington hospital where I called for hours and could not get anyone to help me.

The nurses reminded me of my late mother and her friends that worked in the operating room. They were older and had tons of life experience to go with their years of nursing experience. Most, like my mom, went into nursing as a second career. The director at the Georgetown Hospital came to visit and gave me permission to write about them if I wish. Since she knows it will be a total puff piece, I don't blame her.

My regular physician, Dr. Phil Hoffman, and my other regular physician, Dr. Jim Roach in Midway, called or emailed every day, and they talked to Derek on a regular basis. I am "doctored up" pretty well, and Phil and Jim are important players in how I am revamping my life from here on out.

I am an anti-authority guy, but this is a case where I follow exactly what Derek tells me to do. I trust him and his decisions. I walk multiple times a day (usually up and back the halls of my condo) and do a number of breathing exercises each day. He has me wearing calf massagers to avoid possible blood clots, and I keep them on often and sleep with them. My children know that I don't like a lot of company when I am recovering, but they all check in and are only five minutes away. I've wound up doing some work from home, but starting to realize that could be counterproductive and will stay off work again for the immediate future. Hard for me to shut it down, but I am finding that the quiet and solitude helps me recover more quickly. Also, the office seems to be running better without me.

I have been able to drink protein shakes and clear fluids since day one, but it takes me four hours to drink an 11 oz. protein shake so I only get three a day in. That gives me 105 grams of protein and about 550 calories.

The late famous Louisville attorney Frank Haddad once told me how he had two surgeries. The first time he had a slow recovery, and the second time he trained like a heavyweight boxer and recovery was quick. I followed his lead. Dr. Weiss told me that surgeons worry about an enlarged liver, but mine was absolutely tiny and made the surgery go easier.

I weighed 377 on Aug. 28 when I committed to the program. I got to 355 on the day of surgery. I weigh 346 four days later and should lose about 20 a month for the next several months.

I've taken about a billion tests before and after the surgery, and all look good. I test my blood pressure, temperature and blood sugar multiple times a day at home. All have been excellent. I dropped one of my blood sugar medicines before going into surgery, but blood sugar continues to drop and remains in the normal range. Hoping to drop the other medicine when we follow up on Dec. 10 and eventually get rid of the blood pressure meds or at least start cutting them back. I am taking Lortab for pain, but I keep cutting back the dosage and hope to be off of those by next week. I can't drive until I get off the pain meds, and I really don't want to push it and do something like get pneumonia. I've only had one other surgery in my adult life, and the pain level is about 1000 percent better this time around.

One side effect is that the combination of pain medicine and decrease in water makes me cottonmouthed after about 10 minutes of conversation. My conversations are a lot shorter these days. That will slow up as I drop the medicines. I'm dying to get back on the phone, but I have limited it to family in the near run.

I put a number of organizational structures into my personal and business lives to make this possible, so a lot of what is happening now is going on "autopilot." I had anticipated most of the potential adjusting to life without 80 percent of my stomach. Since I have been so public about this, a lot of people offer "advice," but most are based on experiences with the gastric bypass or the lap band, not the gastric sleeve, which has only been used in the United States for the past five years or so. Few people know about those, and I hope it works as well for others as it has for me. I've read every book on the market about the sleeve. If I continue as I have, I may offer to star in advertisements for them.

Paying for this myself has made me a very conscious health care consumer. It cost $8,500 for the hospital, and the doctor was $5,500. There are people flying to Mexico and other countries to have weight loss surgery who pay more than that. The BLIS insurance was a little more than $1,600.

I suspect that someone with health insurance coverage would pay substantially higher, but I worked with everyone on discounts and was really diligent with my money. I would ask the cost of every test and procedure and why the test was necessary. One was quoted at $5,000 and after I said it was too much, they gave it to me for free.

I never paid attention to the cost of health care services when it was on someone else's dime, but this has been a good lesson overall.

I had put the money away for the surgery, but wound up using my American Express card to pay for it all and now I'm paying it off. The points will allow me to be a Medallion flyer on Delta for another year. I've needed to fly in a first-class seat for the past few years as I did not fit in coach. I look forward to the day when I can comfortably fly in coach without a seat belt extender, but nice to know that I will normally still be in first-class anyway.

A note on why I now am carrying a sippy cup. One thing I have run into is I have to learn how to sip all fluids, like drinking fine Kentucky bourbon, instead of my lifetime habit of gulping it down. I fell into the old habit and found buying some sippy cups, like the ones my grandchildren have used, does the trick. I am going to patent my own model of sippy cup as a medical device. We took a picture earlier today with my new "invention."

I won't be back to working full time before the New Year, but will be easy to find in about a week.

December 2, 2014

I feel good.

They did my heart echo bedside and it went well. I've been walking, and the nurses have been great. I've been off pain meds and everyone comments on how good I look.

Also, I'm eating Jello.

I've been eating and drinking like a race horse, walking the halls and had leg massagers running all day.

I got home from the hospital about 8 p.m. It went incredibly well. All of training and weight loss prior to surgery paid off, and I got through in record time. Still incredibly sore and recovering, but I am doing it at home on minimal pain medicines. I have a difficult time talking as the medicines have dried me out, but great otherwise.

December 3, 2014
3 p.m.

Weight: 354
Blood Sugar: 136
Blood Pressure: 147/100
Temp.: 97.1

It's been a good day. Stayed up since 8:30 a.m. Tested my vital signs at 2 p.m. and all were good. BP is slightly high and I am buying a more professional BP cuff as I am not sure how accurate this one is. 147/92 is my latest reading and that is pretty normal for me, but I was getting better numbers more recently. My body temp was 97.1.

The new BP cuff should be delivered tomorrow. Blood sugar continues to be in the normal range even though I dropped the Metformin and kept the Januvia. Dr. Weiss said it would be a couple of weeks before my blood sugar stayed normal with no medicine, but

I see that day coming.

Took my second Lortab at 2 p.m. Pain has been dramatically better. The goal is to be off the pain medicine by the 10th and I think that will be right on schedule. Left shoulder hurts a little, but not bad. Stomach only hurts when I get up and down. Starting to get diarrhea, which was expected.

Walking on schedule. Not far but frequent. Going to hook the leg massagers up for me to sleep with them on tonight.

They told us to remove the small pump that was sending antacid to my stomach at noon, and my daughter Angela was right on time to help me remove it. It came out without difficultly. That also allowed me to have my first shower of the week, which dramatically improved my inner peace.

On my second protein shake of the day as it takes me a few hours to drink one. Also, I am learning that I like them slightly warm as opposed to ice cold.

Cottonmouth is not as bad as yesterday, mainly because I have not been talking much. My editor dropped off some packages for me and Angela came over briefly, but I've stayed off the phone. That is probably going to remain an issue until I stop the pain medicines.

Glad I made this move. Continuing to move forward.

December 4, 2014
7:30 a.m.

Weight: 349.2
Blood Sugar: 135
Blood Pressure: 164/98
Temp.: 97.4

Asleep at midnight. Woke at 4:45 a.m. with moderate to severe shoulder pain and stayed in bed until 7:10 a.m. (more than seven hours recorded on CPAP). Slept with leg massagers on, which could have contributed to sleeping discomfort, but slept straight through without waking or bathroom run, so they're probably not the problem. Using them again tonight.

7:45 a.m.

Shoulder pain is decreasing as I took pain meds, GasX and I've been up and around some. Just took BP medicines and Adderall. Going to try a different way of sleeping tonight as I may be putting too much pressure on left shoulder, and I may try an afternoon nap. Staying up all day yesterday, doing far more walking than normal and a lot of work on the computer may be too much.

8.30 a.m.

Pain in shoulder is basically gone. Reality is for people who can't handle drugs. Need to drop BP. Suspect it will improve when I get the new BP cuff that I ordered. I will remain diligent about getting more clear fluids as that will help.

I now have my new iPhone set up which has a number of data apps for tracking vital signs, which will be helpful in long run.

As Joe Walsh once said, "I can't complain, but sometimes I still do. Life's been good to me so far."[1]

6 p.m.

Weight: 346.6
Blood Sugar: 137
Blood Pressure: 141/101
Temp.: 97.2

Yes, that has been a three-pound drop in the course of the day. Yes, that is a serious cause for joy on my end.

Dr. Weiss checked in a couple of times via email earlier in the day and asked to be included in these reports that I have been sending to the immediate family. He did not ask me to do the regular readings on my vitals, but I like having the measurements. Like charting an investment fund. In fact, I will chart my weight like a stock when I get a moment. Like I am, he is happy with my progress and happy that I am following his orders, especially about getting up and walking. He put the fear of God (and blood clots into me.) Also, I'm doing the blowing machines. I've been basically in quarantine since I got out of the hospital, but I don't want to do anything that might lead to pneumonia.

I don't like my blood pressure, but it is where it was before I lost the 30 pounds pre-surgery and I suspect it will improve as my weight drops, exercise increases and stress on my body decreases. I'm not supposed to be working, but have been doing so anyway and realized today that was counterproductive. Relaxing and reading this evening and staying off the computer.

Up to three protein shakes today at 35 grams of protein each. I finally got myself around the $3/can cost of the shakes by realizing that it was cheaper than a normal lunch and my other grocery bill is zero this week. Dr. Weiss wants me to get to 200 grams of protein a day as soon as I can get there and shoot for a minimum of at least 100. I made that today and want to do two more shakes to get to 175, and I think that is a worthy goal.

I am fighting cottonmouth, but the combination of pain meds and reduced fluids will cause that. It gets better, but my long conversations are getting a lot shorter.

December 5, 2014
11 a.m.

Weight: 344
Blood Sugar: 112
Blood Pressure: 136/90
Temp.: 97.7

"The stars might lie, but the numbers never do"
- Mary Chapin Carpenter[2]

1. First morning since surgery that I woke up without shoulder pain. In fact, I really don't have any kind of pain. Some discomfort is about it.

2. I have not taken pain meds at this point today. I may take at some point in the day, but not until I think I need them. Want to start weaning off.

3. Only 5.4 hours of sleep. Stayed up too late reading a book about technology companies in Israel (I told Bob Babbage yesterday that only he and I could consider that book "reading for fun," but it's actually a great book) and had an early call this morning. Been sleeping with the telephone next to the bed, but will stop that today as I feel reasonably certain that I don't need it. My sleep patterns are erratic, especially since I have no particular place to go. Shooting for eight hours a night at all costs.

4. Wound up doing more work than I planned on each day this week and going to be relatively disconnected for next few days to stay focused on recovery.

5. I am getting an incredible amount of interest in my book.

6. Dr. Weiss may want me to be his agent. I've had several close friends inquire about the surgery.

7. Dr. Weiss also informed me that my goal was 100 grams of protein a day, not 200. Thank God. I can sip on protein shakes all day and get to 100 grams, but 200 was taking all my effort. I misunderstood his original conversation. Glad he is religiously reading my emails.

8. Going to keep increasing the walking, breathing and exercise. Been a great week, but a blood clot or pneumonia can change that.

9. David Grise seemed amused at the site of me carrying a sippy cup with leg warmers on my legs. I may be starting a new fashion trend.

10. Still fighting the cottonmouth, but it improves. Also, the less hectic lifestyle is appealing to me more than I thought possible.

11. Per my daughter Gena Bigler, it is no longer a sippy cup, but a "self-regulating liquid intake device." I like that.

December 6, 2014
12 p.m.

Weight: 339.6
Blood Sugar: 109
Blood Pressure: 143/84
Temp.: 96.8

A shout out to Dr. Weiss. Since I did the *Huffington* piece, I have a ton of his patients contact me, singing his praises.[3] Been back and forth with Elizabeth Whitt in Richmond, who lost 165 pounds in a year and hit her goal. She told me to tell Derek hi and that he has changed her life.

I only have 10 pounds more than Elizabeth to lose, and I started at a much higher weight. A motivator, that goal is definitely going to happen. I went to college with her father, who was a longtime administrator at EKU. Her dad and I both had lots of hair then. Not anymore.

I've stayed up since my 5 a.m. wake up. Going at a slow pace and thinking that going to the woods like Merton or Emerson is in my future. Deep thoughts are coming from the solitude. Been doing tedious but relaxing things and finally set up my iPhone 6, which runs pretty well. It has some great apps for tracking health info, so I might start going to reports from that soon.

All the organizational structures I implemented before surgery are paying off with a productive, but less stressful lifestyle.

Took a pain med at 5 a.m. and another after I got my shower at 11 a.m. (Shower is not related to pain, but just seemed like a good time to take the meds.) I'm thinking that my reduced amount of sleep may be related to trying to get off the pain meds too quickly and going to take all four today. I've been doing all my other medicines except for Metformin and adding multivitamins in too. Doing my walking, leg warmers and really hitting the breathing machine hard just to change the routine. My biggest fear is getting a cold, flu or pneumonia, and I have gotten like Howard Hughes as I keep myself in a sterile quarantine in the condo. He was afraid of germs, but took it to a little bit of an extreme.

Getting my arms around the idea that I am in recovery, and it takes plenty of time to actually recover, but I feel good and happy with my numbers. I was getting a lot of phone calls yesterday and that started to stress me. Sam Davies wanted to visit, but he understood when I asked him to wait another week or so. We wound up talking via phone.

My cottonmouth comes back if I talk for about 45 minutes (a short conversation for Don), but that is reducing as my sippy cup mastery is keeping me hydrated. Going to read and watch football rest of day.

December 7, 2014
10:30 a.m.

Weight: 336.2
Blood Sugar: 130
Blood Pressure: 141/93
Temp.: 97.8

"I feel good"
-James Brown[4]

Rather than doing three or four reports a day, I am moving to a comprehensive report at wake up and then a shorter follow up later in the day with most of the numbers. No one asked me to do the vitals every four hours (it was Don being Don, going at life with lots of overkill), but I am going to keep testing my vitals at least twice a day and sending them for the very long-term. Numbers have been consistent and good.

I decided on a longer "Sunday Roundup" that gives a complete and total insight into where I am.

Along with planning on living for a long and healthy time, being a role model is a true motivator for doing the surgery. I recognize that doing this correctly is a calling and writing "in the moment" allows me to capture what is going on as it is going on. Like CNN is supposed to do.

Doing a longer report in the morning has become a good exercise for documenting everything, giving me a historical journal to reference and allowing me to focus my thoughts. John F. Kennedy said that "history is the final judge of deeds," and I want to have a complete and total grasp of my personal history when I write about it.[5]

Future reports won't be as long as today's "Sunday roundup" on a daily basis, but getting up and doing a long narrative seems to help. I'll start averaging the numbers by next week or before.

Today's report reminds me of when Laura Babbage started writing about Keen Babbage's daily struggle with cancer on CaringBridge, which we later used as part of their book, *Life Lessons from Cancer*.[6] Having Laura's combination of nursing insights and daily commentary became a "must read" for those of us who care about Keen, but also to a larger audience. I liked how the book came out, too.

I love it when my financial clients give me this kind of detailed insight as it makes it easy to do my job.

Doctors can shake the info out of stats and (increasingly brief) face-to-face visits like I can by looking at tax returns and financial records, but having a story and a narrative makes diagnosis simple. I'm fortunate to have acquired throughout my lifetime a dream team of medical professionals, family and concerned friends, and that is a primary reason I was comfortable having the surgery to begin with.

I have a unique support structure and appreciate it.

1. Current Weight

336.2 weight at wake up

This is the reason I did the surgery, and I'm jumping up and down with joy every time I weigh in.

18.8 pounds lost since surgery on Dec. 1 and 40.8 pounds since Aug. 28.

Average loss of 3.13 pounds A DAY since surgery. I would lose 93.9 a month at the current pace and hit my goal weight of 199 by Jan. 28.

I know it is going to slow, stall or possibly even gain at times long before that happens.

I am psychologically ready for the stalls and the fact that I often get stuck at a number just short of a benchmark, like getting to 301 and staying there for a while. It has caused panic and depression in the past. I understand that weight loss is like the financial markets: You have to stay in the game during the dips and ride it out for the next rise upward.

2. Blood Sugar

130 Blood Sugar (taken before any medicines)

Blood sugar was the secondary reason I did the surgery.

Diabetes had grabbed me and was sucking me into seeing a future of insulin, then insulin pumps, then chopping off limbs, then going blind and in a wheel chair like the famous Kentuckian Ed Pritchard. Then probably an early death like Pritch.

I kept getting a vision in my mind of Pritch whenever I started to doubt the surgery idea. I met him at the end of his life, when he was in bad shape. He died at age 69 so he must have been about 64 when he earned money by representing me on a stop sign violation. He made a terrific impact on the state, but a healthy Pritch who stayed around to age 75 or 77 (normal life expectancy) could have made Kentucky the leader in the nation in education. You don't know what someone is going to contribute in the last portion of their lives if they don't live it.

My AIC averaged to about a 150 blood sugar pre-surgery and had gotten as high as 162 before I went to a very low carb diet as my sugar was all over the place. I had blood spikes and dramatic changes in my mood and temper on a regular basis. Hard for everyone around me. Since surgery, I have been the 21st century version of Perry Como, but fatigue catches me quickly. Let's note: it has only been six days.

I've not had much human interaction post-surgery, but those who have comment on how even my temperament is. Part of it is a more relaxed pace to my schedule, but the consistent blood sugar has to be the primary factor. I'm starting to do some research about diabetes and weight loss surgery and I knew that a lower weight would contribute, but also knew about the concept of "reversing diabetes" after surgery.

There is an internal debate in the bariatric world as to whether the gastric sleeve or bypass is better for eliminating diabetes. I suspect it is like most debates: that the argument is guided by self-interest and their own area of expertise. There is no doubt in my case that the leveling of my blood sugar has been a game changer. I don't know if that changes when I go to actual food, but thrilled about this as much as I am the actual weight loss.

This morning was higher on blood sugar than the past two days, when I had made 112 and 113 in the morning and got to 102 in the daytime, but still in the "normal" zone and dramatically better than pre-surgery. I have not deviated out of the normal zone since I came home at any time of the day, and the numbers don't deviate except in a small range. I may increase my testings and do them on a set basis to get an actual range of deviation.

I dropped Metformin just before the surgery and have not picked it back up. Hard to take and was best for controlling spikes. I have no plans to start that again. I still take Javania every day and suspect I will until I reach a point where my numbers stay below 100 daily on their own. I am sure that will happen long before I get to my goal weight.

3. Blood Pressure

141/93 (average of three readings taken before any medicines)

A little better, but still the vital number that needs to improve. It was better pre-surgery, but went up dramatically in the hospital and slowly inching back down.

My blood pressure was very high the first night post-surgery, and my potassium was very low. I also had some kind of irregular heartbeat (I've never been clear on what happened). A cardiologist was called in. He was very polite, but we did not connect on a personal level, and I did not feel comfortable with his level of expertise.

This is an understatement.

They dropped my Norvasc and replaced it with a Beta Blocker without any insights or conversation with me. You can imagine that did not go over well. I emailed Dr. Phil about the switch, but he suggested, as did Dr. Weiss, that I see Dr. Hal Skinner, Cardiologist in Lexington and get his insights before we go back to Norvasc or something else. Skinner is widely respected and did my stress test in late September, which we needed before the surgery. Dr. Phil and

Derek both say favorable things about Skinner, and our one interaction was good. I don't like Beta Blockers and don't see evidence that they are helping me. I would switch back to Norvasc on my own (I just bought a three-month supply), but will wait until I see Dr. Skinner on the 11th. I see Derek on the 10th, so I am following the playbook that Derek laid out until then.

The cardiologist did an echocardiogram on me, which is the fourth I have done in my life and did one (for $250) at Phil's urging at Lexington Diagnostic Center in 2013. When the tech said that the cost was roughly $5,000, I refused to allow it as I paid for the treatment myself. They brought the insurance coordinator from Georgetown Hospital to meet with us, and she agreed that it was part of my overall payment for the surgery and I would not be charged for it.

Since the cardiologist was a key to my getting discharged and I wanted to go home, I went along with everything, but felt like I was being held hostage and not being informed about important medical decisions on my own body. I got a very comprehensive report about the surgery, which I shared with Dr. Phil and Dr. Jim, but nothing about the $5,000 echo was mentioned in the report.

I have the DVD of my 2013 echo and bringing that to Dr. Skinner on Thursday.

They did the echo while I was in bed the day after surgery and the doctor did tell me that it was a very good read. I told him I had two echoes in the early 1990s after I had taken the drug Redux. Later, I worked with more than 50 Redux victims around the nation from people who developed PPH (Primary Pulmonary Hypertension) after taking the drug. The reason some of my clients had short lifespans is that most of their local physicians missed the PPH diagnosis.

Going back to my writings about only picking top experts, this is the spot in my surgery process where I don't trust someone's expertise, and it's an important person in the process.

4. Body Temp.

97.8

This never deviates from 96.9 to 98.1 (which are ironically the call numbers for two radio stations where I have done work). Looking for any spikes or signs of infection and don't see any. Seems to run at 97.2 consistently during the day.

I do worry about infections and live in fear of catching a cold, the flu or pneumonia. I've lived as a hermit since the surgery and that fear of infection is the driving factor, but I start to get very lonely and desire face-to-face interaction in some kind of short bursts. I have to be out Wednesday and Thursday for doctor appointments and that should allow me to touch the outside world, but don't want to get overwhelmed with too many visitors or visitors that stay for long periods.

I had severe cottonmouth and could only talk for a few minutes on the phone when I got out of surgery. It gets better every day. My normal phone calls last about an hour and when I do those now, I have to lie down afterwards. I could not go that length at all until Friday. Suddenly, I am a "15 Minute Man" (parody of 1950s song)[7] on the phone, and I suspect I need to stay that way until my stamina improves.

Also, since I am not getting any face-to-face interaction, I am starting to not look forward to phone calls, but have done at least two long ones every day since surgery.

The scars on my stomach seem to be slowly healing. It's not hard for me to get around and do physical activity. There's a very slight bit of bruising at the big scar near my belly button, but so minor that I hesitate to even mention. That scar gets the most work as it is large and I occasionally bump into something with that part of my body.

No signs of any kind of irregular healing or infection, and each day it looks less and less like I had been in a knife fight.

5. Sleep

8.2 hours

I fell asleep at roughly midnight reading a book on the couch and went into bedroom around 2:30 a.m. and slept for 6.2 hours after that. My CPAP tracks the hours I spend on it so I get an accurate reading. Also, I fell asleep for roughly an hour in front of the television yesterday afternoon during the Alabama game. Rarely do that, but only had about three hours the night before.

I determined a long time ago that I need exactly seven hours of sleep a night. I've gotten that or more in all but one night, and I'm focusing on making that number work at all costs.

6. Lortab Pain Meds and Running Out of Medicine

I took four yesterday. I have not taken any today, but may need to take some within the hour. Starting to feel some pain, but suspect that my 2,500-word memo is wearing me down. I've gotten up and taken breaks on a regular basis, but will probably disconnect for a number of hours.

I'm balancing my desire not to use them (watched too many people get hooked) with the understanding that using them is going to make me feel better and heal more quickly. Also, I have a practical problem: I am going to run out of medicine.

The instruction said to take four to six a day and I got 30 tablets.

I don't see Derek until Dec. 10 and I was given 30 pills on Dec. 2. If I go at four pills a day, that is 36 pills, and if I up it to do six pills every four hours as instructed on the label, that would be 54 and I would have been out by now.

I hate pain medicine by nature and glad that Derek gave me a lower end medicine like Lortab, but also understand how not having pain allows me to accomplish more overall. It's a tough balance as I went most of Friday without any medicine, and I think the pain and short sleep period on Friday night was a result of that.

7. Seven Protein Shakes and Increase in Fluids

An odd thing happened yesterday. I went from being only able to drink fluids through the sippy cup to suddenly being thirsty and able to drink on a more traditional basis. Also, I got somewhat hungry and looked for energy from my protein shakes.

I drink something called Pure Protein shakes with one gram of carbs and 35 grams of protein. They are very high-end pricewise (but still cheaper than groceries and dining out), but I really like the taste and they are so dramatically convenient as opposed to making stuff in the blender.

I jumped from my previous day high of four shakes to seven and probably could have had eight. I had two today (I've been up for five hours and been writing for most of the time) and drank two Powerade Zero's at 20 oz. each. It took me an entire day to drink three shakes, water and maybe half of a Powerade two days ago.

I can stay on liquid diets longer than most people, and I have no desire to "crunch." Eliminating the thing that reduces hunger in my stomach has worked, along with ending the blood sugar rollercoaster. I never get physically hungry and suddenly things like a big steak or pizza psychologically gross me out (stunning to anyone who knows me). I really am not interested in meat and my only occasional "craving" is for canned green beans, which I have been pretty indifferent about in the past. Looking forward to having some.

I am planning a post-sleeve world that is heavy on organics and introducing the word "vegetable" into my vocabulary.

The good news about my increase in fluids is that it's helping with my cottonmouth issue. I have never had even an upset stomach or even stomach discomfort. Much better than the after effects of my big surgeries. I do take the GasX as gas pain radiates via my shoulders, but that is decreasing.

I had a lifelong battle with diarrhea and then when I went on low carb diets, I struggled with constipation. I had a very difficult time with constipation in the week before surgery, but other than a small bout of diarrhea on day three (which ended in a couple of hours), my bowel movements have been small and regular, with no signs of discomfort or strain. One of those pleasant side effects that no one talks about.

I am hoping that my increased "appetite" is a sign that I am improving and not vice versa. I'm still about 1,200 calories for the day and I doubt I should be concerned, but the sudden change threw me for a bit.

8. Exercise

Derek has been on a mantra about blood clots and I have followed his advice of getting up and walking, but I understand it is the game changer on the long-term battle so I'm developing some comprehensive "business plans" to make this a lifetime habit. Also, time management has become a top priority and I am using the time away from work to develop a rigid schedule.

9. Medicines

Metformin and Lipitor (ironically the two that the drug store gives you for free) are the only ones I have dropped and I picked up some new ones that Derek prescribed for me. I developed an intricate system to make sure I get them all in and don't miss one. Seems to work and I have been diligent about getting in my potassium pills, which I had slacked on in the months before surgery.

As noted, I want to get off the Beta Blocker and somewhere else on blood pressure, but as I track it daily I am not about to reduce or change anything in my medicines until I have a long-term pattern and Dr. Phil is on board with it.

I take them all along with two multivitamins: Vitamin B and Vitamin D. Dr. Jim has had me on the latter for a long time and also doing fish oil and Alpha Lipoid Sustain, an herbal pill that actually had good results in stabilizing blood sugar. I had not taken the fish oil or Alpha Lipoid since surgery as I was unsure if that was something that would slow or damage the healing of my stomach.

Conclusion

I remained thrilled at my progress. I stopped reading all the bariatric message boards, but I seem to be doing far better than the average patient who writes on them.

December 9, 2014
7 a.m.

Weight: 337.8
Blood Sugar: 102
Blood Pressure: 146/86
Temp.: 96.4

1. No meds for blood sugar and 102 may be the lowest morning number since I started.

2. Lack of sleep hitting me today. I need a solid seven hours every night.

My housekeeper Caterina Monsolve is here at moment and can't really take a nap, but focused on early sleep tonight as I have appointment with Dr. Weiss office in morning.

Caterina just offered to come back, pro bono, this weekend if I wanted her to straighten up. I truly appreciate it, but don't need it. She subtly noted that I have been a slob as I am staying here 24/7 even though I have not used the kitchen. Anyway, I have been fortunate to have her in my support system.

3. Looking forward to my doctor appointment in morning. A chance

to get some official measurements and insights. Also, I am going to get another round on Lortab. Still need meds and not going to rush my recovery.

4. Sent out a McNay Report update and got a lot of happy responses with tons of people cautioning me not to move too fast. I think they know the old Don well, but I plan on staying with the program until this is done correctly.

5. Weight loss has stalled, but I expected that to happen as three pounds a day was an insane pace. It will fall back as I have not deviated from the plan in any way. I read a message board post from a guy who had two shots of bourbon eight days out. I wanted to go track him down and punch him. He just wasted everyone's time and money and needed to deal with his addiction issues first. This is a true second chance at life, but only if you allow it to be.

6. All and all, I feel terrific. Also, I am incredibly calm. Everyone who interacted with me has noticed how relaxed I am. It is dramatic. Also, a tribute to the well-defined "business plan" for the surgery and recovering that we are implementing.

December 11, 2014
6 a.m.

Weight: 332.6
Blood Sugar: 115
Blood Pressure: 146/86
Temp: 97.4

1. Sleepy and exhausted after trip to Georgetown yesterday. Felt terrific before and during the meetings, but got very tired very quickly at the end of meeting and stayed that way.

Reminded me of when I had pneumonia in 1998. I went from feeling fine to feeling exhausted almost instantly and without warning,

2. No Lortab yesterday and switched to Tylenol. Think that

withdrawal symptoms are part of problem. Also the lack of sleep in previous days. I have a new prescription for Lortab unfilled, but think I am better off staying off. The combination of three days with little sleep, followed by a 6 a.m. wake up, followed by first trip out, followed by stopping the medicines was probably too much at once, but I had been reducing my dosage anyway and suspect I am feeling it. Like Machiavelli said, it is better to have all bad news at once than dribbling it out, so I am better off getting past the Lortab now.

I don't feel any kind of pain, just restless sleep and exhaustion that feels like a very small case of the flu. My body temperature is normal, and I don't have any coughing or any cold-like symptoms. I'm just exhausted. The pneumonia analogy is my best description.

3. I felt terrific on my visit to Georgetown yesterday, but got extremely tired as I was driven home and stayed that way. Took a nap at 1 p.m. until 3 p.m. Got up and had first food of the day: cream of tomato soup. Small case of diarrhea as I had not had a bowel movement for two days previous, but that stopped quickly and I had some sugar free Jello along with a protein shake later and did not have stomach distress.

5. My weight of 332.6 is a four-pound loss since yesterday. I had a stall for three days, but that changed immediately after the bowel movement. Very happy about that. I felt like my weight loss was continuing well, but glad to have it reflected on scale.

6. In summary, it was a hard day's night, but I have had worse. There does not seem to be anything out of place on my vitals and getting off the pain meds is important to me personally. Glad to see the weight loss and the visit to Georgetown was excellent. Learned a great deal in the two person "class" with my longtime friend Cindy Caywood, and Dr. Weiss was correct about Heather Pile: she is an excellent PA. Both Cindy and Heather are EKU grads, which shows off the excellence of my alma mater where I am serving on the Foundation Board. Heather did a terrific job of answering all my questions.

This "stream of consciousness" journaling about my post-surgery is a new concept for me, but I'm finding it valuable.

December 12, 2014
9 a.m.

Weight: 330.2
Blood Sugar: 119
Blood Pressure: 141/95
Temp.: 97.3

> *"Feeling good was good enough for me*
> *Good enough for me and my Bobby McGee"*
> -Kris Kristofferson[8]

You can't argue with my numbers. They would get me excited even if I had not woken up feeling as good as I did today. BP is the only category out of target range and the weight keeps falling off.

Although I have to remind myself to eat as I don't get physically hungry. I am working some "real food" into the diet every day. Had my first spoonful of cottage cheese since age 10. My daughter Angela gave me a tip for making the cottage cheese taste better and it worked.

Talked to my college roommate Mike Behler late last night, which was terrific timing as I was feeling depressed, exhausted and isolated. In the middle of a long discussion with Mike as to who was the most important member of Cream, Jack Bruce or Eric Clapton (we both voted for Jack Bruce), I circled back to an analogy about the financial markets and weight loss.

I wrote often and frequently in 2008 that the world would have been better off letting the "too big to fail" banks fail, taking the short-term pain and rebuilding. Realized the same analogy with my weight loss surgery. I'm practicing what I preach. Taking a short-term hit for a long-term gain.

Mike is a wheel at the Emory Medical School and knows that I have to be in good hands since Derek is a product of their residency program. It occurred to us that since I went to Vanderbilt, Derek did his residency at Emory, Dr. Jim went to Duke Medical School and Dr. Phil had Tulane and Washington University, my medical dream team touches every great private school in the south. For some reason, that was important to note.

Dr. Phil is off to celebrate his son Ben's 40th birthday. That means that Ben was 14 when I met him and is a measurement of how time flies.

Back to the weight loss report. I really can't call what I am doing an actual short-term hit. I am far ahead of where I dreamed I could be.

It was an off day. Yesterday started slowly, and I felt like a slug all day. Nodded off often, mentally down and lethargic. Barely got off the couch. Unhappy that I had become so tired on my first trip outside the condo on the 10th. I'm wondering when I will be able to go again. I've been hesitant to have visitors or get out as I don't want to catch the flu that is going around or be worn out and not near my home base, like what happened on Wednesday.

I think that psychologically I have to get past that. My Myers-Briggs personality is an X. I am 50 percent extreme introvert, 50 percent extreme extrovert (my wife is the only person I have met with a similar dynamic), and I think the extrovert side is knocking.

I get a lot of people checking in, but when you hit a down cycle, it can be easier not to respond, especially to text or email. People understand if I don't immediately get back to them.

I started doing this daily journal for the first time in my life as a way to record my days for my book and get my medical numbers to my inner circle. Now I see psychologically why people do it.

I'm going to drive myself to the grocery and may do it today. I'm not on the pain meds so I can drive and there is one nearby. I do want to eat as my menu slowly expands (and feel my energy levels rise as I do), but need to go pick the food out. I am following my doctor and dietitian's advice on what I can eat and when I can eat it. I am not deviating.

I tried some things like baby food that is easy to digest, but don't like the taste. I had half of a banana for breakfast and half for lunch yesterday. I have plenty of protein shakes and those fill a lot of needs.

It's been a challenge to learn that I can't eat an entire banana at one time. My portions are small and I eat them slow.

The trick to eating with a gastric sleeve is to reset your mind about portions.

I overdosed on soup the first day. I assumed a can would be a normal portion. About a 1/5 of a can was a better idea. I figured out volume control with the liquids (I am drinking from my sippy cup as I write this) and starting to see it on the non-liquids. My body is going to break old habits, like it or not.

Planning for the time off has gone well. I have the right people in our businesses and we are having an excellent end of the year. My editor has morphed into an invaluable sidekick who has been handling a lot of daily tasks. He is off to Florida in the morning, and we timed it so that we have all things covered while he is gone. He has made the first two weeks go well and I appreciate it. My children are five minutes away, but understand that I usually prefer to recover without people around.

I have the condo set up for comfort and convenience. I have things set up so that I never have to lift or bend and all the advance planning has paid off. I also won't starve. I have five cases of protein shakes and enough Powerade Zero to last a decade. I can't do more than four shakes a day so I am stocked for awhile. I like the taste of those.

It is strange for me not to be actively involved in anything at the moment. The first week I was off, I enjoyed the quiet time, but then I remembered why I liked being on the go. I need to get back into some kind of swing, but balancing the short-term/long-term again. Being out on Wednesday was a setback physically and mentally. I truly enjoyed it, but got so tired at the end that I was miserable for two days.

Glad to be feeling good again today. Not going to stress about it, but I'm logically making some baby steps to introduce myself to the human race again.

Third day with no pain meds and no longer have any in my household. Those are history. Did not even take Tylenol yesterday or today. Don't have any need to.

I also have to recognize that pulling off the pain meds (which I did on my own) probably contributed to my downturn on Wednesday. I slept an incredible amount of time with weird dreams. Last night I had a pleasant dream about the Reds winning the World Series.

Thus, I knew it was a fantasy.

As I started this memo, for today, feeling good is good enough for me. On the other hand, it's even better to be feeling good and 46.5 pounds lighter with normal blood sugar.

I'm going to start moving to one report a day. I'm at a point where doing my measurements every few hours seems like overkill. Little changes in my numbers and the trend is excellent.

This is my first weight loss program in the iPhone era, and the apps and data gathering info are terrific. Without much effort, I have been able to track everything I have eaten or drank since the surgery and a plethora of vital signs. I am going to keep writing the daily journal.

That's the way it is, Dec. 12, 2014, my 11th day since surgery.

December 13, 2014
6 a.m.

Weight: 327.8
Blood Sugar: 134
Blood Pressure: 131/89
Temp.: 96.9

> *"Feel I'm knocking on heaven's door"*
> -Bob Dylan[9]

I'm one of those few people who can take a song about impending death (the original was a soundtrack for the movie *Pat Garrett and Billy the Kid*) and make it one about hope and optimism. I could do a long essay on why entering heaven is a good thing, deserving of joyful behavior, but I digress.

I am happy. I am on the cusp of breaking the 50-pound weight loss number. You can definitely see it, especially in my face (and feet ironically), and I am stunned at how quickly the weight is falling off me. Once I started introducing small amounts of food into the diet, the drop has kicked up to a couple of pounds a day.

Had an upbeat day yesterday. Drove myself to the grocery and got some (on the list) foods that I wanted. Ditching the baby food for the first available taker. Getting out in the sunshine and proving I am mobile made a world of difference in my mood and spirit. Stayed up later than planned and woke up earlier than planned, but as Mr. T used to say, "I ain't got no plan" at the moment. As things are stabilizing, I am starting to get one.

Taking life day-by-day, but did make a plan to get to my wife's parents' house for Christmas. I'm thrilled as I did not have a Christmas plan until now.

Surgery is literally an "Independence Day" for a lot of people, and the lifestyle change is not always embraced by those around them. Change is hard, even if it is positive. That is why you see revolutions in countries that go through rapid advancement. Overthrowing the Shah of Iran was a good example. People can't handle that much change unless they are forced to.

Even if they buy in emotionally and intellectually, when it starts to mess with their holidays or daily living, the weight loss dramatically impacts family and friends. No reason for them to feel guilty; it is human nature. People don't want their happy universe to change.

I made it easier in the short run by living in isolation. I've tried dieting in the past with a house full of people and food, and it is a 1,000 percent more difficult and stressful. I got the concept of environmental control nailed and that is a game changer. Those who are just starting weight loss and fending off outside stressors are struggling. This is a full-pitched war and can only be fought on one front.

The supporting cast for the weight loser is not getting any positive strokes, and the person losing weight gets them nonstop. For some people losing weight, it is the first time in their lives they have gotten positive feedback.

I happened to note on Facebook yesterday that I had lost 46.5 pounds and went to the grocery by myself. My big thrill was having the independence to drive again, but more than 250 people (as of last night) "liked" my weight loss status. This proves that weight loss, not love or money, is the universal language of the world. There is no one overtly opposed to it, although subliminal "aren't you moving too fast" negativity can creep into some conversations. I literally don't have a lot of control over how fast I am moving. It is all on autopilot at this point.

Everyone is happy for you at some level.

I often talk about the parallel between weight loss and sudden money in my books that I have written. I never made the "family and friends" connection on weight loss, but it is the number one reason that people with sudden money blow it all. I suspect the same undermining of family and friends holds true in weight loss.

I think of the books and movie *Carlito's Way* with Al Pacino and Sean Penn.[10] One of the reasons I was captivated by it was I understood the underlying message. I watched a lot of people pulled down by their friends when I was growing up.

I was lucky to have friends who took me to the next level. They still do. Most of my inner circle was formed by the time I was 25 and never deviated. Those who have been added in recent years live up to the standards of the core. Just like my father, I have the ability to bond with people of strong loyalty and character, and it is the greatest gift God has bestowed upon me.

I stayed up to wish a friend, Carroll Crouch, known to my family as TGO (The Great One), a Happy 60th at midnight. He is on vacation in Mexico and had already emailed to check in on my progress. The defining characteristic of my closest friends is that you would pray that your children and grandchildren grow up to be just like them. Certainly true in Carroll's case.

Time to enjoy the moment. Like look at the scale and do a little dance. Maybe a big dance. Numbers are improving. Blood sugar was slightly up, but still in the normal range.

I have been searching for some kind of marking point as to what kind of numbers to hope for or expect. No one wants to give a number and I get that completely.

If I tell you I can get 10 percent on an investment and you get nine percent, you are mad. If I tell you I can get eight percent and get nine percent, you are happy. Thus, I always lowball and I can't find a hard and fast formula anywhere in the weight loss literature. Lots of stuff about six months out, but nothing about the first month. In my wildest dreams, I projected that a 50 (actually 49.2 loss) would happen around the first of the year, not Dec. 13. I am in uncharted territory.

My wife Karen taught me how to scramble an egg. Not six at one time like I was eating a few weeks ago, but just one. Off to enjoy it shortly.

I guess I should just quit projecting numbers and enjoy the ride. I am doing everything my doctors have told me to do and it is working. As great as the weight number is, the immediate stability of my blood sugar is the one that I'm able to feel and appreciate the most.

I am running through my clothes very quickly and learned that suspenders are a good thing. Probably will hit the tailor soon to save some my expensive suits into the next months, but eventually I am going to have to ditch them all. On other hand, one of my goals is to own an Armani suit and that may be what I have on when I do the book launch.

December 14, 2014
6:30 a.m.

> *"What day did the Lord create Spinal Tap, and couldn't he have rested on that day too?"*
> -Rob Reiner in one of my favorite movies, *This is Spinal Tap*[11]

Rather than do a verbose report this Sunday, I want to celebrate that my 326.6 weight today means that I have now lost 50.4 pounds since I started the program on Aug. 28.

There are other numbers and info, but breaking the 50-pound milestone is a spot for solo celebration.

Yay!

Not many people ever lose 50 pounds at any point in their lifetimes and even though it a marker (like Pete Rose, getting 2,000 hits on his way to 4,256) that will long be forgotten, I am going to enjoy the moment.

Next big statistical marker is in 27 pounds when I weigh less than

300 pounds for the first time since 2004.

Have a good Sunday. This news alone makes it a good one for me.

December 19, 2014
6:15 a.m.

Weight: 327.4
Blood Sugar: 102
Blood Pressure: 129/76
Temp.: 96.8

Other than my irregular sleep hours, things have settled into a reasonably predictable pattern. Blood sugar and blood pressure continue to improve. Weight seemed to hit a stall when I got to a 50-pound weight loss and the two pounds I lost on Thursday are back on Friday. I'm doing the right things and been through enough programs to know that the body readjusts in rapid loss situations. Also, I tend to not lose when I am not sleeping well. Not worried about the scale, but it's now a habit to weigh daily.

I've been creative as I bring food back in. My primary focus is making my protein and hydration goals. I've missed on each once or twice, and I really feel lousy when that happens.

I am learning the system. It took me awhile to not eat and drink water at the same time (lifelong habit), but becoming a master of my food chopper. I can puree almost anything and mixing stuff like vegetables and lean meat into a stew tastes good, brings higher protein, lower carbs and fewer processed foods into the mix. I average about 125 grams of protein and get the carbs under 40. Exactly where I want to be.

Eliminating processed stuff like puddings and Jello helps me psychologically as I plan to live in a non-fructose world from here on out. Never had yogurt until the surgery, but definitely love it and one a day gets some protein in.

I buy the most natural brands I can find. Stopped at a big Kroger on Tuesday and it took me two hours to buy $29 worth of food (my grocery and dining bills savings may pay for the surgery, especially when you factor in the $300 a month I am saving on medicines already), as I stopped and read every label carefully. Determined to keep away from fructose, which is everywhere. Michael Pollan wrote that 85 of the 92 items on a McDonald's menu have fructose in it. Not as bad as the Chicken McNuggets which have lighter fluid in them (they really do!), but a good reason to embrace the organic world.

I've been re-reading Gary Taubes' great book *Why We Get Fat and What to Do About It*[12] and his larger work *Good Calories, Bad Calories*.[13] I've also started re-reading Michael Pollan's series of books. Both were great influences a few years ago. (My youngest daughter Angela bought the Taubes' book for me as a Christmas present four years ago. A not-so-subtle hint that I needed help.) Fructose addiction had me in a severe grip. I could not break my Diet Coke addiction, despite numerous efforts, until the week before surgery and suspect I have to be like an AA member and never have one again.

I took my grandson and daughter to the Chop House on Wednesday. My first time in a restaurant since the surgery. Angela had steak and Abijah had every vegetarian thing on the menu (he has never had meat in his 14 years, but went from five-foot-tall to six-foot in the past year). I had an order of deviled eggs. Actually, I had two of the eggs halves and a glass of water that I did not touch. Could not eat anything else and broke my maiden of going out in a social setting again.

Since dining has been my primary form of social interaction, not going out at all was hard from a mental standpoint. Going out to eat seven days a week, like in the past, is not really viable either. I will not be ordering any 16 oz. steaks in the future, but with the holidays coming up, I am going to be around people and food more. It will be a stressor, but an opportunity to adjust.

This process is about getting healthy, not deprivation. One of the reasons I liked the gastric sleeve is that I can eventually eat anything, just in tiny portions. My body lets me know ASAP if I eat too much. I've never gotten queasy or vomited, but I can certainly tell when I am full. Actually, it's not that often. I had a streak when I was not getting enough protein and fluid. Once I got back to focusing on 64 oz. of fluid (which has been very hard) and 125 grams of protein, I felt better and the weight came off faster.

My college roommate Mike Behler is coming up from Atlanta to see me tomorrow. He is going to eat before he comes over and then hang out at the condo. Like all of my friends and family, he has been incredibly supportive. My wife Karen is back to Kentucky from New Orleans, and I catch up to her in Elizabethtown next week before she comes here until New Year's.

I have a strong and definite plan for Christmas and that involves bringing my own food and having plenty of breaks. I won't do the physically taxing sort of things, like a long church service, but will be around both houses (Elizabethtown and my oldest daughter) enough to participate in the holiday. It will still be an adjustment as I have been basically in isolation since the surgery and I will need to deal with the holiday stress. I have plans and a place to escape, but will go with a limited schedule and not push it.

If it were not for fatigue, it would be hard to remember that I had major surgery less than three weeks ago. I've had little to no problems with pain, adjusting to the new eating style and I've been working every day and driving somewhere, even just to the grocery or drive cleaners. My scars on my stomach are starting to not be noticeable and I can wear a belt without it bothering me.

I feel so good that I have to force myself not to remember not to lift more than 25 pounds.

I am noticing the positive impact of having lost the 50 pounds. It's noted in my declining blood sugar (no medicines of any kind) and my blood pressure is slowly dropping. Better yet, I can feel it in how much better I feel. I went to Dr. Skinner's office on Monday and could fit in the chairs. I could not when I went in September and had to stand in the waiting room. A small step, but a giant leap for me. I've never wanted to be a "normal" person, but there are times when doing normal things suits me. I stay very cold all the time. The temp. is on 77 in the condo and I am in heavy sweatpants. A month ago it would have been on 67 and I would be walking around half-naked.

My half-naked body looks a lot better now than it did a month ago (and will look better still a month from now), but I am digressing. An attorney friend who weighs about 275 pounds emailed yesterday about us becoming male swimsuit models. Definitely a career option.

Actually, I have all the career options I can handle. My idea was to work about four hours a day, but I have been sucked into a couple of large, end-of-year settlements and am putting in more like an eight-hour day (10 to 12 was a normal day pre-surgery). My sleep patterns are really whacked out. I try various strategies and Dr. Jim Roach has sent me some ideas, but I need seven hours a night (I've spent a couple of years determining that) and what has happened in the past is if I would get a four or five-hour day (normally via traveling or work), I would "reset" somewhere during the week and get a nine or 10-hour day.

I only track the number that comes from being in bed with the CPAP on as that is my optimum way of sleeping. I have taken Ambien for years and normally with the combination of medicine and my CPAP, I slept soundly through the nights. I had decades of insomnia, but age and sleep treatments seemed to solve that. I had hoped to drop the CPAP and sleeping medicine at some point, but right now they are very important to any hope I have of staying asleep. I fall asleep incredibly quickly. I just don't stay there.

I drank massive amounts of Diet Coke (at least six a day) before the surgery and no caffeine at all now. I assumed that dropping the caffeine would improve sleep, but no luck.

Since I am not getting a lot of good sleep, I jump up wide awake normally around 6 a.m. without an alarm and don't even try to go back. I suspect I get about seven hours sleep a day, but that includes nodding off on the couch in the middle of the day (I have been forced into a European style of taking a long "lunch" break). I catch myself falling asleep sitting up and will nod off at odd times in the evening.

I was a night person, but now all of my energy is in the morning. I also was a huge night eater (I would suspect about 60 percent of my calories came from dinner and nonstop late night snacking), and I have done my best to eliminate that.

I recognize that I am going through a lot of life changes and the stress is manifesting and will even out over time, but the lack of sleep is impacting my mood. One of my neighbors gets up at 6 a.m. and stands in the hall and whistles every morning for about two hours; today may be the day I go punch him.

Well, maybe I should politely ask him to quit first.

I've worked hard to develop routines and schedules, and going into 2015 I will be more system-oriented. I'm hoping that a sense of normalcy helps.

I wrote the first draft of a piece for *Huffington*. I'll finish my edits this morning and get to my editor today so it should be out tomorrow. About prayer and spirituality, topics I don't hit much (like ever), but also about my weight loss and about Dr. Jim Roach, whose upcoming book has inspired me.

A very long piece that I may edit down, but a good reminder that I have been incredibly fortunate to have quality people care about me. My father used to sing (nonstop) a Dean Martin song saying, "You're nobody till somebody loves you."[14]

Dino hit that on the head.

December 20, 2014
8 a.m.

Weight: 324.8
Blood Sugar: 114
Temp.: 97.8
Hours of Sleep: 5.6

I had a two-pound weight loss, a little more sleep and feel good. Dr. Derek told me yesterday I could lift more than 25 pounds now (I am still taking it easy before I go on the power lifting tour) and that opens up a lot for me, especially for things like lifting my suitcase and bringing people presents next week.

I finished my *Huffington Post* column, which I posted late last night in the Healthy Living Section. It tells the story of how Dr. Jim Roach and the power of prayer lifted me through the surgery. The column is racking up big numbers on a holiday weekend.

I have to thank everyone for the prayers and support. Right after I wrote it, I happened to watch a video of the late Teddy Pendergrass wheeled onto the stage at Live Aid in 1985. It was his first public appearance after the 1982 car accident that paralyzed him from the chest down (and ultimately led to his death). The crowd gave a huge and thunderous ovation and Teddy said, "I can feel your love coming right through me." I feel the same way. (If you like deep-voiced soul, listen to Teddy sometime. His career was cut short at its peak, but the guy had some real talent.)

My college roommate Mike Behler is coming from Atlanta to visit. He can admire the handiwork of Dr. Weiss, who did his residency at Emory Medical School where Mike is the guru of financial aid. My beautiful wife is working her way back from New Orleans, and I see her on Tuesday.

Working on hydration and mastering my food chopper as I am focused on high protein, low carb foods without fructose. I'm hitting all my food and water goals. The rest will fall in line if I do that.

December 21, 2014
12 p.m.

Weight: 322.6
Blood Sugar: 132
Temp.: 98.3
Hours of Sleep: 9

My weight dropped two more pounds and I was able to get my longest sleep since surgery. Also, my body temperature is up. It was pointed out that I was averaging in the 96 range, which explained why I have been incredibly cold all the time. Blood sugar is up, but still in the very high side of "normal" range and trends under 100 during the day. I ate before bed last night. Dr. Jim noted last week to watch my early morning blood sugar after that and he is correct. I've been a huge late night eater, but at least I know cause and effect.

All in all, I am very happy with the numbers. Especially the continuing weight loss. 32 pounds in 21 days.

Some of the things that worked yesterday:

1. My focus was on not nodding off all day and getting a normal sleep pattern again. Took some work (especially when the Kentucky basketball team got a huge lead in the game), but I made it. Feel like I hit a "reset" button of some kind.

2. The second focus was on hydration. I drank a lot of fluids early in the day to make sure I got my 64 oz. in. I was not making it in previous days.

3. Counterintuitive: I ate more real food and dropped the protein shakes back. Highest calorie day (1,100) since surgery. Wound up getting to the 125 grams of protein and about 30 carbs and shaking off the weight loss stall. I would like to stay at that ratio. I made my first piece of salmon. All three ounces were terrific. Realize that I needed more food for energy and also more water. I was getting down to the 300 calorie-a-day range. Way too low. Hoping the blood

temperature rise was a result of higher metabolism.

Part of me is horrified that I went up to 1,100 calories and the other part realized that it took 4,147 calories a day to maintain my previous weight. I am way ahead of the curve. I would lose more than five pounds a week on calorie deficit at this pace, and I am not focused on calorie count at all. It just happens to be a measurement in the package.

My focus is going to stay on protein and hydration and not calories.

The fact that I literally recorded every bite and measurement since the day I walked out of the hospital has been a tremendous habit. Dan Sullivan says it takes 21 days to make a habit and today is day 21. Also, he quotes a philosopher who said, "what can be measured can be obtained." Thus, we are measuring like crazy.

Working hard to establish a more rigid scheduling and habit-developing plan for 2015. I am narrowing my focus on the business front and developing daily routines. Most people have them, but I have not for years.

It's a chicken or egg proposition, but I think the weight gain was a byproduct of bad habits or perhaps the bad habits came because of the weight gain. Anyway, I did an excellent job in getting focused and organized for the surgery and the recovery period. Using those same skill sets for the rest of my (longer) life is what I need to make all this work. The "new and improved" Don is going to be a challenge for those interacting with me. It's like when a drinker stops drinking. (I grew up around a lot of drinkers.) The people around them have to adjust to different reactions to previously predictable behaviors, and it is hard on them. I've been on both sides of that fence and fortunate that my family and friends "get it" and have been so supportive.

Gary Rivlin, best-selling author and former *New York Times* reporter is writing a book about New Orleans that releases on the 10th anniversary of Hurricane Katrina in August.[15]

As a really neat gift, he sent a copy of the unedited manuscript for the book. I get to read it months before anyone else does. We talked about my upcoming book, and Gary noted that only Don McNay could get a book out of going to elective surgery. Gary thinks the book will have a big audience. I totally agree on both fronts. I am not only going to lose the weight, I am going to take a 1,000 people along with me and have them lose their weight as well.

That is a true motivator. It helps when the battle is more than just about me.

As for my weight loss, as Buddy Holly said, "Everyday, it's a gettin' closer, rolling faster than a roller coaster."[16]

December 23, 2014
10 a.m.

Weight: 322.4
Blood Sugar: 116
Temp.: 97.4
Hours of Sleep: 5.5

If my surgery would have let me eat last night, I would have. First time I have felt that way since the surgery, but I stayed the course. I need a different way to cope with stress besides eating and I am getting my first test of the new world order. I have stayed on the plan and actually lost weight yesterday, and I plan to continue staying focused on the road.

Up half the night trying to get my Christmas trip organized. It is definitely a dangerous time, but I anticipated it would be and have a series of systems in place to problem solve and cope.

Although there is food everywhere, I do reasonably well in not gaining weight on holidays and will check my blood sugar from road, but won't have an accurate scale. Thus, I won't have another true weigh in until the morning of the 26th. I am bringing protein shakes and my own drinks like Powerade Zero and Crystal Light and will keep everything on record. I have intensely accurate records of every bite or sip of water since the surgery (it is pretty easy with the high tech apps like LoseIt), and I'm not going to deviate.

Traveling for Christmas will be a tremendous challenge, but one I have anticipated for months. I have a plan.

10 p.m.

> *"Well life on the farm is kind of laid back*
> *Ain't nothing an old country boy like me can't hack"*
> -John Denver[17]

Down to 322.4, which is 54.6 pounds lost. A Christmas present to me.

I have to consider today a big break through. A very good day.

I had a ton of trepidation this morning about going on the road to Elizabethtown to celebrate Christmas at Karen's parent's house. I had not driven this far since the surgery and that added to my normal holiday angst. Some people live for Christmas. I live for the day after Christmas. I had to do a lot of plotting and planning to make sure I could handle two very busy days away from the environmentally perfect world that I lived in since the surgery. My first road trip had been on my mind for weeks.

I was totally stressed out, but anxiety was for naught.

I drove to E Town without a problem. I stopped at the Cracker Barrel in Bardstown and had two scrambled eggs as a late lunch. Allowed me to break up the trip and get some walking in.

I like scrambled eggs as a meal as they give me lots of protein and no carbs. I am finding that a combination of about 125 grams of protein and less than 40 carbs seems to be the magic formula for Don. I feel good and the weight seems to come off more quickly when I hit those numbers. As I was told by surgeon Derek Weiss, my worst days came when I got down to about 60 grams of protein. He wants us at 100 grams and 64 oz. of fluid. All of my eating habits are focused on those numbers.

My mother-in-law has been avidly following my journey on Facebook and was totally ready for me. All of the chips and cheese doodles, which are normally around the house 24/7, were strategically placed out of my site. A ton of thought (actually worry on her part) and planning went into what I would eat and how to accommodate me. I won't starve or even need one-tenth of the carload of stuff (like high protein foods and protein shakes) that I hauled down here. They have me totally covered.

I don't seem to be bothered by a temptation for junk food, as I have been when I dieted in the past, but hiding them was an appreciated gesture. Karen and I went to Red Lobster. I had a piece of tilapia and green beans that will last through the next three meals. Jeff Ruby in Cincinnati once justified his steakhouses by saying, "A man doesn't feel like a man eating a piece of Tilapia."

I hate to disagree with Mr. Ruby, one of my late father's closest friends and a man who quotes me on five pages (pages 109 to 114) in his autobiography, but I feel pretty macho right now.

I proved I could travel and stay on the program. That has not always been the case in the past. In fact, it was never the case. Moving into a new environment would cause me to go off the wagon. The great thing about the gastric sleeve is that it makes you stay on the straight and narrow, but I never got to a point today where I needed any reinforcement.

A psychological victory in so many ways.

Got to spend some quality time with my beautiful wife and watch the Game Show Network with her family. I did not realize that Richard Dawson is no longer hosting *Family Feud*.[18] Also, I did not know that he died a few years back either. Or that the current show can get people to act like idiots for the thrill of winning $5,000. I think it would take about $5 million to get me there. Also if Karen, myself or her daughter were contestants, we would clean up. All of us know how to spell Vermont and that seemed to be a problem for the people participating. My daughter and son-in-law lived in Vermont, so maybe they would get more than the lousy five grand. Anyway, I digress.

Tired, but not as tired as I thought I would be. Stayed completely on plan and got more exercise than normal. Won't stay up too late and ought to be able to get some rest.

Probably should not quote Nietzsche during Christmas week, but what does not kill you DOES make you stronger. My next trip to anywhere will not be a stressor. I have a pattern of success to draw on.

Merry Christmas.

December 26, 2014
12 p.m.

Weight: 321.2
Blood Sugar : 144
Temp.: 98.5
Hours of Sleep: 7.9

The highlight of my numbers is that I continued to lose weight over a challenging Christmas holiday. Lots of food around, but I stayed on the plan. More carbs and calories, but within reason.

I think that my high blood sugar, body temperature and hours of sleep are the result of my extreme exhaustion of all the driving and activity. I am just starting to wake up at 10:30 a.m. and feel like one of the characters in the movie *The Hangover*.[19]

I have a lot of end of year activity and really want to write a *Huffington Post* column to help inspire people for the New Year.

Also going to have a protracted meeting with one of my favorite authors tomorrow and the period between Christmas and New Year is always a very busy time for me in the structured settlement business. Many attorneys and adjusters settle cases at the end of the year.

Somehow I hurt my left knee on Christmas Eve. It is a little better today, but I'm only able to walk on it by hobbling around. Better than yesterday. I was in a lot of pain and had to have people help me get in and out of chairs.

I deeply suspect I've slept on it and cut the circulation. I've done that a couple times before when I start writing or working on the computer for multiple hours and become so entranced that I would rub my legs in a funny fashion.

I've noticed things are much better with the knee as I am able to get up and hobble around, and I think being back in my home environment and getting plenty of sleep (I probably got less than four hours a night the two nights that I traveled) helps tremendously. For a guy who is a Platinum Medallion flyer on Delta, I don't travel particularly well. I never have.

It's not particularly swollen and doesn't seem to hurt in any one spot. In fact, my left knee looks smaller than right knee. One of the reasons that I lean towards the lack of circulation self-diagnosis.

Although I'm recovering wonderfully and the holiday trip was a major hurdle, I do have to remember I am still in recovery and will be there for a while to come. I'm adjusting to a very new life, but adjusting pretty well when you get right down to it.

I always look forward to the New Year. I'm a big believer in looking forward instead of backwards. As Satchel Paige once said, "Don't look back. Something might be gaining on you."[20]

From a family, spiritual, emotional and achievement perspective, this had to be one of my best Christmases. Also, while I downplay the commercialism, I got some really terrific gifts this year. Many of them will help me on my weight-loss journey. I had a lot of anticipation anxiety about this holiday and broke through some mental barriers.

I normally don't celebrate New Year's Eve, but have a reservation at Portofino for Karen and I. This year deserves to be honored, and I am a very cheap date (I will just probably get an appetizer) and a great designated driver to boot. Time to start a new tradition. Also, we could walk from the condo. One of the reasons I hated going out on New Year's Eve were the drivers and the pressure to drink heavily. Neither is a factor this time.

Part of my 2015 plan is to take a vacation that has no work connection. I have done three of them in my adult life and one in childhood. I never took time off and neither did my parents. That is changing.

I convinced Karen we need to go to Sarasota on my birthday week in February. I loved to go when the Reds did spring training there, but other teams are around. They have a very nice beach, and we can say hello to my friends Al and Martha Helen Smith who winter there.

Not easy to get me to take time off and have fun, but getting to like the idea.

My 14-year-old grandson Abijah has recently started wearing suit jackets and the kind of shoes (black Allen Edmonds) that his Bapa wears. He looks absolutely stunning and sophisticated, and I am touched by the silent tribute. Also, a motivator as one of my stated goals is to own an Armani. I will be really good role model for him when that happens.

I need to lose another 50 pounds and then I will start to hit eBay. My key to always being well-dressed, even at my highest weights, is, following the lead of my oldest daughter Gena, I am an expert at finding high quality clothing at low prices.

December 28, 2014
3 p.m.

Weight: 321.6
Blood Sugar: 145
Temp.: 97.8
Hours of Sleep: 7

I love going into a New Year. A time to wash away all past sins and start with a fresh sense of excitement and adventure. Based on everything going on in every aspect of my life, 2015 ought to be a landmark year.

I have a 34-year habit of going to the office on New Year's Day. If I am not near my office, I still carve out some time for work. My wife is not crazy about the habit, but it is a psychological thing.

I figure that my competition that stayed home has to play catch up for the next 364 days. I am an extremely competitive guy. I grew up on sports and proud of it. You can train your mind to do anything if you have the right attitude.

I had a fascinating four-hour meeting with Dr. Jim Roach in Midway yesterday, my Integrative Medicine guru and soon to be best-selling author. He has been absolutely with me through every step of this journey and my initial contact to him (he is the person who got me to Georgetown and Dr. Weiss) has resulted in a terrific book called *God's House Calls*, which will be on the market on March 28. I am writing the foreword and RRP International is publishing the book. I helped Dr. Jim on the book and he helped me on my health. A pretty good day with a fascinating man.

I was very worn out after the visit to Midway to see Dr. Jim, but made it back to watch the Kentucky game. I fell asleep during parts of the game. I am used to having incredible energy and almost everyone comments on my work ethic. Thus, having days when I am not channeling that old sense of energy bothers me. Dr. Jim has been helping me find healthy ways to gain that sense of vigor and I feel confident, especially as my weight continues to drop, that I will get to that place of energy nirvana.

I have to remember that I have really not been at that energy level, expect for situations like large mediations and settlement conferences, in the past couple of years. Dragging 377 pounds around and the nonstop litany of weight-related ailments is what finally got me to make my bold move.

On most days, when I pace myself, I feel better than I have in decades, but I'm learning that my limitations are still there. Dr. Jim noted I am not being fueled by six (or more) Diet Cokes a day and, in fact, not drinking caffeine at all. Thus, I am building towards a long-term solution and not a quick fix.

I am fighting the psychological urge for "things to get back to normal" and not going back to my old habit of taking on 48 hours of work in a 24-hour day. One of the reasons I have been attracted to things like settlement planning and journalism is that I love the rush of having a deadline. Changing the mindset is going to be a real battle.

My dear friend and esteemed trial lawyer Bill Garmer once told me (in a moment when I was trying to do 100 things at once) that the most important word in the English language was "No." I think about that often. One of the reasons Bill, like most of the other great trial lawyers, is successful is that he manages his time well and limits the number of people that he works with. He also seems to have balance. Superstar attorneys like Sam Davies, Phil Taliaferro, Gary Hillerich and Peter Perlman have been exercising and eating healthy their entire lives. If you want a roster of the best trial lawyers in the history of Kentucky, those names would be on everyone's list, so there is obviously a correlation.

Maintaining focus and balance is key. Even more important is maintaining a sense of patience, which I have never really had.

My editor was going back through some of the notes for the book last week. We noted that when you look at the detailed plans I had for pre-surgery and for my immediate post-surgery strategy, it should be a textbook for anyone getting bariatric surgery.

I planned every possible detail and contingency, and my medical results have been incredible. Also, I had a true sense of confidence going into the surgery as I knew I had planned every detail and contingency.

The people in my world rose to the occasion. We had an excellent end of the year in business, with little daily involvement from me, and the caretaking for me was first-rate. My family and friends have been there for me. My environment for recovery could not have been better, and these daily memos have allowed me to share my honest thoughts on a daily basis.

Being in that "in between stage" has made me realize that I have not planned out my "next phase" with that same kind of detail and focus.

It's time to get started.

The good thing is that the looming New Year is a natural time for planning, and by the time I get through the holiday, I want to have a "post-surgery" plan as good as my pre-game plan. Also, it needs to a realistic plan. I'm an incredibly ambitious guy and one of my reasons to get healthy is to do things. I have friends in their 70s, 80s and 90s who are making an impact and doing great things. I plan on being one of them. As George Jones once said, "I don't need your rocking chair."[21]

I am not really interested in going back to "normal" in my habits. I recognize this is a time of true rebirth from the physical standpoint. In 2006, both my mother and sister died and my first marriage ended in a nine-month period. I spent a lot of time wanting things to "go back to normal." Once I understood that there was never going to be a "normal" to go back to, things start moving in a positive direction.

Al Smith, the greatest living Kentuckian who knows a lot about recovery after 50-plus years as a recovering alcoholic, understands me pretty well. He called me a couple of weeks ago and said, "My bet is that you are past that surge of enthusiasm and slugging it out day-by-day." Al had a terrific insight. He called on a day when my enthusiasm was lower. My weight loss is now steady and not ridiculous. I was tired of being in the condo every day without face-to-face contact. I was tired of being tired. I've read 35 books in one month and talked on the phone for several hours a day to the point where the combination of talking and decreased hydration zaps my voice.

I can tell you everything happening in the news this month. I hate when I get exhausted without warning and for no particular reason.

The tangible benefits of surgery are all there. Look at my weight, blood sugar and other vitals and you can see I am setting up for a great rest of my life. It's like my football coaches always said: Games are won in July and August, when you are doing three-a-day practices, not in October and November when you are actually playing them. I hated the three-a-day practices (in full pads in 100 degree heat), but I grew up on Vince Lombardi and that relentless pursuit of perfection and preparation brings a sense of confidence and inner peace. I've been more in touch with my spiritual side than any time since 1994 and that has been a great comfort. I drug my very tired body into church on Christmas Eve. I didn't even bring a suit, and I normally don't go anywhere without one.

I knew my wife would like having her husband join the rest of her family in her hometown, but we had planned on my not going and she was fine with that.

If she asks, I can stick with the story that I went to church solely out of love for her, but I also felt like I needed to say thank you to God for the prayers said on my behalf. I suspect God wants more than a one shot appearance from me, but hey, it is a start. As my father used to say, "If God grades on the curve, I am in because I have seen the competition."

I've seen the competition, too. Maybe they should see me.

On the prayer side, these daily "stream of consciousness" memos are my version of talking to God, but my close friends and medical providers get to listen. I like sharing my journey and appreciate the close friends that I trust to share the story with. Everyone has really stepped up for me and I truly feel the love.

I also appreciate that people understand if I don't get back to them on a timely basis. Some days, I am full of energy and some days I run completely out of gas. I never know how it will go and when, and that is very hard on a guy like me who likes to have a plan.

I was able to work on a couple of settlements from home via Skype before Christmas. I was thrilled to be back in action, but those were days when I could feel that I had "overdone" it. Operating on a planned schedule is why the pre-surgery went so well. I need to keep that in mind.

Getting out of the condo has been a big step. The first day I could get in the car and drive was like getting out of prison. Now I am just happy to know that I can.

I was thrilled that I was able to do two days of Christmas at my in-laws and my daughters' houses. My knee was killing me for some strange reason and I was in a lot of pain, but I enjoyed every minute of it. A great Christmas for a guy who normally does not embrace the holiday.

I'm having dinner with my daughter and grandson tonight and lunch with a great friend tomorrow. Dinner with my wife on New Year's Eve, which we rarely do. Trying to get some other friends back on the lunch list after the first of the year. People have noted that my annual restaurant bill (which is the size of many people's mortgages) ought to go down significantly, but I truly enjoy dining out and learned it is not about the food. It is about the people you are with. It is my primary form of socialization and I need that socialization right now.

I lost weight over Christmas and kept my food intake normal. The gastric sleeve doesn't give any other options, but I had no desire to do otherwise. I can go out and have a small appetizer or get a takeout box and eat my leftover dinner over three days.

Actually, my food bill is probably going to go up. I am embracing healthier and organic foods, and fast foods are off the option list. Finding restaurants that fit my new lifestyle does not mean cheap.

Healthy food without fructose is expensive and should not be. A societal issue to address at another point.

Income is the greatest predictor of longevity and the ability to eat healthy food is a divide that separates rich from poor. Which means the rich will live longer and healthier lives. That has been the case throughout history, but additives and fast food may make that divide even wider. Bariatric surgery is available to people who get Medicaid, but not all hospitals accept it and they make the patient go through a ton of hoops to actually have surgery. I'm amazed that anyone does it, but it would certainly change society if it were more widely accepted.

It's only been 28 days, but I can give strong testimony for the wonders of the gastric sleeve. If my weight loss stopped tomorrow, I would have to think that being 55 pounds lighter with normal blood sugar and no blood sugar medicines would be worth the pain and expense of the operation. Since I plan on going at least 125 pounds further, I really am a believer. It is a tool to give an ambitious guy like me a chance to fulfill those ambitious. My stated goal is to get to 199 pounds, but I can also see where losing 200 pounds (177) would be a pretty cool place to get to. I like big goals.

I am working on my game plan. Planning the rest of my life is more complicated than an immediate, goal-driven plan like having surgery and recovering. On the other hand, I know what I want to do and have great role models for the lifestyle. Not many people have that.

I have noted to my family that every year that ends in five (2005,

1995, 1985, etc.) has been a breakthrough and milestone year in business and in life. This "Son of a Son of a Gambler" is looking to 2015 as the next one in my lucky string.

December 29, 2014
8 a.m.

Weight: 323.6
Blood Sugar: 109
Temp.: 96.6
Hours of Sleep: 3.7

My erratic sleep patterns caught me again as it was well after 3 a.m. before I fell asleep. Dr. Jim gave me some ideas on sleep and increasing my dropping body temperature, and I am implementing both. Hoping they help long-term. This morning is tough. Really miss my caffeine or something. Anything.

Super busy these next couple of days wrapping up the end of the year. My wife Karen is here for the week and gets to see the condo for the first time since I converted it into a potential MASH unit for my pre-surgery and recovery. I have a more stylish look planned down the road, but right now it is strictly designed for functionality.

I did set up a strict timeline for my day which gives it some structure as I knock out the end-of-year tasks. Hope I get a decent night sleep tonight.

December 31, 2014
7 a.m.

Weight: 320.8
Blood Sugar: 121
Temp.: 97.4
Hours of Sleep: 5.5

My "wildest dream" goal was to be at 320 by the end of the year. I am .8 of a pound from being there. I feel like I am in a "dream away" infomercial ad. I wake up every morning and expect to be two pounds lighter.

Yay!

"New Year's Eve is for amateur drunks and I'm a professional."
-Dean Martin

My father never went out on New Year's Eve and used the Dean Martin quote often. I deeply suspect that my father, a bookie for the overwhelming majority of his life, stayed home to get ready for New Year's Day, his second busiest day behind the Super Bowl.

Still, he passed the tradition down to his children. I've rarely gone out on New Year's Eve and only been to one of those blow-them-out stupid parties.

I was 19 (drinking was legal at age 18 in Ohio at the time). My buddy almost drove off the road, and I figured it was an omen and have not tried it since. My late sister, who was capable of having a drink on any of the other 364 days, stayed home on New Year's Eve as well.

Last year, I was in New Orleans, where the neighbors gave me the experience of what it must have been like in Baghdad on the first day of the first Gulf War. The fireworks were still going strong at five in the morning, and the sky literally lit up like it was daylight. Hoping things are quieter in downtown Lexington. My neighbors in Hanover Tower are usually in bed by nine on all nights, but I have never been here for a holiday.

I did bend my policy last year, and Karen and I went to Ralph Brennan's restaurant in City Park and were home by nine. Similar plan this year as we go to Portofino at 6 p.m. A very nice restaurant and starting to look at the other upside of my gastric sleeve: I can go to the nicest restaurant in town (Portofino has always been a favorite), and my personal tab will be less than my old one at

McDonalds or Burger King (two places that miss me).

I will probably get a piece of fish for dinner, but I don't drink anything and won't get appetizers, dessert or even a large entry. I'm a cheap date. Even cheaper as I usually pick up the check.

Since Karen and I are in the same time zone, it is time to do some stepping out on the town. We don't get a lot of one-on-one time.

Karen dislikes New Year's more than I do and normally falls asleep well before midnight. I used to stay up to watch Dick Clark, but now that Dick is in the big bandstand in the sky, I have lost all interest in watching the ball drop.

It's my first time in a higher-end restaurant for dinner since the surgery.

My eating has always been night eating, but I am not really capable of eating a lot under any circumstances which is like a blessing from God. Thank you to Derek and my team that made it happen.

This is a major step on the recovery road.

My daughter told me yesterday about a friend who gave the waiter a card so they could get a child's portion or small portion of a meal in a nice place. Cindy Caywood, my dietician guru and friend at Georgetown Hospital, gave the card to me, but I can't see a scenario where I would use it as an option.

To paraphrase the Keyser Soze character in one of my favorite movies, *The Usual Suspects*[22], a snooty waiter who tried to look down their nose at my portion control would get to see what a man of strong will is really like. I want to dare one to try it. I am known to be a strong tipper. Few want to mess with a man with that reputation or one who does not put up with people who like to put other people down.

After years of looking for places with the largest portions, I'm seeking the smallest portions I can find. It also means I am making the mental adjustment. Mastering the mental game is harder than the physical part. Actually the same is true for all of life.

Another reason not to wait up for the ghost of Dick Clark or Guy Lombardo is that I really need some sleep. I've averaged 5.5 hours a night since the surgery and I really need seven. Feeling it big time. Not at my normal energy levels and it's impacting my irritability. I am starting to obsess about it.

A good night's sleep is a good way to start the New Year. I think I am now in a cycle where worrying about sleep is causing me not to sleep.

My wife, who has never missed an appointment in her life, had a 7:30 a.m. alarm yesterday and I woke up four times (I normally never check the alarm at all) to make sure the alarm went off.

I have a lot of underlying night anxiety as I suspect that night eating and high blood sugar were my version of a Michael Jackson-style of knockout drug.

Exercise and lifestyle are obvious remedies that I have to implement in the upcoming year. I'm working on a balanced life. Well, thinking about it anyway.

Trying to schedule some fun time. End of year has been a lot busier this year. Good for my bank account, bad for hitting sleep goals. Today is going to be a busy morning.

A friend/client died from PPH at age 43 in Orlando. Huge outpouring of appreciation for the work Clay and I did for her from her husband, family and friends.

They literally moved me to tears. I am proud that we made her last decade happy. I am sad that she is gone. She was cheering for my weight loss surgery online as recently as last week. I am going to write a column about her and tie it to a lot of things shortly.

Another reason to appreciate life and the New Year. Like my doctors, I get to use my education to help people. Most people would love to be me. Especially the thinner, healthier me.

Since the average person gains about 10 pounds between Thanksgiving and Christmas and I have lost 35 since the surgery on Dec. 1, I figure I am at least 45 pounds ahead of the rest of the world, making it a HAPPY NEW YEAR.

The Second Month

January 1, 2015
6 a.m.

Weight: 320.2
Blood Sugar: 115
Temp.: 97.5
Hours of Sleep: 8.6

> *"The world is quiet on New Year's Day"*
> -U2[1]

> *"Hey, look me over*
> *Tell me do you like what you see?"*
> -an artist currently known as "Prince"[2]
> (When I woke today, my wife got the thrill of hearing me sing this song.)

Excellent New Year's Eve. We had a terrific dinner at Portofino and about 85 percent of my veal meatballs came home with me. Had a couple more for lunch today and still have some left. Our waitress was excellent and we had a great time.

I would have been tempted to seriously eat, but fortunately my gastric sleeve won't let me. The food I did not order looked terrific. Note the weight loss again today, as it was exactly one month ago today when I had the surgery.

That is the beauty of the sleeve over a traditional diet where willpower is not the building block of the system. I don't have any choice but to follow the plan. I don't even care if other people are eating tempting food around me, which was a real problem in the past. I have to ration the amount of food my stomach can accept at one time. Thus, I choose carefully.

Bob Babbage sent me an article from the *Washington Post* about morbid obesity that stated 92 percent of people who start a diet are not going to make it.[3] Especially in the morbidly obese category.

I was jumping up and down with enthusiasm just before dinner as we found late in the day that a book that we published for Suzette Standring, a wonderful syndicated columnist in Boston, won first place in the New England Book Festival.[4] RRP International has had several bestsellers, but this was my first time for critical acclaim as a publisher. It helps that Suzette is a terrific writer.

It is a little bit like Nirvana or Kiss winning a Grammy. A lot of other publishers sniff at our focus on commercial success over impressing the critics, so it is nice to have both.

They can keep on sniffing, but their authors are in second place. Or worse. Thinking about calling a few competitors and mentioning that. And noting their book sales numbers while I am at it.

It was a very nice way to end the year. Especially since we have Dr. Jim's book near the goal line and I have my own book coming out next year.

"I don't like to sleep alone"
-Paul Anka[5]

Karen is an early riser and has not stayed awake until midnight since I met her, so when she went down for the count about 11 p.m., I started channel surfing and wound up on an incredible tribute to Bruce Springsteen on KET. By the time it ended, it was 1 a.m. Never heard the New Year's fireworks outside. Went to bed quietly.

Karen was not woken by the fireworks, but she was by the squeak of my CPAP facemask. She came into Lexington for dinner and is now back on the road to New Orleans, so it was her first time to be here with the CPAP next to my bed since the surgery. The pressures were coming in so hard that it was knocking the mask off my face and making a ton of noise. She can sleep through a nuclear attack, so it had to be loud.

About 4 a.m., I switched to a backup CPAP that I keep perpetually in my suitcase. It is less powerful and I slept extremely well after that. I have a similar one that I keep in New Orleans (I have CPAPs everywhere). Took me a minute to realize that my last good night's sleep happened in Elizabethtown and that was the same backup CPAP.

Suspect that the settings on my nice CPAP near the bed are too powerful for my current weight and the backup, which was set a few years ago when I was about 20 pounds heavier than at the moment, is more accurate. Going to try it this week and keep tracking. If I overcome the lack of sleep hump, I am going to be totally thrilled.

Happy New Year.

January 2, 2015
3 p.m.

Weight: 318
Blood Sugar: 126
Temp.: 97.7
Hours of Sleep: 7.5

Dr. Jim sent an email to me this morning which said, "I hope you did not stay up and watch that football game." Well, actually I did. It ended after 1 a.m. and I stuck through the post-game show till 2 a.m. Then I decided to continue on a long biography of John Fogerty (ask me anything about the music of CCR, anything) and it was after 3 a.m. when I got to bed. Since I am determined to get in seven hours of sleep (switching CPAPs seems to help), it made for a very late start to the day. This is one day where I don't have anywhere to be, so I am using it as a "catch up" day. I need to do a ton of end of year accounting and writing.

I am thrilled about the weight drop this morning. It's the first time my weight is in the teens and knocking on 60 pounds lost. I went grocery shopping late last night. Trying to walk the walk of finding things that are high protein, low carb, preferably low calories and with no fructose. Last part is the hardest in a Kroger. Even things advertised as organic can be marketing ploys. Kroger has an organic yogurt which includes, "organic corn starch." OK. The idea is to get me to buy it over a cheaper brand with non-organic corn starch. I am working hard to not get tricked into things.

It takes me at least an hour to shop for groceries, even though I use the smallest cart and buy about one-fifth of the amount of food that I used to buy. The price is about the same as healthy food costs more.

I am working towards getting my protein and carb goals in (I shoot for 125 grams of protein and less than 40 on carbs) without falling back to my handy protein shakes. I am down to one a day. They are packed with protein, but also with fat and 170 calories. Hard for me to eat 170 calories of food in one sitting, even if I tried, so the move to reduce my protein shake intake ought to keep my calories and fat down over the long haul.

Watching a series of YouTube videos from gastric sleeve patients while I eat a late lunch. Like anything on YouTube, some are terrible, some are mediocre and a couple are excellent.

Hearing how people have lost hundreds of pounds and kept it off is inspiring. It made me realize that a severe issue in the post-surgery process is that I cannot find any weekly support groups to join.

When I asked at Georgetown Hospital, I was told they do it once a quarter and bring in a speaker. That is not a support group; that is a pep rally. Not what I am looking for. If another hospital has one and would let me attend, I would definitely consider that.

I realize that support is a missing piece of the puzzle. Economics probably play into why the weekly support groups aren't encouraged, but this is one where the corporations are missing the big picture. It would be good for the patient and good for the hospital to have people singing their praises on a weekly basis. Or even complaining. It's like a focus group for the bariatric program; you learn what is on people's minds and how to adjust your business model to that.

Anyway, I personally want to find a group to join.

I draw a lot about my journey from two sources. One is my five trips through Dr. James Anderson's liquid weight loss program at the University of Kentucky. One of the keys was mandatory attendance at weekly meetings. It did not need to be mandatory for me. Once I got into a group I connected with, I never missed. We weighed in and got a weekly update on where we were. We shared our ideas and motivated each other. I've been going through my old records (I saved a ton of them over the years), and you can mark when I started to miss my classes as to when my weight started to increase. A direct correlation.

I am sharing my story with the world, which helps at many levels, but it's not the same as being in a group of similar people. Because it was a university-based program, my classmates tended to be highly educated and motivated and many remain friends. A perfect demographic for me. That is the other part. I don't do as well with people who are not as motivated. Sometimes my enthusiasm will inspire others, but I guess I am looking for groups like the ones I had at UK.

My second group I draw from is more from a distance: Watching my friends who have changed their lives with 12-step, AA or other addiction programs. I've written about these groups often as I have seen the amazing difference they have made in people who are very close. I use Al Smith as a role model as he is very open about how AA changed his life 51 years ago, and Al has a wonderful network of friends he developed in the program. I have at least two friends who go to AA 365 days a year. That strategy works and the idea of a group works for me.

Gastric surgery patients are a subset of themselves, different than

Weight Watchers or Overeaters Anonymous. At the same time, they are going through rapid and dramatic life changes due to their changes in body weight. Most of the changes are positive, but some are stressful and complicated. My wife, family and friends are 100 percent behind me and I get a ton of positive reinforcement from writing things like this (and my *Huffington Post* and social media posts), but I have been through other weight loss programs in my life when I did not have family support and it is a lonely battle.

These are people who took a brave and expensive step and I want the others to succeed as much as I want to succeed. Watching my friends in AA, they get back when they give back. I understand the process and would like to like to make that happen for me.

Today's weight was a good day for Don. I really want to get to 294 as the next milestone. It would mean I am under 300 for the first time since 2004. It would mean I am no longer morbidly obese. A major step into a different category.

January 5, 2015
9 a.m.

Weight: 318.2
Blood Sugar: 100
Temp.: 97.7
Hours of Sleep: 6

> *"I'll make you wish there were 48 hour to each day"*
> -Chaka Kahn[6]

> *"Once you get started*
> *Oh it's hard to stop"*
> -Chaka Kahn[7]

> *"Chaka Kahn let me tell you what I want to do*
> *I want you to feel for me like I feel for you"*
> -Rapper at intro to Chaka Kahn's "I Feel For You"[8]

I do a dead on imitation of the "I Feel For You" intro, complete with total command of the lyrics and the dance to boot. When we are in the same city, I sing this for my wife on a regular basis. If she ever divorces or shoots me, my regular performances of the song will be listed as a provocation.

I'm fortunate that my wife understands my crush on Chaka Kahn, which started in high school and never really quit. She tolerates the fact that I have completely mastered "I'll Feel For You" as my singing voice is a very deep baritone and I can do most rappers pretty easily. (I actually do better on 1970s soul singers like Isaac Hayes or Barry White, but the rappers are popular now.)

Thus, I feel good about listening to a series of Chaka as wake up songs, especially since I am by myself. I need to practice the rap part and the dance gives a few seconds of exercise.

The 48 hours to each day part comes up today. I have a true sense of excitement. This is the first true work week of the new year, in the post-surgery world. The weekend was a breakthrough of sorts. I wrote a 3,300-word piece for *Huffington Post* that I am proud of and racking up big numbers.

I easily spent 30 hours in three days writing it, along with a full schedule of other activities, and never seemed to get tired, like I have in the past month. First time I feel like my old energy levels are back.

I am driving to Somerset to see Debra Lambert get sworn in as a Court of Appeals Judge. RRP International Publishing and Digital Media did her website and social media in a campaign where she beat an incumbent, and I was her de-facto campaign adviser as she ran her own campaign without consultants. I did paid campaign consulting before I got into writing my newspaper column, so it was fun to get back in for the first time in 12 years and have an "upset" winner to boot. I thought Debra would always win, but "the experts" thought otherwise. Almost every campaign I was involved with was one where "the experts" thought the other side would win.

Sometimes they were right, but normally no. Rooting for the underdog is what I do.

About 150 miles of riding in the car. Stretching the envelope of what I am capable of each day. Also, I am on Joe Elliott's radio show at 10:35 a.m. in Louisville. He wants to talk about my weight loss. I run from there to the University of Kentucky so I can hand deliver some papers related to Ms. Karen, as they call her in New Orleans, becoming Dr. Karen later this year. I have explicit instructions to put those in the professor's hands and that will happen. Grabbing some lunch and off to Somerset. I have to squeeze some settlement work into the mix. Also, some accounting and tax work. And we are pushing hard on Dr. Jim's book as it needs to be at the printer by Feb. 1.

I feel as well as pre-surgery, and actually better in many respects. My very normal blood sugar has kept my up-and-down temperament more balanced (although I still have my moments) and not dragging around the 59 pounds I was dragging pre-surgery makes a world of difference. Try walking around with 60 extra pounds in weights or dumbbells all day if you want to test my theory.

Normally January is a slower month and last year really was. I stayed in New Orleans last year as I didn't have much going on in Lexington, but this year, I am here for the immediate future. We have a lot happening.

I have ideas about operating at a slower pace, but post-surgery scheduling is an art that needs work. I get a psychological benefit out of being so busy and getting out in the universe, and moving toward a "normal" life is important for my happiness. Trying not to push myself to the level of "stressed out" is always a challenge, and balancing work that I like to do versus work that I need to do is a complicated dance, too.

I'm also keeping myself focused on the bottom line of health and exercise. The second word has not made it into my vocabulary yet. I started looking at gyms in Lexington over the weekend. I really don't like gyms, but would like to start Zumba again and need to get the exercise part of life started. Looking at the usual suspects like YMCA, LA Fitness, etc.

I am at a point where I am no longer stressed about going to a restaurant (I can eat a lot of things, but only three ounces at a time) and back into a normal swing.

January 7, 2015
7 a.m.

Weight: 317.2
Blood Sugar: 115
Blood Pressure: 128/84
Temp.: 96.9

> *"When I'm out in the street*
> *I walk the way I want to walk"*
> -Bruce Springsteen[9]

Dr. Derek has an insightful and talented physician assistant (and fine graduate of EKU) working with him named Heather Pile.

I had an excellent day at Georgetown Hospital yesterday. Heather and I met at length about a variety of topics including my decreasing blood pressure, my decreasing weight, which Kroger grocery is most friendly to my new and improved lifestyle and our mutual admiration of my surgeon. I just sent my first referral to Derek yesterday, but I am confident it will not be my last.

Heather gave me a chart of my weight, which looks like a graph of the stock market in 2008. Straight down.

I am going to start being more diligent in checking my blood pressure. It is showing dramatic improvement and there may be a point where I talk to Dr. Phil about changing my medicines.

My goal is to get 70 oz. of water and 125 grams of protein every day. When I do that, everything falls in line. Heather gave me the go ahead to be reasonably unrestricted in what I eat. The trick is protein first and then other foods, but I have that down. Also, remember not to drink fluids and eat at same time. She warned me that old habits are going to be hard to break and why I should never pick up Diet Coke again, although it remains my only craving.

Derek has some ideas for a gym and Cindy Caywood is working on getting me into Zumba. I would love to nail those projects by the end of the week as exercise is my missing component. I did my last psych exam with Dr. Smith-West yesterday. She likes my attitude. Actually, I like my attitude, too.

As I get "out in the street" as The Boss would say, people are constantly wanting to know "my secret" as the change in my looks are noticeable. They don't quite understand that I am only about one-third of the way along my journey. Being out and about is a good way to help preach the gospel of overall good health. This journey is not just for me, but an opportunity to make an impact. If I start getting other morbidly obese people to check into weight loss surgery, that is a game changer. If I can get them to start being more informed consumers and understand the role of vitamins and supplements in overall health, that is a game changer, too.

Also, as my youngest daughter noted yesterday, being out and about is what I do. I'm the face and brand of my organization. Things go better when I circulate. Thus, I am headed to a breakfast meeting right now and then to a reception in Frankfort tonight. The weather may be zero, but that is not an excuse.

January 8, 2014
2 p.m.

Weight: 316.6
Blood Sugar: 135
Temp: 98.1
Hours of Sleep: 10

"Elvis Is Dead and I Don't Feel So Good Myself"
-One of my favorite book titles by Lewis Grizzard[10]

*"There are too many things waiting in front of me
But right now I am trying to sleep"*
-Don's paraphrase of a Jimmy Buffett song[11]

"Go to sleep Jeff"
-The Wiggles[12]

Yesterday was a complicated day. After sending a 7 a.m. report that I felt great, I went to an excellent breakfast meeting at 9 a.m. and had to leave. Felt incredibly tired and a little stomach distress. Stomach distress has historically been my first sign of illness, but since the surgery, I really don't have any stomach distress. I just wanted to fall asleep right in the middle of the restaurant.

I've had a runny nose since early in the week, and my voice has been rough and irritated. Bad timing as I had a pedal to the metal schedule on the first couple of days and a lot of talking and traveling in cars. Also, a lot of being outside in the cold. I forgot to run my humidifier this weekend, and I think that contributed to the runny nose.

Anyway, I came home and fell asleep immediately on the couch fully dressed in a suit. Probably would have slept for hours, but my phone kept ringing and waking me up. (When I didn't answer, people would assume I had some kind of post-surgery trauma or death and call over and over until I picked up.) Had a lot of start and stop sleep. I could talk, but my voice was very hoarse and I tried to avoid it at all costs.

I was incredibly tired and incredibly grumpy. The people who did manage to wake me up to talk probably wished they had not. The world was coming in through a very negative lens. Also, I think my voicemail is not working properly as people don't seem to be able to leave messages. I am very good on email and even starting to text a little bit.

I did not have a temperature, and in fact my temperature was in the 96 to 97 range all day. I loaded up on my vitamins, but I never miss with those anyway. I slept as much I could through the interruptions, from 1 a.m. to roughly 11 a.m. today. I ate more than normal and loaded on fluids as well. No loss of appetite. In fact, the opposite. I was hungrier than normal.

Anyway, I can't really tell where I am today. It's nearly 1 p.m. and I am just in a state of wakeup. My runny nose stopped yesterday. Not sure about my voice as I haven't spoken to anyone yet and have no desire to do so.

Having some fluids now and making some eggs after I type this. Today was the only day this week when I did not have any appointments, and I just cancelled my lunch appointment tomorrow to give me an open run into the weekend to recover. Slept pretty solidly with two humidifiers all night. I really don't want to talk, but suspect I could better than yesterday. Don't feel awake or asleep. Like in a stage of limbo.

Probably best that I stay away from work. We have a couple of projects that have turned from supposedly simple to incredibly tedious and with my patience so thin, it is best that I avoid them until fully rested.

I tend to heal best as a solo act. I'm not shy about seeking help when I need it, but sleep, nutrition and hydration seem to be the keys.

I suspect my body is telling me that I went at it too hard, and that is not the first time I have ever had that message. Monday and Tuesday were overbooked, but don't know how to avoid days like that. Which client, ceremony, family member, media appearance or doctor's appointment do I say no to?

I'm glad I did the radio show and then went to Somerset, but I could feel my voice going the whole trip and I did not have access to fluids or proper foods. I should have planned the day differently. It was freezing cold and I had too many things to do that day.

I was worn out on Tuesday and my trip to Georgetown Hospital was later in the day. I rushed to get there. I was there nearly four hours, but I won't be back for three months. I don't have to do the shrink visit anymore, which was about 90 minutes. Thus, that kind of day won't happen there again. Maybe I should have asked for a break between people I saw. It was the end of their day and I love all the people so all meetings went long. I should have brought some protein shakes or fluids. I did not plan well. I was miserable by my time home.

Going to wait until I get into a better frame of mind to make any major decisions. Might be back on track when I start feeling better.

There is always a first of the year rush in the financial business. I had planned for that, but now that it is here, I don't feel like I am keeping up with the plans I laid out. Being sick puts me further behind.

Dan Sullivan always pushed us to take planned free time, saying your body would give unplanned free time such as a heart attack. The whole idea behind doing the weight loss is to avoid that heart attack. I don't want to take any more planned time off and especially unplanned like today.

My body is telling me I needed a break. Which mentally frustrates me as I don't want to take a break. I want to do all the things on my list. Especially since I have been off for the month before. I want to be rewarded for my good recovery with a seamless transition back to a new and better world. I am not getting my "recovery bonus," and I am not a guy who is particularly patient.

Anyway, a long rant as I adjust to the post-surgery world. These issues are not related to surgery, but they are. I want to get all of my life "right" as I move into my second half, and somehow balancing my most important resources, time and people (followed by financial stability) is far harder than getting ready for surgery and following instructions post-surgery.

Note I did pass the 60-pound mark. That would be a huge accomplishment if that was the goal line, but it is really only about the one-third marker. It was like in financial services. My goal at age 25 was to make the Million Dollar Round Table. My goal at age 35 was to be the only Kentuckian at the top of the Million Dollar Round Table. It wasn't until I got an award for making the MDRT 25 years in a row that I even remembered it was a goal. Once I focused on a higher number, the other became a mark that I never thought about.

I am happy about 60 pounds, but my first real milestone is 100. I'll be happy when I go under 295 as that will mean I am no longer morbidly obese. All those will happen in due course.

I did well in recovery. I worked on things at my own pace and the people around me stepped up and did an incredible job with me out of the day-to-day picture. Doing a daily memo really helped me mentally.

I went into the end of the year with more enthusiasm for work than any time in the past decade. The surgery did a wonderful job of allowing me to think like the Chinese, in terms of centuries, instead of in terms of fiscal quarters like Americans do. My long-term thinking is becoming longer term. On days when I feel well, I see the big picture.

During recovery, I had time to take my naps in the middle of the afternoon and do work on my own schedule, not someone else's.

I really missed having lunch with my friends and getting out and was thrilled to get to do that again. I go from one extreme to the other, where I am eager to get back into what I was doing pre-surgery and then frustrated when I can't seem to pull it off. Whenever I make a push, there is a setback.

Mentally, I go from running everyone off to feeling intensely isolated and lonely. Sometimes in the same day. In fact, often in the same day.

It's like the line in the John Mellencamp song; I want "someone to thrill me and then go away."[13] (Actually, he was Johnny Cougar back then, but it was still a great song.) It is a mental roller coaster.

Writing all this down and sharing it seems to work for me at some deep level. I've never kept a diary or anything like that before. One of my post-surgery goals was to be totally honest about where I am, day-to-day, and not be afraid to share it. I am incredibly fortunate to have such an understanding group of friends and family who get it and get me. I don't fall into any simple category, but people understand that.

Also, I am thrilled that I know I can send my daily report, good, bad or indifferent, and know that my friends will still be there tomorrow without judgment or hesitation. A lot of people have to posture to make an impression on the world. In fact, most do. The fact that I don't is one of the greatest blessings God has given me.

Today, I am in a down mood. With some rest, I probably won't be so down tomorrow. I wrote to a friend yesterday whose mother is quite ill and wants to give up and quoted Vince Lombardi to her: "Fatigue makes cowards of us all."[14] It really does. If we can figure out where the fatigue comes from, that is a huge start.

Back to Elvis. Happy 80th birthday to the King. I really admired him for many reasons and appreciated his talent and contribution to American history. He also died at age 42 and was a mess when he went out.

I used a line from Elvis in *Life Lessons from the Lottery*: "I believe the key to happiness is having someone to love, something to do and something to look forward to."

As I noted, Elvis had none of those going for him when he died, but he had the right insight in mind. Following Elvis' philosophy and not his last years of how he lived life is a pretty good goal to strive for.

I am off to take care of business. Probably not with a flash, but moving in that direction. Today my business is getting rested and into a positive frame.

For at least 20 years, when someone does something special or extraordinary in our businesses, I send them TCP, which is taking care of penguin, our corporate logo. Thought about designing a necklace with a penguin and a lightning bolt like the ones the King used to wear, but have not gotten there yet.

January 9, 2015
4 p.m.

Weight: 316
Blood Sugar: 108
Blood Pressure: 135/87
Hours of Sleep: 6

> *"And now I'm walking to New Orleans"*
> -Fats Domino[15]

Good day here.

Recovering from the cold I had earlier in the week, but my voice is still very hoarse. In good spirits and the sun is shining. Having a chance to get some rest cures a lot of problems.

I hit 61 pounds on the weight loss. This means I passed Babe Ruth and now I'm tied with Roger Maris. (If you are not a baseball fan, this will go right past you.) When I double Barry Bonds' production, I will be close to where I want to be. I won't need steroids to do it. (I hate to take a crack at Barry as I think he deserves to be in the Hall of Fame, but couldn't help myself.)

Have the OK to travel as of today. Was tempted to hop on a plane and go to New Orleans for the weekend, but they want $1,600 to do that. I may have to wait a week or so. I have mastered the art of flying cheaply (if travel agents still truly existed, I could be one), but I'm low on options to pull that off. I think everyone wants to escape the cold. On the other hand, I am having lunch with my friend Tom Leach on Monday. The Voice of the UK Wildcats can explain why the Cats can't win all their games by 50 points or more. Actually, they should, but they won't. Shows how motivation and psychology are such as a big part of sports and life.

Motivation is what I have going on the weight loss front. Also, like Coach Cal, it's easy to look good when you have a talented team.

Got leads on Zumba classes, a gym, dance classes and Karen has a friend with the *Golf Channel* who offered me tickets to the PGA event in New Orleans in April. Not missing on those. Being inside for so long makes me desire some kind of exercise, and I'm going to follow up on getting some this weekend.

In 1994, Lexington was snowbound for weeks and it was 10-below zero. I had to get out of town. Had a buddy with a Hummer take me to the Louisville airport. Only plane headed south was going to Jacksonville. Took it. Got a deal at the TPC at Sawgrass and played one of the best rounds of my life. With rented clubs. On the big course. Got a birdie on the 17th Island hole, where most of the pros knock it in the water. One of the hardest holes in golf, but my enthusiasm and the lack of wind in January played into it. I figure I am way up on Tiger Woods when it comes to that hole. He is going to have to give me a lot of strokes on the other ones.

Today is Al Smith's 88th birthday. Actually, he celebrated it on the 8th for years, but that is a funny story as his grandmother was related to Rachel Jackson, the wife of Andrew Jackson, so they celebrated Al's birthday on the anniversary of the Battle of New Orleans. Someone looked it up and got the correct day a few years ago. I called him yesterday, on the Battle of New Orleans Day, and with my throat being hoarse and him on a cell phone we couldn't really hear each other, but we talked for 30 minutes anyway.

He went to AA today to pick up his chip for being sober for the past 52 years. He will always be my hero. I continue to want to be him when I grow up. Also, I hope that my book is one-tenth as good as his autobiography.[16]

January 12, 2015
10 a.m.

Weight: 316. 6
Blood Sugar: 111
Temp.: 97.8
Hours of Sleep: 5.1 hours

Monday's are always busy and I'm having lunch with Tom Leach, who I rarely get to see during basketball season. When I lived in Richmond, we had lunch at least once a month and met in Hamburg. Now that I live about 50 yards from him (he lives on the street behind me), it's been more like once a quarter. Looking forward to it.

I used to get stressed when my weight would blip back the other way (I went up 1.6 pounds from yesterday) as it did today, but there are a number of reasons for the shift and none of them are related to food, carbs or calories. I'll just stick to the plan and it will keep rolling.

I am not a patient guy, but this is a situation where patience and understanding are key. When we do everything right, the weight will keep on coming off. It's like investing; you have to stick to the fundamentals no matter what the markets are doing.

Looking forward to seeing Lee Gentry on Wednesday. I was best man in his 1989 wedding and that was in October; in May, I hit my lowest weight (since age 15) of 179 pounds. I probably weighed about 180 for the wedding, and having a shot at that weight, in a tuxedo, gives an idea of what my body shape will be at 199. It makes for some interesting pictures as I show my weight over time.

Actually, we did an intro video for my website last year (that is Greg Stotelmyer, the voice of the EKU Colonels; I am friends with a lot of "voices") that shows the up and down pretty well. We did not intend that as a weight video, but it serves the purpose.

I saw the movie *Wild* yesterday.[17] I am a big fan of Reese since she won the Oscar in *Walk the Line*[18] (and is the daughter of a Vanderbilt professor, but I did not know him when I went to grad school there) and hope she gets another for this movie. Suspect it is her or Julianne Moore. The movie is about her hiking the Pacific Coast Trail from Mexico to Canada.

I am thinking that when I hit 100 pounds lost I should walk from downtown Lexington to Georgetown Hospital to personally thank Derek and the team for making it happen. I am very serious about this. It is about 20 miles and gives me a goal to shoot for. I walked 25 miles twice in high school so I know I can do it again. I like the idea. A physical goal to work for and we have to figure out a route that keeps me from getting run over by a truck.

Much better that I saw *Wild* than something like *The Hangover*, where I might have come up with a different project.

January 13, 2015
6 p.m.

Weight: 316.8
Blood Sugar: 124
Temp.: 97.4
Hours of Sleep: 6.2

> *"I can just see me on a tropical island*
> *Riding the surf and drinking coconut wine*
> *Having me fun with golden girls in the sand*
> *Chasing the sun through an innocent land*
> *Leaving the straight life behind"*
> -Bobby Goldsboro[19]

I think my wife Karen might have a problem with the third line of the song. Actually, she may hate the entire song as few people have a stronger work ethic than she does.

Not many people remember the song (a top 40 hit) and not many remember Bobby. I absolutely hate the song "Honey," his biggest hit (which was written by a guy from Nicholasville, Ky.), but his last hit, "Summer (The First Time)," was a groundbreaking success in the mid-1970s.

I could have used a plethora of Jimmy Buffett songs, but the idea is the same: IT'S COLD AND I WANT TO GET OUT OF HERE!

After a month of being cooped up in the condo recovering from the surgery and another month being stymied by cold weather, I understand why birds fly south in the winter.

Thus, I am making some moves in that direction.

I booked a flight to New Orleans on the 22nd for a few days and working on a trip that will get me to Tampa-Sarasota around my birthday on Feb. 13. Karen is off that week for Mardi Gras and both of us would rather go to a comfy beach than another white tie (and tails and white gloves, thank you) ball. She went to about 40 parades. I went to four, so that is out of my system for another decade or so.

Thinking about driving down. I have friends in Knoxville and Atlanta. It would be my fourth actual vacation since age 10. I am not kidding. I've been to every part of the USA and Canada, multiple times, and been to some cities like Washington nearly 100. All but three have had a business competent to them. Some people would think that is smart tax planning, but actually it is a sign of a guy who never really disconnects from work.

All of my trips were really business trips, and I have tons of documentation to prove it. I don't go to a conference in Las Vegas to have a write off for going to the casino. I go to actually attend the conference. I turn total nerd at those things and go to most of the sessions. If I go with my son-in-law, Clay Bigler, it is even worse. He goes to everything, including the 5 a.m. sessions and stays in the conference rooms sucking in information until the cows come home.

Anyway, a long way to say that in this second chance at life, I am finally recognizing that being able to disconnect is important. I'm not turning into a beachcomber. My idea of roughing it is staying in a hotel where they don't leave a mint on your pillow, but I am starting to think in terms of taking some time off, which is a total shocker to all those who know me.

At least I am intellectually conceiving the idea of taking time off. I picked the 22nd primarily because I could get a cheap flight. Also, the Pelicans are in town twice. Tickets are incredibly cheap as few people in New Orleans appreciate that watching Anthony Davis, especially when you can do it for the price of a ticket to an Ursuline High School game, is an incredible opportunity.

The Pelicans did get rid of the mascot that made young children cry. A big step up, but I hate the new team name.

Looks like the Pelicans are going to get rid of the coach soon, too. Probably a step up, but I am mixed as he lives on the street behind us in Old Metairie. A team with that much talent ought to be winning.

A huge step for me is that I can buy basketball tickets and know I can sit in the seats. That has been a big problem in recent years. Three years ago, Karen had tremendous basketball connections at her school in Lexington and got us seats in first row of the stands. The seats are slightly smaller in the lower section and I could not get in it. That was traumatic as it gets. We went to a Pelican's game last year and I had to wedge myself into the seat and never stand up during the game. Not fun.

I started shopping online at games for seats with folding chairs. No more. Even with only 61 pounds off, those are now in the past.

Being able to go to a game and not worry about fitting in the seats is a game changer. When I was on the Kentucky Educational Television program *Comment on Kentucky*, they used to have to bring a special chair for me.[20] If they ever invite me back on the show, I can sit with the rest of them. Al Smith took a lot of heat for booking a guest that was double the size of the others and I always appreciated that.

I took my numbers this morning. I inched up on the weight, but it is a lifelong marathon, not a sprint, and I am doing all those things that should result in weight loss.

Hoping the Kentucky basketball goes quickly tonight. Watching the late night football messed with my sleep. I did not even care who won and still watched it all.

January 14, 2015
11 a.m.

Weight: 319.2
Blood Sugar: 110
Temp.: 97.4
Hours of Sleep: 5.3

> *"Remain calm, all is well."*
> -Kevin Bacon's character in the movie *Animal House*

> *"Townes Van Zandt, he died too soon*
> *But he's up there with Hank*
> *And they're both fighting the Nashville Blues"*
> -Cory Morrow[21]

Ok, I'm panicking now. Also, it's a very bad sign that I'm listening to songs about (or by) Townes.

Townes was a terrific but self-destructive songwriter who died at age 52, but probably with his substance intake should have died well before then. He has a strong cult following (of which I am one) and a big hit, "Pancho and Lefty," that many others have covered.[22]

Townes was incredibly talented, but a guy with a lot of problems. When I was waiting on James Street to pick me up at the Austin Airport about 25 years ago (Street was an All-American quarterback on the field, but an hour late for everything else), I happened to pick up a copy of *Texas Monthly Magazine* (where my friend Joe Nocera had his first job) and read a long feature on Townes, who was still alive at that time.

I became a fan of Townes, the *Texas Monthly* and the Austin music scene all in one day. Austin is one of my favorite cities. A taste of Texas with the university crowd balancing out the macho redneck stuff. A terrific place. Street and his partner at the time wanted me to live there and work with them, but ultimately I am always going to be quarterback of my own team.

Mike Behler emailed me a note of support and encouragement the other night as he was getting ready to fly to San Antonio for some kind of conference for medical school financial aid gurus, and it may have drifted my mind to Texas. San Antonio is my second favorite Texas city and I reminded him, as I remind everyone who goes to San Antonio, to check out the McNay Museum, which is named for Don McNay who died in World War I. (A very distant relative, but they used to literally roll out the red carpet when I showed up.) His wife was married nine times and it was husbands four and seven who left her the big money. It is one of the most impressive collections of impressionist art in the United States. Don got the name, but he didn't have the money.

The McNay family has an interesting history. We are all related to each other in the United States in some distant way. Joe McNay, same name as my father, is one of the country's great investment gurus. He handled the endowment at Yale and handled the blind trust for Bill and Hillary Clinton when Bill was President. I always follow what he is up to. His son Stuart, who I keep up with on Facebook, was an All-American in sailing at Yale and won the Olympic goal medal. There are McNay's in high-powered positions around the country.

The rest of the McNay's are in jail, or headed that way. You don't find many McNay's holding traditional, middle management jobs.

They are either extreme successes or extreme failures. I guess that is how I got my mind to thinking about Townes.

My weight is up to 319.4. It was 315 on Sunday and after a slow inch upward, it took a big leap this morning. I am trying not to panic and intellectually look at my numbers. It's only been a four-day stall. I'm doing all the right things and can see some wrong things (too many nights averaging five hours of sleep, down on my fluids, not enough trips to the bathroom, my feet feel slightly swollen and I have been working extremely hard) that may be playing into my gain. A little more sodium and cheese than normal. Been dropping back on my protein shakes and I think that is cutting into my fluids. Phone didn't stop until 10 p.m. last night and I ate after that. A four oz. piece of steak and spinach seemed like a good option. I don't remember any fluids after that, but had trouble falling asleep. Lifted some weights for a short period of time and not enough to really regain any fluids.

Logically, the weight gain should not be there. My calories are only 283 and I am getting close to my normal protein numbers. More carbs (about 80 to 100) than normal. Blood sugar is good as is everything else. One of the dangers of weighing every day is having that kind of variance, but I think the daily weigh in and strong record keeping (there is not a morsel of food that has touched my mouth since the Dec. 1 surgery that has not been recorded) keep me intellectually grounded.

But as John Prine said, "My girlfriend said that's all in my head, but my stomach tells me to write you instead" (in a song about Dear Abby).[23]

This has to be a lifelong journey without a time limit. On the other hand, having a specific goal works for me. I feel confident that I am going to make it. Or fail miserably like Townes.

A lot of people wonder why I am so public about all this. There are multiple reasons, but one is that I realize that doing things in a public way is a great motivator. It helps make me a role model. I get several emails a day from people interested in surgery. The mother of one of my clients went to a seminar where Derek spoke on Monday and signed up for the process. (Her insurance will drag it out for several months, and I intend to keep her motivated to the goal line.) I think being a role model has a huge psychological benefit for me. The world has become my support group as I want to show people how to do it correctly.

I can also see why people who are in AA want to do it in private. I have a friend who went to dry out after reading my column in his local newspaper. I was getting ready to stop writing my column in 2007, instead of 2013, when he wrote and told me how I inspired him. I've only met him a couple of times, but he writes often and goes to AA 365 days a year. He refuses to ever go public and I get his reasoning.

This is one of those days when I wish I had an in-person community and support like AA does. Georgetown Hospital went back to one a quarter because enough people were not attending. I get that. A far smaller subset and the good thing about the surgery is that you have to be incredibly self-destructive to cheat on it. It's not like a diet where you can just head to McDonalds. They are not giving me part of my stomach back and no matter how much I order, I can only eat a few ounces at a time.

Also, it is a four-day, four-pound gain. That could be anything, I logically tell myself. But my emotional side is scared of being the weight loss version of Townes: Well-known, admired and dead. Townes fell off because of bad habits, a self-destructive attitude, drugs, drinking, nonstop partying and an attitude summed up in a song: "Waiting around to die."[24]

I'm following my plan and rid myself of bad eating habits (not a piece of fast food or any kind of soft drink has touched my lips since I had the surgery, and I can't think of any other time in my life where I could say that). I have followed my doctors and dietician faithfully. I have tracked everything that I do. I can't gain a whole lot of weight eating 1,000 calories a day when I was at 4,000 or more before the surgery. It takes me three sittings to eat a normal meal.

I've dined out for lunch or dinner or both every day this week. I usually eat the leftover as my next meal. That could be bringing in some sodium, but I track the numbers of what I am eating and they don't seem outrageous. Mentally, I need to get out of the condo as well. I am balancing doing too much and not doing enough, but that has been a 55-year struggle and will be 56 next month.

I'm a confident guy. I understand the financial markets and how when the markets are down, it is a great time to buy. (I can't buy into a second surgery, nor do I want to, but I get the general idea.)

I had about 200 investment clients in 1987 and only four sold out. They lost big. The rest did quite well, including my father and myself, who bought tax-free bonds on the day the market crashed.

Those doubled in the next year.

My clients are mostly annuities and fixed income now, but not a single one cashed in during 2008 and some of us waited it out and bought in during 2009. I lived in a rental house from 2005 to 2009 waiting for a bottom in real estate and bought a nice house at a bargain in 2009. I was rewarded for my patience and long-term view.

Only on weight loss do I let negative emotions sneak in. It's the only place in my life where I have ever had multiple failures and put myself in life-threatening danger.

The rewards are long-term. I get that. Yes, I get that. On the other hand, Townes keeps whispering in my ear, filling me with negative emotions.

I guess I need to listen more loudly to Kevin Bacon.

January 15, 2015
4 p.m.

Weight: 317
Blood Sugar: 103
Temp.: 97.4
Hours of Sleep: 4.9

> *"To be the man, you have to beat the man."*
> -Ric Flair[25]

> *"To be the man, you have to beat Pierce Hamblin."*
> -Don McNay

Today was a good day. Stayed busy all day, helped a family pro bono with their finances (I do terrific work for people with no money, or people with money who don't want to pay me) and feel very productive.

My weight is down 2.4 pounds from yesterday and a couple of helpful hints from friends took me a long way. Back on track.

The comeback reminds us that we can overcome all the bumps in the road.

Today was my buddy Pierce Hamblin's birthday. You can see our picture plastered all over social media. Actually Pierce won't be looking at social media since he doesn't have time for that sort of thing. He's one of the best mediators in the United States, a longtime and popular professor at the University of Kentucky law school and a terrific litigator. I've worked for him and I've worked for attorneys opposing him. You know it is going to be a battle and you always want Pierce in your foxhole.

What Pierce does have time to do, nearly every day, is send me a note of encouragement. When you look up loyalty in the dictionary, you see Pierce's picture. Thus, I gave him a gift that I knew he would prize: a copy of wrestler Ric Flair's autobiography, *To Be The Man.*[26]

Like myself, Pierce is a huge wrestling fan and I got the chance to meet Flair in Erlanger, Kentucky about 20 years ago. (All the wrestlers in that era stayed at the now defunct Drawbridge Inn.) Ric was as opposite as his ring persona as you could get. Very nice. I also met Roddy Piper and a ton of other wrestlers like George "The Animal" Steele, who was actually a literature professor during the week. Piper was just like his ring personality and got arrested that night.

If I can ever pull off a chance for Pierce to meet Slick Ric, I will.

I used to do book reviews for the *Lexington Herald-Leader*. They started as a consolation prize when they ended all the community columnists in 1985, including me. I kept the gig up until I started writing my own column again in 2003, but my last gig at the *Herald* was *To Be The Man*. The book editor knew I was a huge wrestling fan and assigned it to me.

Slick Ric got a favorable review, as he should have. Pierce will always get a favorable review, but his intense concern and loyalty as I go through this weight loss journey have meant a lot to me. There are days (like today) when I feel like George Bailey in *It's a Wonderful Life* and finally start to realize how lucky I am to have true and caring friends.[27]

Slick Ric would say we are "styling and profiling." I use that phrase often as I frequently quote the poetry of professional wrestling in my work.

January 17, 2015
2 p.m.

Weight: 314.2
Blood Sugar: 133
Temp.: 97.1
Hours of Sleep: 9.3

"Sometimes I lay awake at night and wonder

It's 2 p.m. and my day is really just starting to get rolling. My editor came over yesterday and helped me give my condo a massive makeover. It looks great. All of my electronic stuff is now hooked up and it was more physical activity than normal for me.

Not only does the place look good, the activity wore me down, but I did not fall asleep right away. When I did, I hit the jackpot. I slept for 9.3 hours according to the CPAP, but I think the true number is closer to 12 hours as I fell asleep sitting up and reading (I do this often) and then went to bed and put the CPAP on.

It's one of the nicest days in Lexington this month and part of me wants to be out in it. The other part understands that waking up after noon was necessary to get my sleep back on track. I had six consecutive days averaging about 5.5 hours of sleep. I absolutely need seven. After a heavily scheduled week, I left this weekend very unscheduled (my office is off Monday, but I had to cram in an appointment) as I am starting to understand how my body needs a reset button.

I'm headed to New Orleans on Thursday. A quick four-day trip, but plan on making it more of a fun trip, and less of a new location for my work, than in the past.

Dan Sullivan, my entrepreneurial guru in Toronto, taught us to plan our free time first and keep that time sacred. Then plan your work time around those free days. I know a ton of entrepreneurs and few of them follow the system until they get older and a life event, like a heart attack, makes them reevaluate how they do things.

I found Dan in 1994, spent most of 1999 and 2000 traveling to Toronto for his class and made another run at him in 2006. My children knew the sound of his voice from the nonstop tapes that I listened to in the car, but I never got the system down.

The second part I never quite got was even more important: protecting your health means sometimes forsaking fun activities on free days. About midweek, I made the decision that Friday night and Saturday afternoon were going to be devoted to catching up on my sleep. Nothing was going to interfere with that.

"Resetting the clock" is not something I have always done. It's always been kind of a macho thing with me to show off how many hours I put in at work and how I could supposedly get by with little sleep. The bad things happening to my body that resulted in making the decision to do weight loss surgery were the result of decades of making the sleep versus activity tradeoff.

The great thing about my habit, which is becoming strongly ingrained, of tracking a number of statistics about my everyday living is that it is gives me a pattern to look at. I also understand the trade offs. I feel great after my 12 hours of sleep. It reset my averages and even if I don't do anything else today, I'm back on track.

My weight is at its lowest ever, and it was about a five-pound loss since a blip upward last week. Blood sugar is slightly higher as I packed in more fruit and carbs during the week and my morning sugar readings are always higher if I have 10 or more hours with no food.

Like good accounting for money, the record keeping allows me to see trends, make adjustments and make decisions that are pragmatic (like sleeping away my Saturday) but emotionally challenging (I want to be in the sunshine). Also helps me make some long-term plans, just like financial projections do for your money.

One of my buddies called when I was asleep. I am going to catch up with him, get a good night's sleep again tonight and be ready for the rest of life (which I'm projecting to be a long one) after that.

If you think long-term, there will be plenty of time for sunshine. I wrote a tribute to one of my recently deceased clients on *Huffington Post* recently and I used the Tim McGraw song "Live Like You Are Dying." There is also that part of "Live Like You are Living" that you have to work in, too. I talked to my friend's husband yesterday. He is a hurting guy, but she had her post-death planned well, worked around her limitations and took time to make sure that her health came first.

A good plan.

January 18, 2015
4 p.m.

Weight: 314
Blood Sugar: 121
Temp.: 96.2
Hours of Sleep: 3.9

> *"Laughing, laughing with our friends"*
> -John Mellencamp[29]

> *"When you talk to God, they call it prayer. When God talks to you, they call it schizophrenia."*
> -Dr. Jim Roach, in his upcoming book *God's Houses Calls*

Jumping quickly to have brunch with Bob Babbage, one of my closest friends.

We both stay busy and we might get lunch once a year, but it is always one of the best hours of the year. One of the bonds of long-term (35-plus years) friendship is the ability to make each other laugh. Like nonstop. We talked for a bit on the phone yesterday and it was like listening to two Borscht belt comedians at the Friars Club. One funny story after another.

In the live version of "Stairway to Heaven" from the movie *The Song Remains the Same*, Robert Plant cries out, "Does anybody remember laughter?"[30] I couldn't stand the movie when I saw it in the theater in high school and still like the group (and song) a lot better than the movie (I like blank test patterns more than that movie), but it is a prophetic line.

We need more laughter in our lives. Always.

Dr. Jim Roach, who knows a thing or two about integrative medicine, understands the healing power of laughter and of prayer.

He just finished the first draft of his first book, *God's House Calls*, which RRP International is publishing for him. One of the neat things about being a publisher is that I get to see books as they are formed and before anyone else. Sat up and read a good chunk of Dr. Jim's book last night. This will be a hit. Also a book that inspires and moves people.

My weight inches down. Sixty-three pounds is the newest record.

I've added more fruit and carbs to the diet, primarily for balance and digestive reasons, and it is slightly upping my carbs, but they are still in the normal zone. Exercise has not really come into the game and has to. I have a gym scoped out and need to join. I have someone helping me line up Zumba and possibly group dancing (a new skill), and I need to get those into the mix somehow. I've gotten away from some of the things to raise my body temperature and will get back on that today. I had a good night on Friday and a lousy one last night.

Off to work on my one liners. Actually, my buddy has a message to leave on voicemails that I am going to blatantly steal. I think it was Jackie Gleason who wrote that good comics write and great comics steal.

This is one that will get stolen.

January 19, 2015
3:30 p.m.

Weight: 315
Blood Sugar: 124
Temp.: 97.1
Hours of Sleep: 5.3

> *"Anybody here seen my old friend Martin?*
> *Can you tell me where he's gone?*
> *He freed lots of people, but it seems the good, they die young*
> *I just looked around and he's gone"*
> -Dion[31]

> *"We are young, but getting old before our time*
> *We'll leave the T.V. and the radio behind*
> *Don't you wonder what we'll find*
> *Steppin' out tonight"*
> -Joe Jackson[32]

Charles Foster Kane: *"You long-faced, overdressed anarchist!"*
Jed Leland: *"I am not overdressed!"*[33]

I was overdressed today. I had a meeting downtown this morning and decided to walk. It's a beautiful day of about 50 degrees in Lexington, but I dressed like I planned to sleep with the polar bears. I did walk the 2.1 miles back and forth, which is about 2.05 miles further than I have walked in some time. I was shedding clothes like a stripper on a time clock, but thrilled about the effort.

I realized that exercise had to be the next competent in my development. Not just talking about it, but doing something about it.

I was not happy that I had to work on the King holiday. With all of the events of the last year, that was a time when I wanted to honor Dr. King in a big way. However, it was an urgent matter and needed to be cleared up before I go to New Orleans on Thursday. Thus, I suspect Dr. King would be OK with it. Especially since I built an exercise portion into it.

Exercise is truly a psychological nightmare for me. I played team sports every day of my childhood and it was an integral part of my life. When all that stopped, I never found something to replace it. Team sports are more than about exercise. They teach leadership, teamwork, sharing and worked well for super competitive people like me. The idea of walking on a treadmill to nowhere has never connected.

I played football, baseball, basketball, track, golf and ran cross country in the eighth grade. I was pretty good at all of them. Somewhere in my mind, I think I can still do them, even if I have not picked up a ball in decades.

There is that dynamic of wanting to get back to the same level of competitiveness in sports that I had in my youth. My track team in high school won our region all three years I was on varsity and had a couple of legitimate chances to win the state. I came back when I was 28 years old (I weighed about 230 pounds) for an alumni track meet and my class won the 1,600 meters. I put in an excellent time as anchor for the team, and we won when I dived over the finish line on the asphalt.

It's illegal to dive across the finish line, but no one, even the guy who was stride for stride with me, was going to call me on it. Especially since I ripped my shirt and skinned my knees in the process.

I still have the gold medal. I will always have it. The meet proved two points: that I am insanely competitive and have a high opinion of my abilities.

I also still have my C coat that Covington Catholic gives to people who score a certain number of varsity points in their career. I have it sealed by the dry cleaners like a wedding dress and used to think I wanted to be buried in it. Obtaining it was the focus of my high school years.

Which was a long time ago. Like 37 years ago.

Thus, let's get back to the treadmill to nowhere.

> *"When I was a child*
> *I dreamed like a child of wonder*
> *But it's gone, it's gone*
> *Must have found a way out my back door*
> *Must have run away out my back door"*
> -Melissa Etheridge[34]

I hang onto golf as it is the last sport that I can play on a competitive basis. I'll be 56 in a few weeks and I don't see many 56-year-olds playing pro baseball or football. Even the football kickers aren't that old. My body moved on decades ago, but my mind is still waiting for the Cincinnati Reds to call.

My father was an excellent athlete and then was a professional gambler, so the ideas of sports and competitiveness have been intertwined with me since birth. I grew up with the process of prepping for game day, going all out during the game and then the game ends.

The idea of preparation, play the game and go on to the next game has served me well in business. Businesses like structured settlements and journalism take that model into the business world. All I ever wanted, from the time I was a small child, was a career where I did not do the same thing every day. Working nine to five may have worked for Dolly Parton (actually it didn't really work for her either), but it really does not work for me.[35]

It finally occurred to me that I am getting to the heart of my disconnect with exercise. I've always viewed it as preparation for competition, where people who manage their health do things like walking or jogging as part of their overall daily routine. It's like brushing their teeth. They aren't going to get a medal or trophy for it. It is just something they do.

This is very new thinking for me. At least as far as exercise is concerned.

I have a history, throughout my adult life, of going gung ho into an exercise program or sport and then suddenly stopping. I had 80 golf lessons in two years, about 10 last year and none on the schedule for this year. I did Zumba twice a day, got into the masters Zumba program and stopped. I ran one 5K and never again.

I was always the player you wanted to carry the ball to the goal line, but suddenly I am realizing that being in shape is not a goal line. Just day-in, day-out living.

That makes exercise a lot more complicated for me. But it also explains my hundreds of trips on and off the wagon. I'm like Alexander the Great. I want some part of the world left to conquer.

This insight may seem obvious to my friends who walk or exercise with no competitive goal in mind, but this is like the burning bush to me. A truly deep revelation.

I have two options. The first is I start training for some unknown competition and get serious about some kind of goal. I can prep for an Ironman or some long race or see if I can train to play in the American League as a designated hitter. Until I got bifocals, I could still whack the baseball and would occasionally DH in softball.

The second option is to treat exercise like a routine. Like shaving, showering or brushing my hair. I really don't have any hair to brush, so some exercise routine could fill that void.

The actor James Coburn was able to shave his entire face (back when razors were really razors) in less than the 30 seconds it took to make a commercial. Made him famous in the advertising world. Other than that, I've never known any reason to track how quickly or often that I shave. I just do it every day.

This insight has given me a lot to ponder, but I think that maybe I am on to something.

Since I view the weight loss surgery as a chance to be reborn in many senses of the word, it could be that shedding my mental attachment to competitive sports, 38 years after the sports really ended, might be the key to my understanding how to make exercise part of my daily life.

The treadmill to nowhere might be actually be headed towards a healthier life.

Not ready to give up completely on the Cincinnati Reds calling me someday, but it may be time to mentally hang up the spikes.

This is going to be tougher than giving up fast food and Diet Coke, but I have managed to shed them. It could be that the competition is within myself, to see if I can let go of the past and understand how exercise fits into my future.

And not have to win a medal to do it.

January 21, 2015
8 p.m.

Weight: 315.6
Blood Sugar: 119
Temp. 96.9
Hours of Sleep: 5.5

"You are my sunshine, my only sunshine
You make me happy, when skies are gray"
-Jimmy Davis (who was twice elected Governor of Louisiana simply by writing and performing that song)[36]

"And I think to myself
What a wonderful world"
-Mr. Louis Armstrong[37]

It's a busy time of year, but I seem to be more reflective and less reactive. My wife noted that has changed dramatically since the surgery. You can note in my writing and my approach to life in general. I don't get particularly stressed about little things. That also means that I have to be more selective about what I do and who I do it with. It also means that my inbox and to-do list stay in a perpetual state of behind. But I seem to be enjoying the ride a lot better.

Today was an excellent day as I got to have lunch with Peter Perlman. One of the best trial lawyers in the world and one of the most interesting human beings alive. Found out today that he loves classic comics, just like several members of my family. We never talked business for even one second. We did not talk politics either, now that I think about it. We just had fun.

Getting Don to just have fun is really a new experience.

I parked about a half mile from lunch to walk in and Pete walked up behind me. This was good as I needed Pete's help in figuring out the parking meters around the University of Kentucky campus.

I am going back to New Orleans tomorrow for the first time since October. Looking forward to it. I bought great tickets to see the Pelicans play on both Sunday and Monday. I think I have seen eight NBA basketball games since age 10 when the Cincinnati Royals moved and eventually became the Sacramento Kings. Four of those have been in New Orleans. Pelican tickets are easy to get. Even with Anthony Davis on the team.

Karen has an important conference and other presidential duties, but she is doing her best to free her schedule to be with me. I am going to keep up my walking. I am dramatically noticing the difference. I'll have to put in my normal workday from the Big Easy to keep up on work. At least it will be sunny.

I leave from Cincinnati tomorrow and then back on Tuesday afternoon. Taking a longer vacation on my birthday in Florida. I hope. Tried to rent a house on the beach and it turned out to be a foreign money scan. The con people gave me some good tips to work with and I played it out for a round or two to get as much information as I could. It will be a great story someday.

January 22, 2015
4 p.m.

Weight: 315.2
Blood Sugar: 109
Temp.: 97.1
Hours of Sleep: 5

I think my Facebook status says it all:

"On flight from CVG to New Orleans.

Sitting in a normal airline seat without a seat belt extender. First time since Bill Clinton was president.

Feel like I won a gold medal at the Olympics. This opens many new doors for Don."

January 24, 2015
1 p.m.

Weight: 315.6
Blood Sugar: 105
Hours of Sleep: 8
Distance Walked: 1.7 miles

> *"Walking on sunshine and don't it feel good"*
> -Katrina and the Waves[38]

I got out of Kentucky just in time as there was five inches of snow in Lexington. Cold here for New Orleans (about 50), but nice sunshine. Headed out to walk the neighborhood and get my miles in once the Kentucky basketball game is over.

We have a friend from Kentucky visiting tonight and going to The Pelican Club in the French Quarter. Highly recommended. The original referral came from Mike Valentino, considered the King of the French Quarter. It has the quality of places like Antoine's or Arnaud's, but half the price.

I studied the menu and have my dinner picked out ahead of time (fish of the day and goat cheese salad) and even ran the calories, protein and carbs beforehand. That keeps surprises out of the diet.

Another tip I learned from Cindy Caywood: Never go to dinner extremely hungry. Drink a protein shake (my strategy) or eat a snack before going to a nice place.

I needed that yesterday. Went mall walking due to the cold and resisted the food court, but was hungry when we went to Restaurant Cypress. It took every ounce of willpower to avoid the bread and other fillers.

I wound up eating my entire veal entree. First time I have eaten an entire entrée since surgery. More food than planned.

Not going to a place extremely hungry avoids depending on willpower to pull me through.

Ultimately we have to depend on good habits, not willpower, as a long-term strategy.

My weight has stalled in the same range for about 10 days. Lots of reasons, but it's obvious that my carbs are up. My calories stay around 1,200 a day, and I really don't do much to watch those. At least 3,000 a day less than pre-surgery. The portion control comes from the surgery. However, the carbs need to reduce and be replaced by protein.

Very happy to be walking. And see the Cats win again. And that I am not in the Kentucky snow.

January 25, 2015
10 a.m.

Weight: 314.9
Blood Sugar: 101
Hours of Sleep: 9
Distance Walked: 1.9 miles

> *"It's the eye of the tiger*
> *It's the thrill of the fight*
> *Rising up to the challenge of our rivals"*
> -Survivor (Theme of *Rocky III*)[39]

My numbers in New Orleans are very good. I'm eating more and have been out to dinner each night, but it has been high protein, high quality and the protein-to-carb numbers are good. My sleep is dramatically up, blood sugar has been down and I am getting plenty of exercise each day. Been able to relax and have some fun. Had a nice dinner with friends from here and Kentucky last night and got to show them what the French Quarter is like on a Saturday night. It was fairly tame, but we got a wedding parade, a second line parade and a lot of unusual dress.

I should have a bunch of exercise on Sunday. Karen has a conference starting at noon today and outside of her meeting me at the Pelican's game at 5 p.m., I won't see much of her for the rest of the trip. I plan to get out right after I write this, hit a bucket of golf balls and get my walk in. Then I face my next big psychological challenge.

The Pelicans Game(s)

I have tickets to the game tonight and again tomorrow. Karen is meeting me tonight and I am going solo tomorrow. The people of New Orleans have never really supported the NBA (the teams that are in Utah and Memphis started in New Orleans first) and tickets are very cheap and easy to come by. You can sit in the rafters for $5. It costs as much to watch Ursuline High School play as it does to watch the Pelicans.

The problem for me is shaking off the past. My parents started taking me to sporting events before I could walk. I supposedly went to the 1961 World Series at age two and I have been to every other Cincinnati Reds World Series home game (70, 72, 75, 76 and 90) in my lifetime. Sporting events are a favorite thing for me. When I go to a city, I see what teams are playing and if I can get tickets.

The food choices are usually bad as well. Hot dogs, peanuts and a couple of soft drinks are my primary staples and have the positive association of being part of so many happy memories. Then I have the negative triggers.

Almost all of my diets ended at a sporting event.

I was in a program about every two years for awhile (I would lose the weight, gain it back, go back and lose again) and was in the middle of a successful program when my father was diagnosed with terminal prostate cancer in 1992. It was summer when he got out of the hospital the first time and he wanted us to go to a Reds game. I took him, brought a shake in a thermos and drank it before I walked into the stadium. I was not allowed to bring it in. It was a long, hot game and Dad was feeling great and eating hot dogs like crazy. Finally about the fifth inning, I had one too. Then another. Then another. It was like a drug addict falling off the wagon.

I tried to get back into a "shakes only" lifestyle, but was completely off the wagon. I never got back on again. On the last time I tried the program in 2004, I was doing well and was invited to a Kentucky football game. Once again, I fell off with a hot dog.

Thus, the Pelican games on the schedule reminded me of one of the most negative moments in my weight loss history. Not only did I fall off, I was totally stressed out (it was my father's first time out after just discovering he had cancer) and trying to stick to "our product or the highway" philosophy pushed me to my limits. It was one of the worst experiences of my life. I needed a chance to logically think this through.

1) I am not on an "our product, no matter what" kind of program. I am open to a variety of food choices.

2) I can't eat a lot at one time, even if I want to.

3) Basketball does not last as long as baseball or football. I can eat healthy beforehand or have a protein shake right before going in.

4) On the 500 or 800 calorie-a-day liquid plans, I got incredibly hungry if I missed a scheduled feeding time (about every three hours). It is ideal that I eat on a regular basis now, but I can go fairly long periods of time without getting hungry.

5) I was a little shaky psychologically, but here is the kicker: The name of the arena in New Orleans is the Smoothie King Arena. They sell stuff like lemon yogurt. There are some extremely high calorie and high fat items that Smoothie King sells, but they have high protein, low calorie stuff. I've bought it at the airport.

I won't be in a position like Cincinnati, where the options were hot dogs, pizza, beer, peanuts and popcorn.

If all that fails and I get really hungry, Karen won't care if we leave early on Sunday. She is supportive and the arena is about a 10 minute drive from the house. On Monday, I am going solo. I can come and go as I want.

This sounds like I am over-thinking the situation, but actually I am not. Going to a sporting event was something I had to deal with. It's one of my favorite activities in the world and the key to the surgery was that it would open me up for more positive experiences, not restrict them. This is one where working through the next two days, like having my airline seatbelt buckle without an extender, knocks down an old demon.

Knocking out demons is a key to making this a lifelong success.

Fitting in the Seat

My last experience at a Pelicans game was similar to one that I had with the University of Kentucky basketball game. We had great tickets, but I couldn't fit into the seat. Seats closer to the floor of the arena tend to be a little smaller than those higher up (they can cram a few more seats in a row that way).

Had the same thing happen in New Orleans last year. Fortunately, there are not a lot of fans at a Pelican game and I could move to a different seat with more room.

This year, it will be a big moment when I sit in the normal seat like a normal person. I've lost 10 inches around my waist and it is New Orleans, the most obese city in the United States. If I don't fit in these, I won't fit in anything.

I'll fit. And slay my psychological sports team phobia. A milestone on the road to weight loss success. And a chance to prove I still have the "Eye of the Tiger.""

January 26, 2015
11 a.m.

Weight: 313
Blood Sugar: 109
Hours of Sleep: 8.5
Distance Walked: 1.5 miles

> *"Beautiful coastline*
> *Warmed up weather*
> *Let's get together and do it again"*
> -The Beach Boys[40]

Today is my last full day in New Orleans and I plan to replicate much of what I did yesterday. While the rest of the country has had blizzards and snow, it is sunny in New Orleans, mid-50s, with zero chance of rain. About 10 degrees colder than yesterday, but hard to complain.

Yesterday I got out and hit some golf balls, did some walking and had terrific seats for the Pelicans game and a great victory. Plan on doing much of the same today.

Dr. Weiss sent an email and suggested that maybe my weight loss stall was due to lack of food intake and not having enough to burn during the day. I think he is correct and especially on the fluid intake. I had pretty much stopped drinking water lately, and I'm back on track with that today. Had more calories than normal (1,400), but weight dropped to my lowest number and I felt better, even though I went hard all day.

I think we are onto something.

It has been a relaxing weekend. You can see that by my dramatic increase in sleep, which is working its way back to a long-term average near seven hours, which is where I want to be. Also, my blood sugar has been excellent. I will have to "sleep quick" tonight (an old Texas expression that I picked up from James Street) as I will get back from the game late and then up at 5 a.m. to catch my flight back to Cincinnati tomorrow. It looks like Wednesday is going to be busy, but I feel rested and ready for it.

I have been eating healthy in the Big Easy. Not that hard as they have a ton of seafood and unlimited number of choices. I am not drinking anything besides unsweetened ice tea. That keeps the calories down.

I wound up not eating anything at the basketball arena, which was another milestone. I was not particularly hungry and our seats near the court were far away from the concession stands. A lot of "non hot dog" style of concession that I was not interested in and went to dinner after the game. I had permission to eat at game, but did not have any real interest.

Doing it all again would be another great day.

January 28, 2015
8 a.m.

Weight: 311
Blood Sugar: 125
Temp.: 96.9
Hours of Sleep: 2.9
Distance Walked: 3.1 miles

> *"Moving on up, we've finally a got a piece of the pie"*
> -Theme to the television show *The Jefferson's*[41]

My first day back in Lexington resulted in a new record on weight loss. 311 or 66 pounds since I started. I broke the three-mile mark in walking, mostly in airports. Instead of taking the train between terminals, I walked to each place. It meant that I was the last person to pick up my luggage in Cincinnati, instead of the first, but the luggage was waiting for me.

The long travel day which started with a 5 a.m. wakeup, going to sleep after 2 a.m. and back up early today was poor planning on my part (I could have slept longer than 2.9 hours and should have), but traveling midweek and switching time zones doesn't work well with me. Also, I had several long phone calls waiting on me and that kept me very late getting the time needed to be ready for today.

I need a buffer day to recover, but here at end of January, with a number of tax-related items due, clients waiting to see me, the telephone ringing all day and night and a book we are publishing due at the printer on Feb. 1, a recovery day was not really an option. In fact, I really need to double clutch it today.

Ironically, I'll probably catch up during the Super Bowl, normally a very busy day. When Karen and I are in the same city at the same time, we normally have a small party, but nothing this year and I really don't care about the teams playing. I can watch it while I do other things.

Vacation and rest are important. As is pacing myself during the day. I have a history of working to the point of burnout and doing my best to make some boundaries. I had a client call on a nonessential question at 9 p.m. last night. I said they had to wait a day and call during business hours. They were more than happy to do it once I asked.

I would not have asked a few months ago. Then I would have been up even later, and truly exhausted today. Right now I am tired, but feel pretty good. I had a ton of sleep over the previous four days.

My next trip is actually on my birthday, Friday, Feb. 13, and I come back on the next Friday, Feb. 20, so I'll have a weekend to recover and get organized before the phones start rolling. A lesson learned.

My blood sugar is lower when I get normal amounts of sleep. Easy to see the correlation.

It is also easy to see the correlation with eating more. Thus, I have more energy and the interest in exercise and getting in more fluids.

Happy with the new weight number. I may be happier that I got so much walking in. I am focused on making sure that happens each day. Moving on up.

January 29, 2015
8 p.m.

Weight: 313
Blood Sugar: 125
Temp.: 97.8
Hours of Sleep: 7
Distance Walked: 1.75 miles

> *"Now, Andy did you hear about this one?*
> *Tell me, are you locked in the punch?*
> *Hey Andy, are you goofing on Elvis?*

Hey baby, are we losing touch?"
-REM[42]

A busy day as a busy week rolls along. I did the numbers early this morning, but just getting around to writing.

LoseIt, the iPhone app I have used to record every morsel of food that has touched my mouth since Dec. 2, had a contest going to see how many people could give up soda for the month of January.

I fully expected to win as I have not had a soft drink of any kind since sometime in November. I quit drinking soft drinks to get ready for the surgery and don't plan to start again. Like ever. It is my understanding that the carbonation will do bad things for a person with gastric sleeve surgery and even if that is not true, I want to believe it is true (so don't tell me differently).

I drank about six Diet Cokes a day in the years before the surgery. It probably was more like 12 at some point. I drank them from the day they came on the market in 1985. I steadily gained weight during that time period and was fully convinced that they spiked my blood sugar, did not cause me to lose weight and were totally addictive. It was the one thing I could not completely give up.

Until now. It is still the only thing I occasionally have a craving for. Mostly out of habit. I used to drink one immediately upon waking up. Doing a lot of coffee and herbal tea these days. That seems to work out just fine.

Thus, I felt like I should have gotten a medal and won the contest. I have not touched any soft drink of any kind. Instead, I came in tied for fourth. The contest had a number of rules that I adhered to (like faithfully recording every bite of food), but a few non-related items in the mix where apparently I fell behind.

I guess I should be happy. There were hundreds of people involved and I came in fourth. On the other hand, I feel like comedian Andy Kaufman. One of his first roles was on the Redd Foxx variety show, and there was a recurring skit where Andy would come in second in a Fonzie lookalike contest to a man who looked like Redd Foxx (much older than Fonzie, different skin color).

I happened to be a huge Andy Kaufman fan, as is my youngest daughter Angela Luhys. We saw Jim Carrey's terrific performance as Andy on the day that *Man on the Moon* hit the theaters several years ago.[43]

Even more special, I got to watch Jerry "The King" Lawler put Andy Kaufman in a pile driver during a wrestling match in Rupp Arena. Thanks to my good friend Bob Babbage, who was on the Rupp Arena Board of Directors at the time, I had excellent seats and was close enough to see that Kaufman actually needing an ambulance was all part of an act. I still thought it was great showmanship.

Back to the Redd Foxx show. Andy's character knew he looked more like Fonzie, but the contest was rigged.

I don't think the LoseIt contest was rigged, but I did stay off the soda all month. They ought to send me some kind of cute reward. On the other hand, going 70-plus days for literally the first time in life without a soft drink is quite a feat. I plan to go about 7,000 more.

It's pretty cool. Just like Fonzie. He was cool, too. Another milestone on the road to good health.

January 30, 2015
9 a.m.

Weight: 312.2
Blood Sugar: 119
Temp.: 97.8
Hours of Sleep: 6

> *"We both were growing older then*
> *And wiser with our years*
> *That's when I came to understand*

The course his heart still steers"
-Jimmy Buffett[44]

"I'm growing older, but not up
My metabolic rate is pleasantly stuck
So let the winds of change blow over my head
I'd rather die while I'm living than live while I'm dead"
-Jimmy Buffett[45]

Happy Birthday to Dr. Jim Roach. The soon-to-be author of *God's House Calls: Finding God Through My Patients* is finishing the final edits for the book while he celebrates his birthday in a place where he is likely to hang out with Jimmy Buffett.

Actually, Jimmy spends a lot of time in New Orleans and we were in the same shop together last year, but I did not recognize him until after he left. We've never met, but have mutual friends and I have seen him in concert. Thus, I feel like we are buddies.

My wife claims that I think of everyone as my buddy. She is probably correct. A trait I picked up from my father. He knew everyone and those who did not know Dad missed out.

Actually, Dr. Jim has allowed me to reflect on the greatest "house call" that God has given me: the ability to have interesting and very loyal friends.

Dr. Jim is actually a prototype of who my close friends are. Most of my friends are my age or a little older and have been in my life for a long time. Most have long and stable relationships. Jim married Dee Dee on July 3, 1976, and they look like they are still on their honeymoon. My friends are successful in their chosen professions, but usually got there with some bumps along the way. All are extremely smart.

I met them when they had humble beginnings, but they make it to the top.

The other trait my friends have is that I could call any of them at 3 a.m., tell them I needed help and all would be there for me. Very few people can make a statement like that. They know it operates both ways, but in a world of disconnected people who go on "dates" by texting across the same table to each other, the fact that I have such loyal support is one of the reasons I have done so well with the weight loss. I have people lifting me up on days when I get in a rut.

I need to be around for a long time to come, just for the fun of spending time with them.

I just heard from my old friend Keith Yarber. His upbringing is as humble as they come. His father died when Keith was very young and his mother worked as a waitress at Jerry's restaurant to support him. I went to her funeral in Mount Sterling. It wasn't packed because Keith moved from being a high-powered radio executive to the tremendously successful publisher of *Tops in Lex* magazine, devoted to his wife and children; it was packed because Keith's mom touched a lot of people along the way.

Back to Dr. Jim. He told me he has a tan and great hair cut now. I have neither. He also understands that life is a balance between work and fun. I've always focused more on the work and less on the fun. I'm fortunate that my work is fun, but I have been reading for years about successful people disconnecting and taking time off. This is the first year that I have actually been doing it. I'm getting ready to walk to a lunch meeting, rather than race to one in a car. I don't schedule myself as tightly as I used to, but learning to work with great focus, then to disconnect completely.

My productivity is higher than ever as I am rested and in better health when I take on a project. Dr. Jim's life story is based on a similar model. He took the risk of redesigning his medical practice when it was tremendously controversial to do so, has risen to the top of his profession and lives a structured and organized life.

He is cranking out the final part of his book while sitting at the ocean. We all want to live like Jim. Then he will come back and treat his patients with a combination of enthusiasm and empathy. One of those people I am lucky to have as a friend.

Some final notes as I walk toward lunch.

Yesterday was a fascinating connection with my roots.

I'm named for Don Donoher, one of the greatest college basketball coaches in history, who was best man in my parents' wedding. Before Don was a coach, he and my father played on the same special services basketball team in the army. Dad was a terrific player who never went to college. Don went back and captained the Dayton team that won the NIT and then led small town Dayton as a coach to the NCAA finals where they lost to John Wooden's UCLA team, which had Kareem Abdul-Jabbar as its center.

After he left Dayton, Bobby Knight hired Don as an assistant at Indiana and Don was an assistant coach for the 1988 Olympic Team. Thus, he has an Olympic gold medal. The basketball arena at Dayton is named the Donoher Center and is a frequent spot for NCAA tournament games. My nephew Nick and I went to the NCAA regional finals there in 2006 (the year that George Mason upset everyone), and it was so neat to be in the building named for my namesake. Also great timing as I stopped and had dinner with my mother on the way back from Dayton. She suddenly died a couple of days later and it was the last time I saw her.

Yesterday, Bobby Knight and Don stopped in the Montgomery Inn Boathouse in Cincinnati for lunch. I have not seen Don in decades, but he asked Vicki Gregory, one of the owners and daughter of the founder Ted Gregory, about me and talked about his friendship with Dad. Vicki connected with me via Facebook, and Don and I went back and forth via her. It was a public Facebook conversation, but Steve Wolf jumped in. He is a CBS basketball analyst and had been a college star at Xavier. I went to grade school with him, and his father, who had coached the Detroit Pistons and Cincinnati Royals in the NBA, was our coach. I have seen Steve on television, but not connected in decades either. Steve was a good friend of my sister

Theresa and asked me to tell her hello. I have not had the heart to tell Steve that she died in 2006 as well. Steve is on television tomorrow so I may wait until Sunday to break it to him.

Long story short, my family members live in the hearts of their friends, years after they are gone. I was lucky to learn that kind of devotion and loyalty at home and lucky to have so many people who are there for me.

Also if you know Dr. Jim, wish him a Happy Birthday. If you don't know Jim, drink a Margarita or something like that (unsweetened ice tea is as wild as I get these days) in his honor.

January 31, 2015
12 p.m.

Weight: 311.2
Blood Sugar: 111
Temp.: 97.8
Hours of Sleep: 5.8
Distance Walked: 2.5 miles

> *"Layla, you've got me on my knees*
> *Layla, I'm begging, darling please*
> *Layla, darling won't you ease my worried mind"*
> -Eric Clapton[46]

> *"I'll find my way*
> *Through night and day*
> *Cause I know I just can't stay*
> *Here in Heaven"*
> -Eric Clapton[47]

I've been reading Eric Clapton's autobiography.[48] For the early part, it was an incredibly boring book (Eric did lots of drugs, Eric slept with hundreds of unknown women when he was on the drugs, etc.) and had little about his music, but when it shifted to his battles with first drugs, then alcohol (he switched from one addiction to another), it was during his efforts to get clean that he made a couple of fascinating revelations.

One is that he got down on his knees, during his second trip through rehab, and started praying to a higher power of no particular religious affiliation and he has done so every day since then.

Secondly, he kept a diary. During his worst, he wrote that he was determined not to sugarcoat his experiences, so that anyone else going through a similar experience would have something to relate to.

That struck me hard. The lyrics that I picked, "Layla" and "Tears in Heaven," are about intensely personal stuff. "Layla" is a plea to Pattie Boyd, who was married to Eric's friend George Harrison at the time. (Pattie later married and divorced Eric. Great song, but the romance was doomed from the word go.) The song was a hit when Pattie was still married to George, but there was no hiding where Eric was on the issue.

"Tears in Heaven" was even more personal. Eric's four-year-old son got away from the nanny at the mother's 53rd floor apartment in New York and fell out of the window. On the list of the most stressful things that can happen to a person, losing a child is number one. I have many clients who have lost a child and I suspect that "Tears in Heaven" is almost a theme song. It gives them comfort that someone else has walked in their shoes.

There are points in Eric's book that made me uncomfortable because they involved other people (he outed a favorite singer of mine from Broadway and her one disco hit for a venereal disease, and I could have gone the rest of my life without knowing that), but he does less tattletaling than most celebrity biographies do.

As I move forward, I feel connected to two of Eric's points. One is a connection to a spiritual being, even if it is not always specific. Most importantly, I want to be as honest and straightforward in my writing as I can get. There are millions of people fighting obesity, and I am already seeing people inspired to deal with their health after seeing what I am doing. That will multiply in the upcoming years and I need to give them the good, the bad and the ugly.

Although this is all about me, it's really not. I want my journey to good health to be the thing that moves others to do the same. I am in a unique position to be a role model and embrace the opportunity. It keeps me motivated when I have my good and bad days. I think it is my calling.

Yesterday was a good day. The sun was shining and when I met a friend for lunch a mile away, I walked there and walked back. Note that I am a guy who used to drive his car to the mailbox at the end of his driveway.

It was a long driveway, with a steep hill, but I have certainly come a long way in how I view exercise. I missed one day of exercise in the past 10, and that was my worst day. No matter what happens today, I am getting out and doing it.

A few weeks ago, I was looking at expensive gyms and training facilities. I am still working on lining up things like Zumba and dance, but recognize that just getting out and walking, which I can do for free anywhere, seems to be a big step forward. More and more, it is becoming something I want to do and enjoy, rather than something I have to do.

An important mind shift.

Shifting minds is what I want to do with my weight loss project.

THE THIRD MONTH AND BEYOND

February 1, 2015

It's noon. I just came back from a two-mile walk in the rain. You would have never heard about walking anywhere from me a couple of months ago.

A proud moment. I'm averaging nearly two miles a day and it is rapidly becoming a habit. My worst days are the ones when I don't get the two miles in.

The Bose headphones that my wife got me for Christmas have been a game changer in getting me to exercise.

I am a happy man overall.

It's Super Bowl Sunday in the rest of the world, but for Don McNay, it is the two-month anniversary of when I had my weight loss surgery. I got up in the middle of the night and wrote a little story about it on *Huffington Post*.[2] Since I posted in the middle of the night and did not submit to an editor, there are some mistakes in it. I didn't write it for the rest of the world as much as I wrote it for me. I wanted a long-lasting record of what we have accomplished by this date.

It's a little like watching a band record a live album. A lot of things are done for the long-term audience.

Anyway, I really don't care who wins the Super Bowl today and not even sure if I will watch. I have things to do and this is a good day to do them.

I do want to thank everyone for what has been accomplished. This is truly a situation where I am getting by "with a little help from my friends."[3]

The big celebration will hit when I pass the 100 pounds in weight loss goal. It will be here sooner than you think.

Thank you and Happy Super Bowl. It is a manufactured holiday invented as a way to advertise, but I guess that is as American as the Fourth of July.

My Weight Loss Super Bowl

> *"You know we're just struttin' for fun*
> *Struttin' our stuff for everyone*
> *We're not here to start no trouble*
> *We're just here to do the Super Bowl Shuffle"*
> -The 1985 Chicago Bears[4]

Super Bowl Sunday marks an important anniversary for me. Exactly two months ago today, Dr. Derek Weiss of Bluegrass Bariatric in Lexington performed gastric sleeve weight loss surgery on me at Georgetown Community Hospital.

This is part of my business plan for an upcoming book, and the plan is working.

I started my recovery, which included walking around the hospital a few hours after surgery almost immediately and was discharged the next day. I had no serious complications and after a few weeks off of work, I've come back better than ever.

Therefore, I have some reasons to celebrate my weight loss Super Bowl.

Concerning health issues:

-My weight has dropped from 377 to 311 pounds. A loss of 66 pounds.

-I was diabetic before I started the surgery. I have not been since the day after the surgery. I threw away the two blood sugar medicines that I was taking for diabetes the day after the surgery and my blood sugar stays in a normal range and never varies. That saves me more than $400 a month in medications.

-My blood pressure is steadily dropping. I take medicine for that, but probably not much longer.

-My ankles and feet don't swell. My shoe size is about half of a size smaller.

-I have more energy and personal happiness than ever.

-My mood stays very balanced and even. The blood sugar spikes are no longer sending shockwaves to the people around me.

Lifestyle issues:

-I've lost 10 inches around my waist and four around my neck collar.

-I can sit in a normal coach airline seat (I couldn't before).

-I can sit in a normal coach airline seat without a seat belt extender (I couldn't even get near that before).

-I can crawl on the floor with my grandchildren. I had to be pulled off the floor previously.

-I went to two NBA basketball games and could sit in normal seats.

I've had times in recent years where I did not fit into seats in sports arenas.

-I won't be gaining thousands of calories at this Super Bowl, as I have in the past. I can have normal food, but my stomach only holds a tiny amount of it. My focus will be on low carb, high protein snacks, like meat. No chips and no soft drinks.

- I will probably never have another soft drink. Since I was knocking out six Diet Cokes a day or more, this is a huge step.

-I have not been to a fast food restaurant since the surgery. I also have not had any bread. They allow me to have some bread with the surgery, but I am not interested in the carbs.

New habits I picked up:

-I have written down every morsel of food that I have eaten or drank on an iPhone app named LoseIt. Everyone seems to have their favorite app or something like Fit Bit. I happened to get this one first, it does what I want it to and I have no desire to change.

-Immediately upon waking up, I weigh myself, take my blood sugar, body temperature, blood pressure (not every day) and how much sleep I had the night before.

-Lately, I have added my steps for the day, which LoseIt also tracks. I focus on getting two miles of walking in each day. This is 1.9999 miles longer than it was two months ago.

To quote Jimmy Buffett, "if it suddenly ended tomorrow, I could somehow adjust to the fall."[5] I am a lot healthier, and everyone around me tells me I am much happier. I'm pretty laid back for the first time in my life.

On the other hand, I am not even at the halfway point. My business plan calls for me to lose 175 pounds and that is what I am going to do.

By next year's Super Bowl.

They say it is hard to repeat as Super Bowl champion, but in the weight loss Super Bowl, I plan to rack up two in a row. Then a lifetime after that.

February 3, 2015

Weight: 312.4
Blood Sugar: 125
Temp: 96.8
Hours of Sleep: 6.4
Distance Walked: 3.2 miles

> *"Follow me, I'm the Pied Piper*
> *And I'll show you where it's at"*
> -Crispian St. Peters (No, I've never heard of this guy either, but the song was a huge hit in 1966)[6]

> *"Something touched me deep inside*
> *The day the music died"*
> -Don McLean[7]

Feb. 3, 1959 is one of those historic days in Don's world. It was exactly 10 days before I was born and Don McLean captured the moment in one of the greatest songs ever written in "American Pie." It was the day "the music died," when Buddy Holly, Ritchie Valens and the Big Bopper died in a plane crash in an Iowa cornfield.

I know a lot more about the crash than I probably need to. I've read numerous books and stories about the crash. I know how Dion and Waylon Jennings turned down the seat on the plane that Ritchie Valens ultimately took. There was a local television guy in Lexington, Bob Hale, who was slated to be the disc jockey for the show that never happened in Clear Lakes, Iowa. When he was in Kentucky, I spent hours talking to him about the day. I've seen all the biographical movies and remain a huge Buddy Holly fan. An example of how you can make a huge impact in a short period.

Since it happened exactly 10 days before my birth, I grew up thinking that I had some kind of cosmic predestination to carry on the tradition of the three. Maybe I could sing like Buddy Holly, entertain like Ritchie Valens and have the physical build of the Big Bopper.

With the weight loss program, I will wind up being built more like Buddy and less like the Bopper when it is over with.

My *Huffington Post* piece about my two-month progress spurred a lot of interest around the country, but primarily with my friends. One of my friends from Seattle emailed this morning and told me that my progress has inspired her to look into fitness. My son-in-law Clay Bigler has lost about 30 pounds with an intense diet and exercise routine. I thought I would pass him on the trip to 199, but he has become a rapidly moving target. I've had two of my friends sign up to consider bariatric surgery, and one of my friends is doing a diet called the "Trim Healthy Mama" which I need to look into. It apparently involves Stevia which I have started using.

I never heard of Stevia until the television show *Breaking Bad*, but became a big fan of the show and the stuff.[8]

Thus, the fact that so many people around me are interested in diet and exercise reminded me of the "Pied Piper" song. One of the best things about what is happening to me is what is happening to those around me.

I keep up the walking every day. Even when it is incredibly cold and windy, I keep up the walking. It takes 21 days for something to be a habit (this memo is into day 62 and fairly ingrained at this point), and I am working hard to make sure it sticks.

My biggest complaint about my weight loss program is that it does not have a support group. The reason that AA and other 12-step groups work is that the support of the group goes both ways. Thus, I am thrilled when people are following my lead on healthy living, even if they are doing it at a distance.

February 5, 2015

Weight: 309.8
Blood Sugar: 121
Temp.: 97.2
Hours of Sleep: 6
Distance Walked: 3.1 miles

> *"I'm gonna soak up the sun*
> *I'm gonna tell everyone to lighten up"*
> -Sheryl Crow[9]

> *"Nobody OD'd, nobody burned a single building down*
> *Nobody fired a shot in anger*
> *Nobody had to die in vain*
> *We sure could use a little good news today"*
> -Anne Murray[10]

I saw Anne Murray at the Kentucky State Fair in the early 1980s. Not exactly like watching a KISS concert (it started low key and went lower), but a nice show. She had a lot of hits in her day.

I guess with the weather changing, I could have started with the lyrics from "Snowbird," which was her biggest hit.[11]

The one thing I have learned is to take some true free days. Looking forward to some fun in the Florida sun next week as I turn 56.

Disconnecting from the rat race is good for all of us. I used to hide where I was traveling, but now I figure that the hackers already know what flight I am on and what credit card I used. Thus, I will be on the sunny beaches of the gulf side of Florida and going to see Al and Martha Helen in Sarasota during the trip.

I got the good news that my weight is at 309.8. I called Karen and woke her when I got off the scale. First time I made the single digits since the first year of George Bush's term. They didn't have iPads or Facebook then. I had a little bit of hair. It was a long time ago.

February 9, 2015

Weight: 310.6
Blood Sugar: 124
Temp.: 97.2
Hours of Sleep: 8.4
Distance Walked: 4 miles

> *"Been stuck in airports, terrorized*
> *Sent to meetings, hypnotized*
> *Overexposed, commercialized*
> *Handle me with care"*
> -The Traveling Wilburys[12]

> *"Remember to manage your attention, not just your time."*
> -Dan Sullivan's post on Facebook this morning

Every now and then, Facebook reaches out and gets you back on track.

The last week of my 55th year on earth has been a busy one. Going all day, every day, including weekends for the past two weeks. Six factors were in play:

1) Self-induced stress from self-induced deadlines
2) Confusing activity with accomplishment
3) Managing my attention poorly
4) The timing of the several scheduled events. There was no way to avoid being busy or going hard all week and weekend.
5) The fact that I always try to do inordinate amounts of work before I leave town for vacation or business. Since I make all the top tiers at the airlines and hotels, I lived in a constant state of stress which has impacted my health, weight and mood over the years. I run in this relentless quest to have things organized before I go anywhere.
6) The fact that I can't seem to "do an all nighter" like I used to.

I have this deep, long held fear that business and life will collapse when I am out of pocket.

Ironically, what being off work for the weight loss surgery taught me is that life and business go on pretty well when I am not around. In fact, maybe better. My team thrived without my micromanagement in December, so maybe I should just go away for long periods of time and let them do their thing.

The Dan Sullivan quote was one of those wake up calls from cyberspace. I stopped and made a list of all my tasks. The list is not that long and most of them are not that urgent. Several can be delegated to others, several can be delayed and several aren't really tasks at all.

Then I realized the other part. My primary focus has to be my health, but I have started "falling off the wagon" in sending the daily reports and maintaining accountability.

If you don't hear from me for a day or so in the future, send an email and remind me. I need the help.

The last two weeks have been stressful and I won't be able to do detailed reports while on vacation next week.

An excuse, not a real reason. As Dan noted, this needs to be the primary focus of my attention.

I've been faithfully tracking my numbers each day and getting in good walking days like the one yesterday. I got some excellent advice from my dietician guru Cindy Caywood on Friday.

Derek gave me a ton of insights via email yesterday, and along with my daily interactions with Dr. Jim (the first copy of his new book is on a UPS truck from South Carolina to here) and others on this email, I am getting the kind of world class advice that maybe one in a million people could get.

I am going to lose 175 pounds. Then I am going to tell the world how to do the same thing.

A pretty good primary focus.

Throw in trying to be a good husband, father, grandfather, friend, writer, civic leader and businessman, and the next 56 years of my life are going to be pretty busy. The key is recognizing that very few things have to be done in the next five minutes. And not to worry about it when I can't make the deadline.

I guess that is a paraphrase of the serenity prayer. Which is starting to sink in.

> *"Lefty he can't sing the blues*
> *All night long like he used to"*
> -Townes Van Zandt[13]

The line from "Pancho and Lefty" keeps rolling through my head in my post-surgery existence. I happen to be a left-handed person, and since the surgery the one thing that has dramatically changed is my temperament.

My wife and I spend hours discussing the dramatic change, and one of the things that many people notice is how unusually calm I am. My youngest daughter noted that I have developed a true sense of inner peace. Things that used to get me jumping up and down don't bother me.

I thought that maybe it was the lack of sugar and multiple Diet Cokes that made the change. Then I realized that those were recent additions to my life. Well, maybe they were always there, but I did not note how badly they impacted me.

I suspect that having my blood sugar even out has to help my mood, but I realized the other day that I have done the "jumping up and down" thing all my life. Long before my blood sugar was an issue.

Some of my friends who go back with me 35 or 40 years can attest. I tended to morph into my mother's personality under minor stress. She would scream about silly things. However, I also morphed to my dad's personality when the heat was truly on. He was always in charge when the stakes were high.

I am the guy you want in a true crisis. I never lose my cool and can see the bigger picture. That is what has made me good at things like mediations and political campaigns. I was also a high-powered chess player in high school (and then quit it completely). I can do big stuff well. The bigger the stakes, the better I perform.

Throw me the ball with the game on the line and I hit the shot. Throw it to me when the game is meaningless and I may miss the backboard. If we are under nuclear attack, I am the guy you want in your foxhole. The same guy that used to jump up and down screaming if a red light lasted too long.

The other thing I have always had is that ability to kick into another gear at the deadline. That is why fields like investments and journalism appeal to me. Everything has to be done with that adrenaline rush. Suddenly, that is gone. I don't get the rush. Or the physical "hangover" after I do it. I stay a lot more even-keeled.

Since the surgery and recovery, I tend to stay in the "bigger picture" mode. This week was really the first time that I have started to get back to being stressed by little things and frustrated that I did not have a desire to do an "all nighter" to catch up the schedule.

Then I am starting to see the pattern. I do not need an all nighter if I am organized during the day. I am planning my day and focus better. This was a week where my focus was challenged. I was letting a lot of minor issues get in the way and it was upping my stress level. Deciding what is major and what is minor is the key. It's not always the case of responding to who yells the loudest. It took an hour for me to write this. There is part of me that thinks I could have used the hour to keep on dealing with minor issues and knock a few off the plate. The other part realizes this was the best hour I spent in the past few days. I have my thoughts and priorities reorganized and there is something about "talking it out" in print that seems to work for me.

February 10, 2015

Weight: 311
Blood Sugar: 119
Temp: 97.2
Hours of Sleep: 6
Distance Walked: Less than a mile

The Fat Shaming Scandal

> *"Sad, so sad*
> *It's a sad, sad situation*
> *And it's getting more and more absurd*
> *Oh it seems to me*
> *That sorry seems to be the hardest word"*
> -Elton John[14]

Bryn Mawr College apologized. Is that enough? Did they violate HIPAA? Did they just do something incredibly insensitive or is it worse?

It appears to many observers Bryn Mawr College, an all-female college, completely violated its students' privacy by going into their health records and offering the "opportunity" to be in a weight loss class because of their BMI.

Some of us are still outraged at the news that broke last week. As a recovering fat person, I never needed anyone to point out to me that I was overweight. I was in the morbidly obese category, and it wasn't like it was news to me. They certainly didn't have to comb my medical records to clue me in. If I wanted to join a weight loss class, I did. Many times.

According to a UCLA study and numerous other research projects, the majority of people who diet do not keep the weight off long-term.

Until I did the gastric sleeve weight loss surgery, I was morbidly obese. I had also tried every diet program in the world, numerous times, and none of them were successful.

Thus, Bryn Mawr College decided to call out their supposedly overweight students and put them in a position of likely failure. What a great way to build their self-esteem!

I'm writing a book about my weight loss journey and living the journey. I'm granted a lot of positive self-esteem from the other good things that have happened in my life, but that is not always the case for overweight people.

There are people who feel like they have a license to take pot shots at those who are overweight. How many times do you see a television news program that feels compelled to show overweight people, obviously without their consent, walking down the street?

There is a word for people who make fun of those who have different physical characteristics than them. It's called bigotry, and in 21st century America, bigotry for any reason is wrong.

At an all-girls college, the idea of "shaming" students into losing weight is unbelievable. College students are teens or barely post-teen. I'm of the theory that we are at an impressionable age our entire lives, but especially during those years when we are being educated.

I've done a ton of research and many personal interviews with people who have had or are considering weight loss surgery. I don't know how to quantify it, but it is obvious that society makes life much harder on overweight women than overweight men. I've never suffered professionally, or really personally, from being obese, but I've talked to numerous women who get overlooked in the professional world because of their weight.

It's like the line in the Janis Ian song, "At Seventeen": *"And those whose names were never called, when choosing sides for basketball."*[15]

People never get over the hurts of discrimination and being picked on, or picked out, because of their weight.

I am particularly stunned since Bryn Mawr is an all-girls school. I read Carl Bernstein's book *A Woman in Charge: The Life of Hillary Rodham Clinton* several years ago, and one of the things that jumped out was that Hillary going to an all-girls college allowed her to take a leadership role (she was student body president) and gain the self-esteem and skill sets that might not have been available at a coed college in the 1960s.[16]

Thus, the Bryn Mawr attempt to do some self-esteem crushing goes against a basic premise for their existence.

Maybe Bryn Mawr should do a weigh in and add that to admissions criteria along with academics.

Elton John said that "sorry seems to be the hardest word." Actually, that is pretty easy to do. They are hoping this all blows over and life goes back to normal. What is harder is finding some evidence that the people at Bryn Mawr truly understood the gravity of what they did.

February 11, 2015

Weight: 310.6
Blood Sugar: 119
Temp.: 97.2
Distance Walked: Less than a mile

> *"They said it really loud*
> *They said it on the air*
> *On the radio"*
> -Donna Summer[17]

My best medium is the radio. I know every song ever written from the time I was born until I was about 30. I have an excellent radio voice, a couple of stints on the air when radio was hot and anchored election night coverage for a decade. I've been on hundreds of times and a guest on almost every major show, except Rush and Hannity.

Thus, when the lottery gets hot, this bird goes back to his favorite nest.

Whenever the lottery goes up to a jackpot level, I start doing media appearances around the country and often around the world. My books shoot up to the top of the charts and I have a 15-minute run of fame. At least once a year.

This year, it is this week. A busy week as I am leaving town for my birthday on Friday and wrapping up work before I go, but I stayed up past midnight to do a show on *KABC* in Los Angeles last night and on the station I grew up on, *WLW* in Cincinnati. Two of the great AM radio stations in the country in one day. An early happy birthday for Don.

Tonight my children and grandchildren will come over for cake. I won't eat much, if any, but I tap the cake in a move that I got from the Hyman Roth character in *The Godfather II*.[18] (After a decade or so of watching me, all my children do the same.) I love doing my *Godfather* move.

Getting to spend a week with my beautiful bride starting on Friday is a great birthday gift. The idea of us spending non-work, uninterrupted time is completely foreign to us. Yes, I did a call on a structured settlement on our honeymoon and did take a call from *CNBC* (who did not use me on air) on our last vacation, but this time is going to be different. I might do a report or so on this, but we have a busy schedule planned and I won't have a scale. We are missing Mardi Gras, but Karen has done about 30 parades, high-powered events and parties, and getting out of town is a rare chance for us to get quiet time. She looks hot in her bathing suit, but she looks hot in about everything.

I wrote a column about self-esteem yesterday for *Huffington*, but Karen does not suffer from low self-esteem and never will.[19] She did not have me from hello. She had me when I saw her across the room and spent two months plotting how to make her my steady.

For the trip, the focus goes on healthy eating and exercise. A lot of seafood and walking on the beach. Bought some new swim trunks. I won't wear them for long as they will be too big by summer, but time for me to get out in the sun. I'm pretty worn out from staying up so late to do the *KABC* interview, but the host Peter Tilden was well prepared and did an excellent job, and the producer had been at another station that used to book me frequently, so we have a good relationship.

I realized last night that I have been in the media in Los Angeles more than any other place but Louisville in the past four years. That includes Lexington and I have never been on anything in New Orleans. I'm bigger in New Zealand, Italy and South Korea (where I have been on national shows).

Call 1-800 Mr McNay if you win the lottery tonight. I will walk you through what to do next.

February 16, 2015

Weight: 309.8
Blood Sugar: 109
Hours of Sleep: 9.2
Distance Walked: 2.2 miles

"Vacation, all I ever wanted
Vacation, have to get away"
-The Go-Go's[20]

"Little surfer, little one
Made my heart feel all undone
Do you love me?
Do you, surfer girl?"
-The Beach Boys[21]

1977-78 was my freshman year in college, and it was an epic year where the weather got to 25-below zero and stayed there for several weeks. The heat in our dorm room averaged about 44 degrees, and I played The Beach Boys nonstop to try to change my mental attitude. Mike Behler was my best friend and roommate then. He remains my best friend despite hating The Beach Boys stuff. I threw a little Jan and Dean in to mix it up, but the idea was to quit thinking about the cold.

I turned 56 on Friday the 13th and had a better idea. I went to the gulf coast of Florida for a week. Actually, a week plus one day as I extended my trip to Saturday after seeing how horrible the weather is supposed to be in Kentucky. (I moved my flight back quickly when I saw the first weather reports.)

I have "survivor's guilt" to a minor extent. The weather is slightly cold (low 60s), but absolutely sunny as I read about my family and friends fighting the worst winter storm in a decade.

Karen and I are having a terrific time. We shut off all work for the week and focused on a lot of healthy behaviors. We eat right, exercise and get lots of sleep. One of the rare times we get to be together by ourselves and that has been fantastic. We have a nice condo about a block from Clearwater Beach, and we walk for miles on the beach. Many of the neighbors are drinking heavily, but I am drinking protein shakes and Powerade zero. (Karen did have wine with Valentine's Day dinner.) We have been cooking ourselves a little and going to seafood places when we go out. My protein-to-carb numbers are fantastic. We have one scheduled dinner, with Al and Martha Helen Smith in Sarasota, that we are really looking forward to tomorrow, but otherwise we have no schedule at all. We got up to see the sunrise, even though we don't have an alarm or even a clock in the room. We spend a lot of time not doing anything. This is a totally foreign concept to Don.

Karen's school is off for Mardi Gras and I had arranged to completely disconnect from work this week. With the holiday and terrible weather, this was the week to be away from work anyway. I had no idea when we picked it. I was in New Orleans the other time it snowed in Kentucky, so I have not seen real snow since a year ago. As my father would say, you have to play the great cards when they are dealt to you.

The entire idea of doing this vacation, the third true vacation of my entire life, was to have some true "disconnect" time to focus on recharging and healthy behaviors. I have a friend who takes two weeks in December. He and his wife go to Mexico with the primary goal of exercise. One of those great ideas that allows him to hit the start of the new year fresh. I've always felt guilty taking time away from work. What would happen if a client called? (I work with a group of talented people, and the key is not for everyone to take vacation at the same time.)

I never liked having employees who wanted lots of vacation time and tended to pick people who racked up extreme amounts of hours like I have done. I'm rethinking that. The key is like playing football. You take time off to rest up for game day and then you go at it with 100 percent focus on the day of the game.

A happier way of life and definitely a healthier way to live. Also very different for me.

The odd thing is that taking time off for the weight loss surgery made me realize that disconnect time was possible. Then we won the lottery on the weather. It is colder than normal here, but I think most of the United States would take 60 degrees and sunny at the moment. I probably won't get to use my fancy swimming trucks that I bought for the trip (and they will be too large in a few months), but we timed this perfectly.

I spend a lot of time post-surgery listening to my entrepreneur guru Dan Sullivan. He has you plan your free and vacation days first and then your work time after that. Totally the opposite of how most of us do things. I planned the vacation idea months in advance. I made sure that all projects were completed or scheduled in a different time slot. I did not bring any work with me, although I am a guy who reads annuity journals for fun. Karen is reading a novel. Not about running a school. I have never seen that before. We picked the spot early and even had dinner reservations for birthday and Valentine's weeks in advance. A little bit of pre-planning that allowed for low stress. Off to get my walk on the beach in. My numbers reflect a good strategy and taking vacation is an idea that I am not going to resist as an employer, or person, in the future. Those in our organizations need to remind me of that when I do resist in the future.

"The weather is here, wish you were beautiful."[22] (One of my favorite Jimmy Buffett songs, but actually I mean the opposite to the people who get this email.) Also, a birthday shout out to my friend and dietician guru Cindy Caywood. A fellow, well-educated EKU grad, she is smart, truly cares about her patients and has taught me a lot.

February 25, 2015

Weight: 308.6
Blood Sugar: 114.4
Temp.: 97.2
Hours of Sleep: 6.7
Distance Walked: 2.1 miles

Karen and I had a terrific vacation. It was the first time since we started dating in 2010 that we ever had an entire week by ourselves, and the first time that neither of us did any kind of work on the trip. Since I don't even drink soft drinks, it was not a wild and partying kind of vacation, but I never did those vacations anyway. On the other hand, I never really did any kind of vacation. Our offices, clients and faculty understood the importance of this one completely. They were terrific in not contacting us for any work-related stuff. I appreciated it as it was a sacrifice on their part, but it also shows how well they do what they do without my tendency to micromanage. My obsessive pre-surgery work habits and carrying 377 pounds meant that I never did anything fun. As I have noted many times, the surgery is like being born again in a non-religious sense and being a fun guy is part of it.

Or at least a healthy guy.

I walked more than four miles a day on the beach and Karen did about seven. We relaxed, ate healthy at nearly every meal (tons of seafood) and understood the true meaning of why vacations are so important to all aspects of life. The last thing I did before I caught my plane in Cincinnati was bring along my winter coat. I usually leave it in the car when I go south. Also, I paid $64 more to have my car in covered parking. Two terrific decisions.

The people in Kentucky had record cold and snow. The negative 32 degrees in Richmond was the coldest spot in the United States one day, and Kentucky was completely shut down while I was gone.

It was also record cold in Clearwater and Tampa, but that was more like 40 degrees. With the wind coming off the ocean, it was cold and having the winter coat allowed me to get out and do my walking and enjoy it immensely. Karen bundled up in some of my clothes and hers and made her walk, along with an earlier walk that I usually missed.

As noted, I got nearly eight hours of sleep a night. That seems to be a game changer. Getting proper sleep makes everything else fall into place. I wound up in Florida for a few more days to avoid the bad weather, but Karen had to go New Orleans. Gave me a chance to read and reflect. I doubled down on my healthy behaviors.

A lot of my thoughts were about pushing towards excellence. A concept that everyone gives lip service to, but few ever truly implement. It's like Jack Welch used to preach at General Electric: You need to be in the top tier at everything you do. Also, you need to say no to things that take away from your focus and overall objective. Health is a focus, but not my obsession. Developing a true balance between health, work and family is the real focus. I'm developing good systems and time management to make those happen. I read several books on time management recently as I recognize that the foundation for the rest of my life is going to depend on always keeping that focus on balance and excellence.

It's about keeping the "to-do" list short and the circle tight.

If I am learning anything, it is vision and patience. Until the year or so before surgery, I always had a lot of vision, but little patience. Now both are here in Technicolor. Good systems, delegation and time management allow you to get to a phase of excellence in life and have that feeling of satisfaction when a job is done well. I've told two people who have done exceptional things in my businesses to take a few minutes and appreciate the moment. It's a terrific feeling when a project or job is done to a high degree of excellence. Since I have never been one to "enjoy the moment," I have not always appreciated when others around me have pushed to the highest level. Or thanked them. I'm getting better at that. Anyway, I am proud. I am moving on my journey towards a long and healthy life. On the other hand, I am even prouder of what I am doing with the time that I am getting.

There is a line in Carl Sandburg's book *Abraham Lincoln* that I read when I was eight or nine years old.[23] They were talking about my wife's home city of Elizabethtown. It said, "They call it E-Town to save time, but they never knew what to do with the time once they saved it." At age 56, I'm starting to figure out what to do with the time.

March 5, 2015

Weight: 305.4
Blood Sugar: 115
Temp: 97.4
Hours of Sleep: 6.6

> *"I'm just sitting here watching the wheels go round and round"*
> -John Lennon[24]

My biggest excitement is that my weight started dropping again. It had been in a semi-stall for about three weeks, but I have lost seven pounds in the past 10 days. I have a pretty good balance of getting my protein numbers in about 150 grams and keeping my carbs low. That particular combination, along with eating every three hours, seems to work for me,

I'm eager to weigh less than 300 pounds. An incredible milestone and one that I would have never dreamed possible a year ago. On the other hand, I am not going to change any of my habits or processes to goose it along. The weight loss is happening on a gradual basis. At first, I thought February was a slow month since I "only" lost eight pounds. Which means I would lose 96 more pounds in a year at that pace. All indications are that March will be bigger than that, but if not, eight pounds gets me under 300 by the end of the month.

It took me awhile to be able to understand how much weight I have lost. I took my daughter Angela to the Merrick Inn for her birthday on Monday. I stopped in the men's room and almost did not recognize myself in the mirror. It took me a minute. They know me there and usually have a special chair without arms on it discreetly waiting when I come in. I did not really need the special chair this time. I can sit in booths and in chairs with arms and never worry about going to a sporting event and not fitting in the seat.

As much as I like the huge improvements in my health, such as controlling my blood sugar with absolutely no medicines, to quote Sonny and Cher, "it's the little things that mean a lot."[25]

March 25, 2015

Weight: 301.4
Blood Sugar: 130
Temp.: 97.9
Hours of Sleep: 6.5
Distance Walked: 2 miles

When I look at the numbers above, I feel wonderful. My sugar is higher lately, but my sleep, walking and body temperature have dramatically improved. I ought to be happy.

Then I realize that I have the Early Wynn Syndrome.

Early Wynn was a Hall of Fame baseball pitcher. He started in 1939 and retired in 1963, missing a couple of years to serve in World War II.

He got exactly 300 wins. He was a terrific pitcher, but never the same after he was injured in 1961. He went 7-15 in 1962 to get to 299 wins, but then had seven starts over nine months in his attempt to get his 300th win. It became an embarrassment for this terrific star, who held on to get that last milestone under his belt.

He finally backed into getting his 300th win. He left a game leading five to four after five innings, and a reliever went the rest of the way so that Early could get the win. Wynn immediately retired after that and became a great pitching coach. Wynn was not particularly proud of his milestone, but it became important to many that he hit it. 299 is a terrific number and he would have easily won another 20 or 30 if he had not missed time to serve in the War.

I feel like Early. Getting my weight below 300 pounds has become an obsession.

I got to 301.8 on March 12. In the 13 days since then, I have bounced around in the 301 area, sometimes going back to 303 or 304.

I weigh early and I weigh late. I have days when I walk seven miles and I have days when I don't walk at all. I go to zero carb days and then I go to higher carbs. I try not drinking as much fluid and then I pound the fluids down. I stopped dance lessons as my teacher and I have different business philosophies, but I was hitting those hard and can do a pretty mean waltz and hustle now.

This is getting to me. A lot of my friends check in, waiting to see the 300 mark broken and a lot are shying away from the topic. I suspect

Early Wynn had the same problem. It is the elephant in the room. Logically, it should not make any difference. I did not get too concerned about going from 308 to 306. Also, this is a lot different than Early in that 299 is not a final destination point. 199 is the publicly stated goal and getting to about 225 ought to be doable based on normal projections for the surgery. I don't really count my calories, but I suspect it is impossible for me to have a day above about 2,000 calories. My body won't let it.

Somehow, I have to get my mindset changed. There is a certain amount of desperation setting in and I'm really in the early part of my lifelong journey.

It may be better if I stop thinking about it. I suspect that weighing myself five or six times a day is not helping me mentally.

I really need to stop thinking in terms of a set weight number, and especially one that is really a stop along the way, but I am so programmed, like an Early Wynn, to making a hard number that it is hard to stop thinking like that. If I had it to do over again, I would never have named the book *Project 199* as aiming to a number, instead of better health, was the wrong idea for a goal.

I can argue this all day long, but until I weigh less than 300 I will not be happy. On the other hand, I will. I am going to get past 200, too. I make my goals even if bitch and moan about them.

March 29, 2015

Weight: 299.8

I took everyone's advice. I stopped weighing myself every day. Then I made it to the scale a few minutes ago. I broke the 300 barrier. I'm at 299.8, with a picture to prove it.

An interesting irony. I was reading a *NYT* article about Bill Clinton right before I weighed. The last time I weighed less than 300 pounds, it was in the Clinton Administration.

It's like breaking the four-minute mile. (An old reference for those of you who follow track and field.) It was one of those "impossible" barriers that just became possible.

April 19, 2015

Weight: 295.8

> *"Old habits like you are hard to break"*
> -Hank Williams, Jr.[26]

For those who are wondering, it is projected that I will lose more than 100 pounds by the Fourth of July.

Independence Day in a true sense.

My blood sugar is 117.4 without medication and I walk an average of about 1.5 miles a day, but that can be inconsistent based on scheduling and weather.

I average 147 grams of protein a day, about 1,700 calories a day and take very little in sugar and starch. I average about 6.5 hours of sleep a night and working hard to get that to seven. I have not had a soft drink, diet or otherwise, since November nor any kind of alcohol or carbonated drink.

I eat organic as often as possible, reduced my beef and increased my other proteins. I still drink about two or three protein shakes a day, but they are a convenient way to make sure I am eating about every three hours and keeping my protein numbers up.

Dr. Jim Roach has given me a regimen of vitamins and supplements that I follow religiously (a key was to put all of them in weekly organizer boxes so that I just have to grab the organized handful at set times) and I certainly have more energy that anytime I can remember.

Ten inches off my waist and my BMI is less than 40, which means I am no longer morbidly obese.

At least four of my friends have contacted Dr. Weiss about doing the gastric sleeve, and I will inspire many more. Actually, a lot of people in my life have reduced or given up soft drinks or sugars since I started. I was never much of a drinker (and never smoked) and I see no reason to start those ever again. My only serious craving is diet soft drinks and that happens when I am out of my element, like traveling or at a sporting event. I have not fallen off, but it remains the one thing that reminds me that I am actually on a weight loss program.

Dr. Weiss told me I would lose about 10 pounds a month, give or take, and that seems to be on target. If I try to goose it forward (like I did when I was stuck at 301) or completely ignore the scale (as I have lately), I still hit about 10 pounds a month.

The key is developing good habits. Not insane habits like trying to do an Ironman race, but good habits.

I'm proud lately because I have kept up an intense social and work schedule and that won't stop for at least another month. Normally that is the type of thing that gets me off a diet, and it has made carving out walking times a little more challenging. I do things like park on the other end of parking lots and walk steps instead of elevators trying to get my steps in and it seems to work.

It is really fun to get out and do as many things as I have been doing and have the confidence that I won't "fall off the wagon." Mainly because the surgery doesn't allow me to go crazy and I am learning skill sets.

I went to the Reds game last Sunday. Got my protein and water in before the game, sat through an 11-inning game, had one hot dog and a couple of bottles of water to pull me through. That would have been a couple of dogs and four or five Diet Cokes last year.

I've been to a number of dinners and banquets lately where I have no control over the food. I make sure I don't come in hungry, skip the breads, wine, desserts and usually the salad (if I eat the salad, I can't eat the protein) and that seems to work. I don't feel deprived and the people around me aren't awkward about eating in front of me. In fact, they are usually happy to have a shot at my wine and/or dessert.

I have had a busy local travel schedule and a busier schedule over the upcoming weeks, and I don't feel compelled to fall back into "stress eating" which has been a lifelong habit. I am getting confident that my good habits and skill sets are keeping me on track.

If they don't, the gastric sleeve will. On those days when I want to go crazy, I can only eat a small amount.

Which brings me to another topic: *Project 199.*

There is a great internal debate as to whether I should keep that as the book title or goal. As one of my friends pointed out, books and movies frequently change titles before release and some even do after release. Then there are others around me who think I should stick with the title that I started with and think that maybe I am trying to back off of the goal of losing 178 pounds.

I'd love some other feedback. I'm ultimately a man who makes up his own mind and is not easily swayed by anything, but one of the reasons I have been so busy lately is our structured settlement business has kicked back into full gear, along with the publishing. One of the reasons we have kicked into gear is that I am actually open to outside advice, strong systems and not micromanaging every detail. I am still working on that habit, but have come a long way and it helps that I have so much newfound energy.

I see both arguments and am open to new arguments.

I think titles are important and when I had my syndicated column, one of the rare things I negotiated into my contract was that the newspapers had to use the title that I gave it. I use a lot of songs and quotes to start my pieces as the title is a jumping point.

A great movie about stock car driver Junior Johnson was called *The Last American Hero* after the terrific Tom Wolfe story that inspired it.[27] It used the Jim Croce song "I Got a Name"[28] as its theme right about the time Jim died, and somewhere along the way, they changed the name to *Hard Driver* and then they changed the name to *The Last American Hero* again. I think that the multiple names confused people.

On the other hand, I had a friend who is a big-time writer tear up his book when it was 90 percent finished and start all over. Since a book is there for eternity, you want it to be correct. And since you want to grab an audience right away, you want a title that catches people.

My *Son of a Son of a Gambler: Winners, Losers and What to Do When You Win the Lottery* was a huge hit with Jimmy Buffett fans, but the average person did not understand it.[29]

Anyway, my friends who are adamant that I keep *Project 199* are afraid that I am wimping out by not putting a number on it or that I am going to quit. Now that my habits are becoming ingrained, it would actually take some effort to quit, and I like how I feel and the accomplishment of moving forward. Also, I have made this so public that being a role model is an overwhelming goal. I am focused on getting past the 100 pounds lost number. Very focused. That is a rare category, like hitting an eagle in golf or 50 home runs in baseball. Not many people do it and it is a symbol of a terrific achievement.

One hundred seventy-five pounds is more like hitting a hole in one in golf or hitting 70 home runs; it is a once in a lifetime achievement.

If I live a long and healthy life and get to do as many things as I have been doing lately, I don't think the number is all that relevant, but I would love to wind up at 199. I definitely see it as doable.

I've always set "impossible" goals and made a lot of them happen. On the other hand, I've never been one who always enjoys the journey. The goal becomes an overwhelming obsession and then I go on to another. When I started in financial services, I wanted to make the Million Dollar Round Table by age 25 and I did. I made it another 30 times since then, but never really cared and quit sending in the forms after I hit 25 in a row. The first was focus, the rest of it was habit and skill sets. The same thing happened when I was the only Kentuckian at the time to make the Top of the Table and I wanted it by age 40. Once I got there, I never cared, but my production stayed at that level.

I like measurements and making the scale the only measuring stick was the wrong focus, but also the one focus that everyone can grasp. The fact that my blood sugar and blood pressure are so good is actually better, but harder to grasp.

Anyway, I am open to ideas and suggestions.

May 8, 2015

Weight: 290
Blood Pressure: 126/82
Hours of Sleep: 6
Distance Walked: Averaging 1 mile

> *"Reggie Jackson is Mr. October and Dave Winfield is Mr. May."*
> -George Steinbrenner

> *"By May the 10th, Richmond had fell*
> *It's a time I remember oh so well*
> *The night they drove old Dixie down*
> *And all the bells were ringing"*
> -Robbie Robertson[30]

For some reason, I have always lost weight in May. This goes back to when I was on the track team in high school and has been fairly consistent. Like Dave Winfield, this has always been my big month. I'm losing about a pound a day right now and even lost three pounds on a weeklong trip to New Orleans. That takes a certain amount of planning and discipline as I ate in high-powered restaurants almost every day. Right now, I have lunch appointments in Lexington scheduled for almost every work day in May.

That I am operating in the "normal" world and losing weight is a huge psychological victory.

The weather is sunny and I get out and about more. Also, the focus gets on not eating as much. My financial and structured settlement business gets dramatically busier from May to the end of the year. I wish I knew why most of the activity happens in the last half of the year, but all I can tell you is that after 34 years, it happens that way every year. My oldest daughter Gena has a birthday on May 18th and the office joke is that nothing happens until we get her birthday properly celebrated.

Thus, I am in a busy work routine, but the biggest focus has been on developing regular routines in every aspect of life. Many good habits are now coming to me automatically.

Walking is one habit that has become a little more hit and miss. That needs to be the next area of improvement and the outside heat needs to be off the list as an excuse. I started focusing hard on record keeping as the new month kicked off and that has helped tremendously. I was starting to slip and my weight loss was starting to flatten.

Going back to the Mr. May theme, one advantage of May is that I have a positive attitude about it. I know it has always been a good month for weight loss, even in years when weight loss was not a priority. It's like a lot of things you do in life: there is a self-confidence that results when you have had a track history of good things happening in the past.

"Keep on the sunny side"
-The Carter Family[31]

"I used to be hell on wheels
Back when I was younger man

Now my body says, 'You can't do this boy'
But my pride says, 'Oh, yes you can'"
-Toby Keith[32]

I saw a research study in the *Washington Post* this week that I absolutely hate. It is titled "Researchers have found a really good reason not to be an optimist."[33]

I am sure there is some scientific reason that says that people shoot too high in their ambitions and should be "more realistic."

I just know that does not work for me. The bigger the goal and ambition, the more likely I am to achieve it. I originally called my book *Project 199* on the idea that I would lose 175 pounds. I have not given up on the idea that I might lose 175 pounds. Six months into it I lost 87 pounds and I'm dropping a pound a day at the moment. It's just that I think focusing on a weight loss number is the wrong goal.

I had a checkup with Dr. Phil Hoffman this week. The fact that my blood sugar was so great was news of joy. Despite being the father of a rock star and a famous comedian, Phil is not a particularly excitable man, but he was almost jumping up and down when he saw my lab results. My blood pressure is excellent, even as I cut back on the medicines. I feel better than I have in my adult life and I handle stress and life better. The number is a marker, but the game changers are on other fronts.

I've known a lot of people whose lack of optimism have done them in. It seems like I spend a lot of my life explaining to people that they can do something, when life and other people have tried to beat them down. I was fortunate to have parents who taught me to believe I could do anything.

Including lose an incredible amount of weight and get my body in great shape at age 56.

If you have a good plan, good advisors and people around you, good routines and a vision of how it will all look at the end, anything is possible.

I'm glad I believe that. Even if some scientist says it is not true, I still believe it.

An insurance agent named John Savage used to speak at the Million Dollar Round Table each year, and he always said, "I have visited 31 countries, and I have yet to see a statue of a cynic."

A man who was once a close friend and then fell away killed himself yesterday. I had not talked to him in the past couple of years, but when you kill yourself, you've lost all hope for things in this world. A slight bit of optimism might have kept his wit and wisdom with us for a while longer. I understand depression and have been there many times and think that getting to a positive place is better than any of the pills they can hand out.

I wish I had a few minutes with my friend and let him know that setbacks are usually bumps in the road. Sometimes they seem like mountains, but all of them can be climbed.

Off to achieve great things.

A man who has truly achieved great things for our nation is former Jimmy Carter Cabinet Secretary (and former New Orleans Mayor) Moon Landrieu, and I wrote an interesting piece about him for *Huffington Post* this week.[34] Especially interesting as we did the lunch in my favorite Italian restaurant and I had broiled crab. Moon kept popping Onion Rings on my plate, but it still came in less than 400 calories. I did get a meatball at Vincent's, another New Orleans Italian favorite, the next day, but staying on the game is more of a habit and the positive results bring on more positive reinforcement.

June 4, 2015

Weight: 285.2
Blood Sugar: 102
Blood Pressure: 126/82
Hours of Sleep: 5.9
Distance Walked: 2 miles

> *"Good times, these are the good times*
> *Leave your cares behind, these are the good times*
> *Good times, these are the good times*
> *Our new state of mind, these are the good times"*
> -Chic[35]

I have not sent the update lately. Normally that is a sign that things are going badly, but in my case, it is the opposite. Things are great. I've been staying extremely busy on the McNay Financial front and I am developing good structure and routines.

It's was one of "God's House Calls" that I got to spend so much time with Dr. Jim Roach early in the year as we were publishing his best-selling book. Jim is a fascinating man, but one of the things he does exceptionally well is manage time. He keeps an organized and disciplined schedule, but allows time for total balance in his life. He exercises, sees his patients, spends time with his family and gets out talking at churches each week. He is never rushed, but he never wastes time either. It all plays hand-in-hand. He has terrific health, but one of the reasons he stays in such good shape (along with following his own advice on proper food and nutrition) is that good actions have become habits. He takes well thought out breaks and vacations.

As I get thinner, I get better organized. That has helped business tremendously, but also means I take more breaks and vacation time. Which makes me more rested and productive. It's meant that I have had to narrow my focus. I only do a few things and a few projects, but do them well.

It's harder to contact me and expect an immediate response. On the other hand, if I set an appointment, I get to it on Lombardi time, which is 15 minutes early. I never realized how much I cancelled meetings or appointment pre-weight loss, but I don't do it now. I feel good every day, but also it is a result of not over-scheduling and staying focused.

When I interact with someone now, I am fully engaged. I plan things out far in advance and actually delegate. From a business standpoint, the surgery was an unexpected gift in how I approach everything.

I need to get in shape as I think the Reds are going to need me soon. I reported in uniform on Sunday, but they were able to win without using me. They have lost every game since then. Someone asked my age and I think I am younger than Satchel Paige. It's hard to know as Satchel lied about his age.

As I lose weight, I give my clothing to charity. It means I have been wearing the same (new) stuff a lot, but of the mindset that the old stuff goes for good.

July 21, 2015

> *"Why me Lord?*
> *What have I ever done*
> *To deserve even one of the pleasures I've known?"*
> -Kris Kristofferson[36]

I've lost more than 100 pounds in six and a half months past my gastric sleeve weight loss surgery. I weighed 377.7 pounds and was probably higher than that. (I stopped weighing myself at some point.) Now I weigh 275 pounds and dropping more every week. I used to have diabetes and a host of other illnesses. I don't now. I've never felt better in my 56 years on the earth.

I've been able to turn around a lifetime of poor eating, bad obesity genetics and indifference to physical activity and get a second chance at life.

A chance some of my heroes never got.

The "why me" question does not consume me, but it comes up. I've spent a lifetime helping injured people handle their money and come to the conclusion that bad things happen to good people for no particular reason and the inverse is true. A good person will die in a car wreck while the drunk that hit them walks away without a scratch. I count on God and the justice system to balance it all out someday.

I'm not sure why I got the second chance and others did not, but I am going to make the best of the opportunity given to me.

I stay keenly aware of survivor's guilt. There is a concept called "blood money" where a person who receives money from a death or an accident tries to blow it as fast as possible. Deep in their minds, they think that life will be "back to normal" if their money is all gone.

It doesn't work that way.

With injured people, many lose a loved one and then lose their money as well. A double tragedy that I witness too often.

In the weight loss world, many of us who have been fat all our lives start to think that things can never change. I truly believe that I can do anything that I set my mind to doing.

Obesity was messing with my "you can do anything you set your mind to" theory. I tried everything. I went through one medically supervised program six different times. I had to go face-to-face with my deepest fear: Surgery.

Surgery was the only answer.

I was always terrified of surgery until I had to have emergency surgery in 2011. Living through that reduced my resistance, but weight loss surgery was still a no-no in my world. I finally reached a point where I recognized that I could take a chance on dying quickly or die slightly less quickly from the boatload of obesity related problems on the horizon.

> *"Loneliness can get you down*
> *When you get to thinking no one cares"*
> -Paul Anka[37]

Obese people are a group that society can discriminate against with impunity. The message from the clips is "let's make fun of the fat people." They know the fat people are not going to fight back, and this experienced journalist knows that picking on someone is good for ratings.

Fat people take that mental beating throughout their lives.

Fat people are never the popular kids. Even though obesity is usually a product of genetics, income and environment, it is often foisted on obese people that it is their lack of willpower and self-discipline causing the obesity.

I inherited my obesity from obese family members. I also inherited my height, high IQ, blue eyes and male pattern baldness. It's all part of the package. I'm a man with a very strong will and my history in other life endeavors proves it. Once I understood that willpower had nothing to do with weight loss, surgery became a logical option. A medical solution to a medical problem.

I have gotten by with the help of my friends. And family. I see a lot of people battle their loved ones when they try a weight loss program or life change. Mine have been with me 110 percent.

> *"And we can build this dream together*
> *Standing strong forever*
> *Nothing's gonna stop us now"*
> -Starship[38]

Going from 377 pounds to 275 pounds is a miracle. I'm on the road to a place I've never been before and should lose 50 or 75 pounds more in the next year. All of my habits have changed.

I went from barely moving to frequently walking more than 10 miles a day. I came in second in my age category (50 and over) in a 3K run. I don't drink alcohol, soft drinks or anything carbonated and I rarely hit a fast food place.

I threw away my diabetes medicine two days after surgery and my blood sugar has been perfect. Little things rarely stress me and everything stressed me pre-surgery. I have fun and my work productivity has skyrocketed as I don't get tired as easily.

I can fly coach and fly with a normal seatbelt. I can fit in movie theater seats. I can walk in any clothing store and find apparel my size.

I'm reducing my blood pressure medicine and on the road to ditching my CPAP, which has been a constant companion for 20 years.

Many of you know your AIC rating for blood sugar. Mine was 7.8 before the surgery. Now it is 5.1, which is in the normal range and I don't take any medicines. I would have been happy to have the surgery just to get the blood sugar under control. Losing more than 100 pounds has been a bonus.

> *"Tell me Lord if you think there's a way*
> *I can try to repay all I've taken from you*
> *Maybe Lord I can show someone else*
> *What I've been through myself"*
> -Kris Kristofferson[39]

Some of the answer to the "why me" question has been hitting me over the head since the process started.

My call is not about survivor's guilt, it is about giving back.

I went into the weight loss surgery process knowing I would write about it. I already have a high profile from my other writing and media appearances and no qualms about sharing my most intimate details with the free world. Some people keep their weight loss surgery a secret. Not me. I want to help others be able to do what I have done. Which is get a second chance at really living.

I thought I would just write about it and let others find their path to the health. Now I am becoming more of an activist. Health insurance should pay for weight loss surgery for all Americans and make it easier to qualify. It is more of an upfront cost for the insurer, but the long-term savings are dramatic.

Impacting legislation and telling my story are activities on a global basis, but life really happens one-on-one. I've had several friends get interested in the surgery and I helped them start the process.

My first appearance in public after my surgery was the January swearing in of Kentucky Court of Appeals Justice Debra Lambert. My company did the website and helped her with social media in her successful campaign.

David Gambrel is an elected official in Lincoln County, Kentucky and a friend from when I was in college at Eastern Kentucky University. He was part of Justice Lambert's ceremony. David noticed my weight loss and I told him about the surgery. We went back and forth via email and messaged about it. Like other weight loss patients have done for me, I have been there to answer his questions and guide him through the process.

Last week, David had the same surgery, using the same surgeon that I used. I was in Chicago, but texted with his wife literally day and night through the next two days, as I walked him through the same walk that I had done. He is at home from the hospital and seems to be doing well. He sent me a text giving me his permission to write about him and that we have a responsibility to help others.

Yes we do.

In about seven or eight months, I want do a story about how David has lost 100 pounds, like I did.

Why me?

I suspect it is because I have the forum, attitude and motivation to make my weight loss journey a guide for many other people's journeys in the future.

So far, my strategy is one for one. And I am 100 pounds lighter.

I have a lot to be thankful for. And a lot of giving back to do.

EPILOGUE

My journey to become a Brand New Man took place over roughly 18 months. Here is an update on some of the people that you got to know through the book:

I was honored to be Al Smith's guest when he was named to the Kentucky Public Service Hall of Fame in November 2015 by the University of Kentucky Martin School of Public Policy and Administration. Al turns 89 in January 2016 and will celebrate 53 years of sobriety.

Karen Thomas McNay remains President of the Ursuline Academy in New Orleans and is scheduled to receive her doctorate from the University of Kentucky in May 2016. Her proudest achievement is that her alma mater defeated my undergraduate alma mater in football and basketball this year.

Angela Luhys is the Executive Director of Kentucky Guardianship Administrators, based in Richmond, Kentucky. Her 15-year-old son, Abijah Luhys, is brilliant, good looking and, at six-foot two-inches, is now taller than his grandpa-author.

Gena Bigler wrote her first book, *Frugal Spending for Rich Living,* in 2015 and appeared at the Kentucky Book Fair.[1] Clay Bigler continues to be one of the top structured settlement consultants in the United States. Their children Adelaide Bigler and Liam Bigler (ages seven and four) are focused on planning their future careers as movie stars, scientists and athletes.

Gary Rivlin's book, *Katrina: After the Flood,*[2] that I got to read in a rough draft form while recovering from surgery has won a number of accolades and awards, including being named one of 100 most notable books for 2015 by the *New York Times.*[3]

Joe Nocera moved from the Opinion Page to the Sports page of the *New York Times* in November 2015 and his highly anticipated book, *Indentured: The Inside Story of the Rebellion Against the NCAA,* will be released on Feb. 16, 2016.[4] At a key point in the process, Joe gave me some wise and well-needed advice about when and how to finish *Brand New Man.*

Deb Elam, who has been such an inspiring role model and cheerleader in my weight loss journey, continues to do incredible things in her role as one of the most accomplished African American females in the United States. She and her significant other, my friend Cary Grant, have a nonstop travel schedule which includes trips to the White House and with numerous other world and business leaders. Deb is President of the GE Foundation and Chief Diversity Officer for GE. It was widely noted in the New Orleans media this year when Deb was selected to as the first African American to receive the Outstanding Alumnus award at Ursuline Academy in the 288-year history of the oldest all girls' school in the United States. I also have to note that Deb made a generous donation to fund a leadership scholarship at Ursuline and that my wife Karen, the president of the institution, was thrilled by Deb's generosity. Deb checks in with me at least weekly on social media to track my journey to fitness. I truly appreciate it.

David Gambrel, the elected Property Value Administrator in Lincoln County, Kentucky, was inspired to have weight loss surgery with Dr. Derek Weiss on July 20 after first seeing me at Debra Lambert's January 2015 swearing in ceremony. As of Dec. 12, 2015, David has lost 72 pounds and we are planning an event in Lincoln County in 2016 to celebrate the weight loss for both of us.

Stacy Tuttle had the gastric sleeve surgery in Louisville on Aug. 18 and has lost 45 pounds. The Tuttle Tots race will take place June 18, 2016 in Carrollton, Kentucky. The McNay team plans to return to defend their championships.

Adam Turner is the Executive Director of RRP International Publishing, which has recently published two noteworthy books,

God's House Calls by Dr. Jim Roach and *Beans, Biscuits, Family and Friends: Life Stories* by Bill Goodman.[5] RRP International also designed the web page for well-known Louisville attorney Gary Hillerich.

Bill Garmer was elected Vice President of the Kentucky Bar Association.

Cindy Jester Caywood is now the Director of the Bariatrics Center at Georgetown Community Hospital.

Dr. Lisa West Smith is now with the Department of Psychiatry and Behavioral Neuroscience at the University of Cincinnati.

Dr. Derek Weiss remains the head of Bluegrass Bariatric Surgical Associates in Lexington, Kentucky.

Dr. Jim Roach remains one of the nation's top experts in Integrative Medicine and has made countless media appearances in 2015.

My children and grandchildren and I attended the Nutcracker Ballet at the Lexington Opera House in December where Caterina Monsolve's 12-year-old daughter Paula danced the lead role of Clara in a performance by the Kentucky Ballet Theatre.

After having lost contact for more than 25 years, I reconnected with my half-brother Joey McNay in December. A story that will be told in another book or forum.

After taking pictures and assisting me during the interview with his daughter Elizabeth, which became a *Huffington Post* article and allowed me to feature Elizabeth in this book, I asked Marc Whitt to assist RRP International and Dr. Jim Roach in doing the public relations for the launch of *God's House Calls,* and he did a terrific job. Even better news happened later in the year when Marc was named Director of Philanthropy Communications at the University of Kentucky.

Chas Walsh, the best man in my father and stepmother Lynn's wedding, died this year after a legendary career in the casino industry. His daughter Susan Walsh is a Pulitzer Prize-winning photographer for the *Associated Press* at the White House.

Peter Perlman was named to the Hall of Distinguished Alumni at the University of Kentucky and moved his law practice into the same office as his two former associates Tom Herren and Chuck Adams.

Gary Hillerich was named Personal Injury Lawyer of the Year, 2015, Louisville, Kentucky by Best Lawyers.

On Dec. 12, Sheila Hiestand successfully completed her first race, The Reindeer Romp in Louisville, after injuring her knee during the Ironman competition. She is training for another Ironman race in 2016.

-Don McNay
Dec. 15, 2015

ACKNOWLEDGEMENTS

"I can fly higher than an eagle
For you are the wind beneath my wings"
-Bette Midler[1]

"I am a part of all that I have met."
-Alfred Lord Tennyson[2]

"Victory has a thousand fathers."
-John F. Kennedy[3]

I decided to write this book before I did anything related to actually becoming a Brand New Man. I knew that writing a book would give me a sense of accountability and allow me to stay focused on my mission as I relaunched my life. Good health is a cradle-to-grave process, but I really needed to make the most of my second chance.

My weight loss process is one where I have love, support and cheerleaders. They give me an incredible boost of energy.

And a whole lot of people to thank.

First and foremost is my family: My wife Karen Thomas McNay; my daughters, Gena Bigler and Angela Luhys; my son-in-law Clay Bigler; my brother Joey McNay; my nephew Nick McNay and his wife Tina; my stepmother Lynn McNay; and my grandchildren, Abijah Luhys, Adelaide Bigler and Liam Bigler.

As noted, my daughter Angela contributed a great deal of material for the book and was my primary caretaker in the months after the weight loss surgery. My daughter Gena and son-in-law Clay Bigler were there for me as well. Karen checked in every night from New Orleans and a special shout out goes to my terrific stepmother Lynn, who stepped up and served as a second reader and copyeditor.

Also, my mother and father-in-law Byrle and Walker Thomas, Sr.; sister-in-law Teresa Thomas Young; brother-in-laws Shane Young (County Attorney in Hardin County, Ky. and was voted Prosecutor of the Year in 2015) and Walker Thomas, Jr.; Uncle Leon Thomas, a highly decorated Vietnam War hero; stepchildren Max Kirby, Emily Kirby and Zach Kirby; and my stepsister Dobie Deemer.

Include nieces and nephews Lyndsay Jo Francis, Aaron Thomas, Celia Thomas, Eli Thomas, Hope Thomas, Jack Young and Matt Young, and I have a family unit larger than the Brady Bunch. That family grew even further when in December 2015 I reconnected with my brother Joey, better known to the world as Puck Dunaway, for the first time in about 25 years. I've yet to meet his wife Ericka McIntyre, but we are avid Facebook friends.

Adam Turner is Executive Director of RRP International Publishing and Digital Media, where he rules over the editing, production and marketing of books for authors such as Bill Goodman, Dr. Jim Roach, Suzette Martinez Standring, Keen Babbage, Clay Hamrick and Laura Babbage, along with being the most important person, from start to finish, in the books that I write. He also has built a budding digital media and website creation business and is a really nice guy to boot. I can't thank him enough. Jessica Shelton served as an intern for Adam and contributed to some of the early versions of the manuscript, and Ryan Alves served as an additional editor.

From the world of best-selling authors, a special shout out goes to two heavy hitters, Gary Rivlin and Joe Nocera, as well as my mentor Al Smith. They gave me excellent and sometimes pointed advice. Learning from true experts is a theme of the book, and you can't find three better writers and journalists than those three.

Financial genius Carroll Crouch of Lexington is a longtime friend and a terrific photographer. He took the "after" picture of me for the back cover and the "gambler" picture of me in the book.

I'm lucky that some of the greatest attorneys in the history of Kentucky are also some of my closest friends. They include Samuel

Davies, Gary Hillerich, Peter Perlman, Bill Garmer, E. Andre Busald, Lee Gentry, Sheila Hiestand, Greg Bubalo, David Grise, Phil Taliaferro, Richard Hay, J.T. Gilbert, Pierce Hamblin and Brian House.

I shared the details of my journey with friends via email and especially through social media. Some pop up in the reality show, but a lot of them make their mark quietly and subtly in this book. My medical dream team and weight loss heroines have their own chapters. Dr. Rebecca Hammond in Berea, Kentucky has been a valuable friend and advisor for several years. Friends like Bob Babbage, Mike Behler, Keith Yarber, Deidre Gettings Brumfield, Kevin Osbourn, Marc Whitt, Liz Roach, Adrienne Banks, Tiffany Nash, Moon Landrieu and Yvette Hourigan contributed ideas and concepts to the book.

I wish I could remember the names of the nurses and staff that I dealt with at Georgetown hospital, but I was highly medicated at the time. They did an incredible job, as did the teams that Dr. Jim Roach, Dr. Derek Weiss and Dr. Phil Hoffman assembled in their offices.

I was lucky to have excellent medical and fitness advisors throughout my life that kept me alive long enough to be a Brand New Man. They include Dr. Ralph Caldroney, the late Dr. Daryl Pauly, Dr. Patricia Blackwell, Dr. James Anderson, Dr. Bill Wachs, Dana Merkley, Steve Carroll, Neil Burns, Dr. Byron Westerfield, Rhonda Goode and Onieta Walden Stewart.

I wrote several articles about the weight loss journey on *Huffington Post* and one of them, about how I used BLIS to insure my surgery, caught the attention of Antonia Namnath, who is the tireless founder and President of the Weight Loss Surgery Foundation of America (www.wlsfa.org) and invited me to speak at their convention in May 2016. A huge meeting with Carnie Wilson as a headliner. I've gotten to work with WLSFA board member Laura Van Tuyl and they do a terrific job in operating an all volunteer organization.

I touch on the concept of fat shaming briefly in *Brand New Man*, but the WLSFA goes at the topic with full intensity and force. One of their projects is to have people take an oath against fat shaming. The oath says:

I chose…

-To fight fat shame and stigma everywhere
-To share compassion and understanding to all affected by obesity
-To give others the courage to enjoy life free from obesity shame and bias
-To use my voice to educate about the epidemic disease of obesity
-To demand insurance coverage for all medical treatment of obesity

I say AMEN to every one of those points.

Alex Brecher runs a great online resource called BariatricPal.com. I visited it daily as I was getting prepared for surgery and got to know Alex via his daily insights on Linkedin.

Others who have helped my journey to become a Brand New Man came from a life of developing great friendships or my recent fascination with CrossFit. Some started out as total strangers who became interested in what I am doing.

People who should be pointed out are:

Deb Elam, Cary Grant, State Senator Robin Webb, Evan Sloan, Jeff Chasen, Vickie Gregory, Rhonda Hatfield-Jeffers, Terry Gregory Andrews, Dean Gregory, Tom Gregory, Kaye Spalding Peterson, John Y. Brown III, Lincoln Brown, Marisa Anders, Debbie Fickett-Wilbar, David Kramer, Larry and Bonnie Doker, Rob Dollar, Dex Hopkins, Ben Welter, Erica Spitz, Savannah Osbourn, Verna Landrieu, Paula Hayes, Eva Gillespie, Judge Debra Lambert, Robyn Davis Sekula, Hans Poppe, Joe Elliott, Jennifer Highland, Michael and Norma Kimble, Kelan Grffin, Kathie Blash, Kendra Steele, Kathie Petrey, Bill and Annette Daniels, Richard Hay, Teresa Campion Bowerman, Jay Prather, Carla Wade, Anne Litton, Elyse Litton, Dwayne Litton, Allison Ball, Jim Vanover, Kirk David, Nick

Perlick, Len Press, Lil Press, Ken Kurtz, Neil Middleton, Susie Walsh, Jay and Farrah Vaughn, "Cadillac" Charlie Shanks, "The Music Professor" Jim LaBarbara, Dr. Debby Herbenick, Al and Patti Cross, Monique Morial, Lezlei Swanson Kelly, Nancy and Paul Collins, Nancy and Phil Hoffman, Dr. Michael Taft Benson, Keven and Liz Moore, Dave Baker, Connie Kreyling, Whitney Greer Sisson, Donna Davis, Harry Moberly, George Phillips, Caterina Monsolve, Sheila Holdt, Mark Neikirk, Theresa Currier Thomas, Mark Buerger, Martha Helen Smith, Greg Stotelmyer, Liz Croney, Tom Leach, Wes Browne, Denise Gray, Kathyn Jackson, Charlie Fortney, Jessica Byrd Wilson, John Wilson, Alan Stein, John Eckberg, Judy Clabes, Nancy Oeswein, Samantha Swindler, Stephenie Steitzer Hoelscher, Skip Daugherty, Carl Kremer, Jody Hanks, Steve DiMartino, David Gambrell, Kelly Gambrell, Chris Tuttle, Ron and Kelly Deitz, Randy and Jennifer Cox, Heather Pile, Lisa West-Smith, John Sam Steele, Renee Brake, Yvonne Yelton, Martha Eastman, Rick Robinson, Helen Gulgan Bukulmez, Nick McDowell, Sarah House, Marc Ehrhardt, Jim Gormley, DeeDee Roach, John Doug Hays, Judge Jack Kennedy, Rhonda Jennings Blackburn, Renee Shaw, Kathy Childress, Andi Mullins, Kenneth George, Betty Gettings, Jim Vanover, Gina Vessals, Kathyn Cody, Nate Spitz, Andrea Strassburg, Heather Kiser, Amber Allen, Bonita Black Rivera and Ray Rivera, Senator Alice Forgy Kerr, David Helmers, Sandra Slatten Sams, Lisette Valentino Turpin, Michael Valentino, Mike Tucker, Judge Kathy Stein, Stokes Harris, Eric Brandenburg, Mary Pat Behler, Connie Crowe, Chris and Aimie Burlile, Chuck Beal, Adam Collins, Barry Peel, Noel Rodriguez, Tina Workman Harris, Pam Trimm, Dawn Marie Bacon, Len Blonder, Jordan Baker, Dennis Smith, Jennifer Whitt, Regi Schindler, Kim Brown and a whole lot of other people.

Having such a wonderful and talented support system is what made my journey to becoming a Brand New Man possible.

(P.S. I threw in the line from Alfred Lord Tennyson to stun Peggy Bertlesman, my English teacher at Covington Catholic High School, by proving that I could still remember "Ulysses" all these years later.)

BIBLIOGRAPHY AND REFERENCE SOURCES

When we started the book writing process, there was a protracted internal debate as to whether we should include footnotes and a bibliography. It is my personal journey, not an academic dissertation, but one that drew upon a lot of references and resources along the way. Doing research and gaining insights gleamed from a wide variety of sources is a key to why my journey has been a successful one.

Thus, I provided footnotes when appropriate and put together a bibliography of books that were read, referenced or drawn upon during the process. To make it easier for anyone looking to become a brand new person, I have separated the bibliography into categories and sections.

Books You Must Read

How I Raised Myself from Failure to Success in Selling by Frank Bettger
Napoleon Hill: The Rare Teachings of Napoleon Hill by Patrick Doucette
The Autobiography of Benjamin Franklin by Benjamin Franklin
The Checklist Manifesto: How to Get Things Right by Atul Gawande
Profiles in Courage by John F. Kennedy
What They Don't Teach You at Harvard Business School by Mark McCormick
Katrina: After the Flood by Gary Rivlin
A Pirate Looks at Fifty by Jimmy Buffett
The Essays of Ralph Waldo Emerson (Collected Works) by Ralph Waldo Emerson
The E-Myth Revisited by Michael E. Gerber
Team of Rivals: The Political Genius of Abraham Lincoln by Doris Kearns Goodwin

Dispensing with the Truth: The Victims, the Drug Companies and the Dramatic Story Behind the Battle over Fen-Phen by Alicia Mundy
Fight Club: A Novel by Chuck Palahniuk
The Power of Positive Thinking: 10 Traits for Maximum Results by Norman Vincent Peale
Never Going Back: Winning the Weight Loss Battle for Good by Al Roker
The Magic of Thinking Big by David J. Schwartz
Why We Get Fat: And What to Do About It by Gary Taubes

Books about Addictions

Addiction to Alcohol
Alcoholics Anonymous: The Big Book
Dry: A Memoir by Augusten Burroughs
The Alcoholism and Addiction Cure: A Holistic Approach to Total Recovery by Chris Prentiss
Kentucky Cured: Fifty Years in Kentucky Journalism by Al Smith
Wordsmith by Al Smith
Five O'Clock Comes Early: A Young Man's Battle With Alcoholism by Bob Welch and George Vecsey

Addiction to Drugs or Narcotics
The Man with the Golden Arm by Nelson Algren
Incomprehensible Demoralization: An Addict Pharmacist's Journey to Recovery by Jared Combs
Clean: Overcoming Addiction and Ending America's Greatest Tragedy by David Sheff
American Pain: How a Young Felon and His Ring of Doctors Unleashed Americas Deadliest Drug Epidemic by John Temple

Addiction to Food
The Twelve Steps and Twelve Traditions of Overeaters Anonymous

Gambling Addiction
One of a Kind: The Rise and Fall of Stuey "The Kid" Ungar, The

World's Greatest Poker Player by Nolan Dalla
Born to Lose: Memoirs of a Compulsive Gambler by Bill Lee

Other Addictive Behaviors

All That Is Bitter and Sweet: A Memoir by Ashley Judd
Dancing for the Devil: One Woman's Dramatic and Divine Rescue from the Sex Industry by Anny Donewald

Celebrity Obesity and Celebrity Weight Loss Surgery

How Sweet It Is: The Jackie Gleason Story by James Bacon
Losing It: And Gaining My Life Back One Pound at a Time by Valerie Bertinelli
Shine: A Physical, Emotional, and Spiritual Journey to Finding Love by Star Jones Reynolds
Kicking & Dreaming: A Story of Heart, Soul, and Rock and Roll by Ann Wilson
Gut Feelings: From Fear And Despair To Health And Hope by Carnie Wilson and Mick Kleber
I'm Still Hungry: Finding Myself Through Thick and Thin by Carnie Wilson

Books about Weight Loss Surgery

The Emotional First + Aid Kit: A Practical Guide to Life After Bariatric Surgery by Cynthia L. Alexander
Successful Weight Loss with the Gastric Sleeve by Guillermo Alvarez
Losing It: My Journey of Losing 150 Pounds in a Year with the Gastric Sleeve by Anne Andrews
Gutting It Out: Bariatric Surgery Beyond the Numbers; From a Man's Perspective by Jim Bates
The Big Book on Bariatric Surgery: Living Your Best Life After Weight Loss Surgery by Alex Brecher and Natalie Stein
The Big Book on the Gastric Bypass: Everything You Need to Know to Lose Weight and Live Well with the Roux-en-Y Gastric Bypass

Surgery by Alex Brecher and Natalie Stein

The Big Book on the Gastric Sleeve: Everything You Need To Know To Lose Weight and Live Well with the Vertical Sleeve Gastrectomy by Alex Brecher and Natalie Stein

Weight Loss Surgery: Bariatric Surgery by Kim Browne

Bariatric Weight Loss: The Truth by Michael Connelly

The Success Habits of Weight Loss Surgery Patients (3rd Edition) by Colleen M. Cook

Battle Scars: My Journey from Obesity to Health and Happiness, Fifteen Years and Counting! by Stephen Cremen

Just Don't Do Gastric Bypass by Mary Elder

Legacy 1.0: A Bariatric Memoir by Alan Falk

Half-Assed: A Weight-Loss Memoir by Jennette Fulda

Gastric Sleeve Changing Body, Changing Life by Linda Guill

Weight Loss Surgery: The Definitive Guide to Lose Weight And How Surgery Can Help by Charles Hope

Through Thick & Thin: The Emotional Journey of Weight Loss Surgery by Warren L. Huberman

Weight Loss Surgery for Dummies by Barbara Thompson, Brian K. Davidson and Marina S. Kurian

Stranger Here: How Weight-Loss Surgery Transformed My Body and Messed with My Head by Jen Larsen

Before and After: Living and Eating Well After Weight Loss Surgery by Susan Maria Leach

Okay...I've Gone Through Weight Loss Surgery, Now What Do I Do?! by Joanne M. Moff

Weight Loss Surgery: The Real Skinny by Nick Nicholson M.D. and B.A. Blackwood

The Sleeved Life: A Patient-to-Patient Guide on Vertical Sleeve Gastrectomy Weight Loss Surgery by Pennie Nicola

Exodus from Obesity: The Guide to Long-Term Success After Weight Loss Surgery (2nd Edition) by Paula F. Peck

Weight Loss Surgery: The Stranger in the Mirror by Ellie Salser

I'm Healthy, Just Big: The Story of My Gastric Bypass Life Change by Nate Washington

Ultimate Gastric Sleeve Success: A Practical Patient Guide to Help Maximize Your Weight Loss Results by Dr. Duc C. Vuong

Medically-Related Books

ADD and ADHD
Driven to Distraction: Recognizing and Coping with Attention Deficit Disorder by Edward M. Hallowell, M.D. and John J. Ratey, M.D.
Succeeding with Adult ADHD: Daily Strategies to Help You Achieve Your Goals and Manage Your Life by Abigail Levrini and Frances Prevatt
More Attention, Less Deficit: Success Strategies for Adults with ADHD by Ari Tuckman
Fighting ADD ADHD with Food by Jon Bennett

Big Medicine and Medical Errors
Medical Errors and Medical Narcissism by John D. Banja
Serotonin by Syd Baumel
Wall of Silence: The Untold Story of the Medical Mistakes that Kill and Injure Millions of Americans by Rosemary Gibson
Catastrophic Care: How American Health Care Killed My Father — and How We Can Fix by David Goldhill
On The Take: How Medicine's Complicity with Big Business Can Endanger Your Health by Jerome P. Kassirer M.D.
Blind Eye: The Terrifying Story Of A Doctor Who Got Away With Murder by James B. Stewart
Internal Bleeding: The Truth Behind America's Terrifying Epidemic of Medical Mistakes by Robert Wachter and Kaveh Shojania

Cancer, Co-Dependency and Depression
Life Lessons from Cancer by Dr. Keen Babbage and Laura Babbage
Codependent No More: How to Stop Controlling Others and Start Caring for Yourself by Melody Beattie
Down Came the Rain: My Journey Through Postpartum Depression by Brooke Shields

Diabetes
American Medical Association Guide to Living with Diabetes: Preventing and Treating Type 2 Diabetes by AMA

The First Year: Type 2 Diabetes: An Essential Guide for the Newly Diagnosed by Gretchen Becker
The Diabetes Diet: Dr. Bernstein's Low-Carbohydrate Solution by Richard K. Bernstein
Dr. Bernstein's Diabetes Solution: The Complete Guide to Achieving Normal Blood Sugars by Richard K. Bernstein
The Insulin-Resistance Diet: How to Turn Off Your Body's Fat-Making Machine by Cheryle R. Hart and Mary Kay Grossman
Diabetes For Dummies by Alan L. Rubin

Exercise and Grief
The Rise of Superman: Decoding the Science of Ultimate Human Performance by Steven Kotler
I'm Grieving as Fast as I Can: How Young Widows and Widowers Can Cope and Heal by Linda Feinberg
Unremarried Widow: A Memoir by Artis Henderson
The Last Lecture by Randy Pausch and Jeffrey Zaslow

Healthy Living
The Book of Secrets: Unlocking the Hidden Dimensions of Your Life by Deepak Chopra
How Doctors Think by Jerome Groopman
Because It Feels Good: A Woman's Guide to Sexual Pleasure and Satisfaction by Dr. Debby Herbenick, PhD
The Blood Pressure Cure: 8 Weeks to Lower Blood Pressure Without Prescription Drugs by Robert Kowalski
The Red Queen: Sex and the Evolution of Human Nature by Matt Ridley
Eight Weeks to Optimum Health by Andrew Weil

Health Insurance and Health Care Reform
Health Care Reform and American Politics: What Everyone Needs to Know by Lawrence R. Jacobs
Beating Obamacare: Your Handbook for the New Healthcare Law by Betsy McCaughey
The Patient Protection and Affordable Care Act by Barack Obama
Health Care Reform Simplified: What Professionals in Medicine, Government, Insurance, and Business Need to Know by Dave Parks

Diet and Obesity

Dr. Anderson's Antioxidant, Antiaging Health Program by Dr. James W. Anderson

Dr. Anderson's High-Fiber Fitness Plan by Dr. James W. Anderson

The Simple Diet: A Doctor's Science-Based Plan by Dr. James W. Anderson

Atkins Diabetes Revolution: The Groundbreaking Approach to Preventing and Controlling Type 2 Diabetes by Robert C. Atkins

Dr. Atkins' Nutrition Breakthrough: How to Treat Your Medical Condition Without Drugs by Robert C. Atkins

Dr. Atkins' Health Revolution: How Complementary Medicine can Extend Your Life by Robert C. Atkins

Missing Microbes: How the Overuse of Antibiotics Is Fueling Our Modern Plagues by Martin J. Blaser

Wheat Belly 30-Minute (Or Less!) Cookbook by William Davis

The 4-Hour Body: An Uncommon Guide to Rapid Fat-Loss, Incredible Sex, and Becoming Superhuman by Timothy Ferriss

Quit Digging Your Grave with a Knife and Fork: A 12-Stop Program to End Bad Habits and Begin a Healthy Lifestyle by Mike Huckabee

Drop Dead Healthy: One Man's Humble Quest for Bodily Perfection by A.J. Jacobs

Hope, Help, and Healing for Eating Disorders: A New Approach to Treating Anorexia, Bulimia, and Overeating by Gregory Jantz

The End of Overeating: Taking Control of the Insatiable American Appetite by David A. Kessler

Fat Chance: Beating the Odds Against Sugar, Processed Food, Obesity, and Disease by Robert Lustig

The Low-Carb Cookbook by Fran Mccullough

Grain Brain: The Surprising Truth about Wheat, Carbs, and Sugar-- Your Brain's Silent Killers by David Perlmutter and Kristin Loberg

Good Calories, Bad Calories: Fats, Carbs, and the Controversial Science of Diet and Health by Gary Taubes

Handbook of Eating Disorders by Janet Treasure

Body Stories: Research & Intimate Narratives on Women Transforming Body Image In Outdoor Adventure by Dr. Lisa West-Smith

The Diet Drug Redux
Redux: The Revolutionary Weight Loss Drug by Marilyn Larkin
Battling Goliath: Inside a $22 Billion-Legal Scandal by Kip Petroff

Books from the World of Business

Communications
You Are The Message by Roger Ailes
The Culture Code: An Ingenious Way to Understand why People Around the World Live and Buy as They Do by Clotaire Rapaille
How We Decide by Jonah Lehrer
The Signal and The Noise: Why So Many Predictions Fail-but Some Don't by Nate Silver
What Stays in Vegas: The World of Personal Data—Lifeblood of Big Business—and the End of Privacy as We Know It by Adam Tanner

Law
The Predators' Ball: The Inside Story of Drexel Burnham and the Rise of the JunkBond Raiders by Connie Bruck
Who Gets What: Fair Compensation after Tragedy and Financial Upheaval by Kenneth Feinberg
What Is Life Worth?: The Unprecedented Effort to Compensate the Victims of 9/11 by Kenneth Feinberg
You Can't Teach Hungry ...Creating the Multimillion Dollar Law Firm by John Morgan
The Seventeen Traditions: Lessons from an American Childhood by Ralph Nader
Winning the Insurance Game: The Complete Consumer's Guide to Saving Money by Ralph Nader
Good Guys and Bad Guys: Behind the Scenes with the Saints and Scoundrels of American Business (and Everything in Between) by Joe Nocera
The Man to See by Evan Thomas

Leadership
Getting Things Done : The Art of Stress-Free Productivity by David Allen

Dawns with Dexter: How Finding the Right Mentor Will Change Your Life Forever by Ron Ball

Leadership by James MacGregor Burns

Creativity, Inc.: Overcoming the Unseen Forces That Stand in the Way of True Inspiration by Ed Catmull and Amy Wallace

Influence: Science and Practice by Robert Cialdini

Good to Great: Why Some Companies Make the Leap...And Others Don't by James C. Collins

The 7 Habits of Highly Effective People: Powerful Lessons in Personal Change by Stephen Covey

The United States of Wal-Mart by John Dicker

The 4-Hour Workweek by Timothy Ferriss

The Winner-Take-All Society: Why the Few at the Top Get So Much More Than the Rest of Us by Robert Frank

Tribes: We Need You to Lead Us by Seth Godin

Affluence Intelligence: Earn More, Worry Less, and Live a Happy and Balanced Life by Stephen Goldbart and Joan Indursky DiFuria

Mastery by Robert Greene

The 48 Laws of Power by Robert Greene

The Hard Thing About Hard Things: Building a Business When There Are No Easy Answers by Ben Horowitz

On Becoming Fearless...in Love, Work, and Life by Arianna Huffington

Third World America: How Our Politicians Are Abandoning the Middle Class and Betraying the American Dream by Arianna Huffington

Steve Jobs by Walter Isaacson

Brilliant, Crazy, Cocky: How the Top 1% of Entrepreneurs Profit from Global Chaos by Sarah Lacy

Don McNay's Greatest Hits: Ten Years as an Award-Winning Columnist by Don McNay

Pizza Tiger by Tom Monaghan

The End of Power: From Boardrooms to Battlefields and Churches to States, Why Being In Charge Isn't What It Used to Be by Moises Naim

The Art of Asking: How I Learned to Stop Worrying and Let People Help by Amanda Palmer

EntreLeadership: 20 Years of Practical Business Wisdom from the

Trenches by Dave Ramsey
The Productive Person by James Roper
Not Counting Tomorrow: The Unlikely Life of Jeff Ruby by Jeff Ruby and Robert Windeler
Lean In: Women, Work, and the Will to Lead by Sheryl Sandberg
How to Invest Your Time Like Money by Elizabeth Grace Saunders
Good Self, Bad Self: How to Bounce Back from a Personal Crisis by Judy Smith
Never Own Anything That Eats While You Sleep by Dan Sullivan
The Laws of Lifetime Growth: Always Make Your Future Bigger Than Your Past by Dan Sullivan
The Pursuit: Success is Hidden in the Journey by Dexter Yager and John Mason

Money

Wealth in Families by Charles W. Collier
Why Smart People Make Big Money Mistakes And How To Correct Them by Thomas Gilovich and Gary Belsky
The Intelligent Investor: The Classic Text on Value Investing by Benjamin Graham
Thou Shall Prosper: Ten Commandments for Making Money by Rabbi Daniel Lapin
The Opposite of Spoiled by Ron Lieber
Inherited Wealth: Opportunities and Dilemmas by John L. Levy
Life Lessons from the Lottery: Protecting Your Money in a Scary World by Don McNay
Son of a Son of a Gambler: Winners, Losers, and What to do When You Win the Lottery by Don McNay
Wealth Without Wall Street: A Main Street Guide to Making Money by Don McNay
Happy Money: The Science of Happier Spending by Michael Norton and Elizabeth Dunn
The Courage to be Rich: Creating a Life of Material and Spiritual Abundance by Suze Orman
Annuities For Dummies by Kerry Pechter
Financial Peace by Dave Ramsey
Broke, USA by Gary Rivlin
Irrational Exuberance by Robert Shiller

Marketing to the Affluent by Dr. Thomas Stanley

Stop Acting Rich: And Start Living Like A Real Millionaire by Thomas J. Stanley

The Millionaire Next Door: The Surprising Secrets of America's Wealthy by Thomas J. Stanley

The Wisdom of Crowds: Why the Many Are Smarter Than the Few and How Collective Wisdom Shapes Business, Economies, Societies and Nations by James Surowiecki

Nudge: Improving Decisions About Health, Wealth, and Happiness by Richard Thaler and Cass Sunstein

The Soul of Money: Transforming Your Relationship with Money and Life by Lynne Twist

Why Smart People Do Stupid Things with Money by Bert Whitehead M.B.A., J.D.

Predictably Irrational: The Hidden Forces That Shape Our Decisions by Dan Ariely

A Piece of the Action: How the Middle Class Joined the Money Class by Joe Nocera

Your Money or Your Life: 9 Steps to Transforming Your Relationship with Money by Vicki Robin

Maxed Out: Hard Times in the Age of Easy Credit by James Scurlock

10 Habits of the Rich by Cameron Taylor

Triumphs of Experience: The Men of the Harvard Grant Study by George E. Vaillant

Books about Celebrities

Starstruck: The Business of Celebrity by Elizabeth Currid-Halkett

Fame Junkie: The Hidden Truths Behind America's Favorite Addictions by Jake Halpern

Everyone Loves You When You Are Dead: Journeys into Fame and Madness by Neil Strauss

Celebrity - Addiction

Johnny Cash: The Life by Robert Hilburn

Cash: The Autobiography by Johnny Cash

Clapton: The Autobiography by Eric Clapton

Careless Love: The Unmaking of Elvis Presley by Peter Guralnick
Hotel California by Barney Hoskyns
Does the Noise In My Head Bother You? by Steven Tyler
I'll Sleep When I'm Dead: The Dirty Life and Times of Warren Zevon by Crystal Zevon

Celebrity - Inspirational
Tuesday with Morrie: An Old Man, a Young Man, and Life's Greatest Lesson by Mitch Albom
Lips Unsealed: A Memoir by Belinda Carlisle
Yes I Can: The Story of Sammy Davis, Jr. by Sammy Davis, Jr.
Knockout Entrepreneur by George Foreman
Me, Inc.: Build an Army of One, Unleash Your Inner Rock God, Win in Life and Business by Gene Simmons
Wild: From Lost to Found on the Pacific Crest Trail by Cheryl Strayed

Celebrity - Music
The Soundtrack of My Life by Clive Davis
Society's Child: My Autobiography by Janis Ian
Soul Picnic: The Music and Passion of Laura Nyro by Michele Kort
The Music Professor: A Life Amplified Through Radio & Rock 'n' Roll by Jim LaBarbara
Eric Carmen: Marathon Man by Ken Sharp
Girls Like Us: Carole King, Joni Mitchell, Carly Simon --And the Journey of a Generation by Sheila Weller

Books Related to Diet and Food

The Vegetarian Low-Carb Diet: The Fast, No-hunger Weight Loss Diet for Vegetarians by Rose Elliot
The Sugar Fix: The High-Fructose Fallout That Is Making You Fat and Sick by Richard Johnson
In Defense of Food: An Eater's Manifesto by Michael Pollan
Eat Right for Your Type by Peter D'Adamo
Get the Sugar Out: 501 Simple Ways to Cut the Sugar Out of Any Diet by Ann Louise Gittleman

Cheeseburgers: The Best of Bob Greene by Bob Greene
Well Fed: Paleo Recipes for People Who Love to Eat by Melissa Joulwan
Food Rules: An Eater's Manual by Michael Pollan
The Omnivore's Dilemma: A Natural History of Four Meals by Michael Pollan
Fast Food Nation: The Dark Side of the All-American Meal by Eric Schlosser
The Zone Diet by Barry Sears

Books Related to History

200 John F. Kennedy Quotes by Robert Taylor
We Are The Builders of Our Future: Success through Self-Reliance by Ralph Waldo Emerson
The Way to Wealth by Benjamin Franklin
Mythology: Timeless Tales of Gods and Heroes by Edith Hamilton
The True Believer: Thoughts on the Nature of Mass Movements by Eric Hoffer
The Letters of John F. Kennedy by John F. Kennedy
Beans, Biscuits, Family & Friends: Life Stories by Bill Goodman

Biographies
The Passage of Power (The Years of Lyndon Johnson) by Robert Caro
My Life by Bill Clinton
The Bully Pulpit: Theodore Roosevelt, William Howard Taft, and the Golden Age of Journalism by Doris Kearns Goodwin
Einstein: His Life and Universe by Walter Isaacson
Mornings on Horseback: The Story of an Extraordinary Family by David McCullough
Truman by David McCullough
Destiny and Power: The American Odyssey of George Herbert Walker Bush by Jon Meacham
The Rise of Theodore Roosevelt by Edmund Morris
Dreams from My Father: A Story of Race and Inheritance by Barack Obama
Plutarch: Lives of the noble Grecians and Romans by Plutarch

The Triumph of William McKinley by Karl Rove
Being Nixon: A Man Divided by Evan Thomas
Benjamin Franklin: An American Life by Walter Isaacson
Ike's Bluff: President Eisenhower's Secret Battle to Save the World
by Evan Thomas
Robert Kennedy: His Life by Evan Thomas
The War Lovers: Roosevelt, Lodge, Hearst, and the Rush to Empire, 1898 by Evan Thomas
The Right Stuff by Tom Wolfe

Motivational and Self-Help Books

Life Lessons from a Dog Named Rudy by Dr. Keen Babbage
Willpower: Rediscovering the Greatest Human Strength by Roy
Baumeister
The Sweet Spot: How to Find Your Groove at Home and Work by
Christine Carter
Kentucky Footnotes by Byron Crawford
Bold: How to Go Big, Create Wealth and Impact the World by Peter
Diamandis and Steven Kotler
Stumbling on Happiness by Daniel Gilbert
Eat, Pray, Love by Elizabeth Gilbert
*David and Goliath: Underdogs, Misfits and the Art of Battling
Giants* by Malcolm Gladwell
*Navigating Life's Transitions: Connecting Your Means to Your
Meaning* by Joshua Kadish and Nicole Mayer
The Success Principles(TM) - 10th Anniversary Edition by Jack
Canfield
How Will You Measure Your Life? by Clayton M. Christensen
The Selfish Gene by Richard Dawkins
Abundance: The Future Is Better Than You Think by Peter H.
Diamandis and Steven Kotler
*The Number: What Do You Need for the Rest of Your Life and What
Will It Cost?* by Lee Eisenberg
The Tipping Point: How Little Things Can Make a Big Difference by
Malcolm Gladwell
*Carry On, Warrior: The Power of Embracing Your Messy, Beautiful
Life* by Glennon Doyle Melton

The Upside of Irrationality: The Unexpected Benefits of Defying Logic at Work and at Home by Dan Ariely
The Six Pillars of Self-Esteem by Nathaniel Branden
Transitions: Making Sense of Life's Changes by William Bridges
Thinking, Fast and Slow by Daniel Kahneman
Life Mapping: A Journey of Self-Discovery and Path Finding by Monika Moss

Books Related to Sports

Coach: Lessons on the Game of Life by Michael Lewis
Indentured: The Inside Story of the Rebellion Against the NCAA by Joe Nocera
The Inner Game of Stress: Outsmart Life's Challenges and Fulfill Your Potential by W. Timothy Gallwey
It's Not About the Bike: My Journey Back to Life by Lance Armstrong
Moneyball: The Art of Winning an Unfair Game by Michael Lewis
Born to Run: A Hidden Tribe, Superathletes, and the Greatest Race the World Has Never Seen by Christopher McDougall

CrossFit
Crossfit: The Ultimate Crossfit Training & Diet Guide by Russell Arkons
Crossfit (Crossfit, Crossfit for Beginners) by Chase Burrows
Training for the CrossFit Games by Douglas Chapman
Learning to Breathe Fire: The Rise of CrossFit and the Primal Future of Fitness by J.C. Herz
Embrace the Suck: What I learned at the box about hard work by Stephen Madden
Inside the Box: How CrossFit ® Shredded the Rules, Stripped Down the Gym, and Rebuilt My Body by T.J. Murphy
Starting Strength by Mark Rippetoe
Cross-Training for Dummies by Tony Ryan and Martica Heaner

Dancing
Zumba: What Zumba Is and How You Can Lose Weight and Improve

by Amanda Britton
Every Man's Survival Guide to Ballroom Dancing: Ace Your Wedding Dance and Keep Cool on a Cruise, at a Formal, and in Dance Classes by James Joseph
Social Dance: Steps to Success by Judy Patterson Wright

Exercise

Get with the Program!: Getting Real About Your Weight, Health, and Emotional Well-Being by Bob Greene
Make the Connection: Ten Steps to a Better Body—and a Better Life by Bob Greene
The Coregasm Workout by Dr. Debby Herbenick
Finding Ultra: Rejecting Middle Age, Becoming One of the World's Fittest Men, and Discovering Myself by Rich Roll

Football

Everybody's All-American by Frank Deford
Hogs, Horns and Nixon Coming: Texas vs. Arkansas in Dixie's Last Stand by Terry Frei
Darrell Royal: Dance With Who Brung Ya by Mike Jones
The Blind Side: Evolution of a Game by Michael Lewis
Run to Daylight!: Vince Lombardi's Diary of One Week with the Green Bay Packers by Vince Lombardi
The Essential Vince Lombardi: Words & Wisdom to Motivate, Inspire, and Win by Vince Lombardi
The Lombardi Rules: 26 Lessons from Vince Lombardi--The World's Greatest Coach by Vince Lombardi
When Pride Still Mattered: A Life of Vince Lombardi by David Maraniss

Golf

The Inner Game of Golf by W. Timothy Gallwey
Life Lessons from the Golf Course: The Quest for Spiritual Meaning, Psychological Understanding and Inner Peace Through the Game of Golf by Clay Hamrick
The Touch System for Better Golf by Bob Toski
The Big Miss: My Years Coaching Tiger Woods by Hank Haney

Books that are spiritually related

Proof of Heaven: A Neurosurgeon's Journey into the Afterlife by Eben Alexander, M.D.
Dion: The Wanderer Talks Truth by Dion DiMucci
Man's Search for Meaning by Viktor Frankl
Beyond the American Dream by Millard Fuller
Christians in the Marketplace by Bill Hybels
A Grief Observed by C.S. Lewis
The Seven Storey Mountain by Thomas Merton
God's House Calls: Finding God Through My Patients by Dr. Jim Roach
The Man Comes Around: The Spiritual Journey of Johnny Cash by Dave Urbanski
The Purpose-Driven Life: What on Earth Am I Here For? by Rick Warren

FOOTNOTES

Dedication

1) Tyson, Peter. "The Hippocratic Oath Today." *PBS*. 27 Mar. 2001. Web.
2) Browne, Jackson. "Doctor My Eyes." *Jackson Browne*. Asylum, 1972. CD.

Introduction

1) Brooks & Dunn. "Brand New Man." By Kix Brooks, Don Cook and Ronnie Dunn. *Brand New Man*. Arista, 1991. CD.
2) "Vince Lombardi Quote." *BrainyQuote*. Web.
3) "Sisyphus." *Encyclopedia of Greek Mythology*. Web.
4) "Quote By William Faulkner." *Quotery*. Web.
5) Leary, Denis. "Life's Gonna Suck." By Denis Leary and Chris Philips. *Lock 'n Load*. A&M, 1997. CD.
6) McNay, Don. "Picking Experts and the Quest for Great Weight Loss Surgery." *The Huffington Post*. 28 Nov. 2014. Web.
7) Young, Neil. "This Note's For You." *This Note's For You*. Reprise, 1988. CD.
8) Keith, Toby. "I Wanna Talk About Me." By Bobby Braddock. *Pull My Chain*. Dreamworks, 2001. CD
9) "Robert Frost Quote." *BrainyQuote*. Web.
10) Buffett, Jimmy. "We Are the People Our Parents Warned Us About." *One Particular Harbour*. MCA, 1983. CD.
11) Buffett, Jimmy. "My Life (In Four Hundred Words or Less)." *A Pirate Looks at Fifty*. Random House, 1998. Print.
12) Buffett, Jimmy. "Changes in Latitudes, Changes in Attitudes." *Changes in Latitudes, Changes in Attitudes*. ABC Dunhill, 1977. CD.
13) Buffett, Jimmy. "Margaritaville." *Changes in Latitudes, Changes in Attitudes*. ABC Dunhill, 1977. CD.

Weight Loss Heroines: Sheila Hiestand

1) Parr, John. "St. Elmo's Fire (Man in Motion)." By David Foster and John Parr. *St. Elmo's Fire Soundtrack*. Atlantic, 1986. CD.

2) Boel, John. "Ironman Competitor Hopes Third Time's the Charm." *Wave3 News*. 22 Aug. 2012. Web.

3) Green Day. "Wake Me Up When September Ends." By Billie Joe Armstrong. *American Idiot.* Reprise, 2005. CD

4) The Lovin' Spoonful. "Do You Believe in Magic." By John Sebastian. *Do You Believe in Magic*. Kama Sutra, 1965. CD.

5) Springsteen, Bruce. "Brilliant Disguise." *Tunnel of Love*. Columbia, 1987. CD.

6) *The Verdict*. Dir. Sidney Lumet. Screenplay by David Mamet. Perf. Paul Newman. 20th Century Fox, 1982. DVD.

7) Reno, Mike and Wilson, Ann. "Almost Paradise... Love Theme from Footloose." By Eric Carmen and Dean Pitchford. *Footloose*. Columbia, 1984. CD.

The Economics of Obesity

1) "A Quote from The Temper of Our Time." *Goodreads*. Web.

2) *Scarface*. Dir. Brian De Palma. Screenplay by Oliver Stone. Perf. Al Pacino. Universal, 1983. DVD.

3) Frizzell, Lefty. "If You've Got the Money I've Got the Time." By Lefty Frizzell and Jim Beck. *Listen to Lefty*. Columbia, 1950. CD.

4) Williams, Geoff. "The Heavy Price of Losing Weight." *US News Money*. 2 Jan. 2013. Web.

5) *Animal House*. Dir. John Landis. Screenplay by Douglas Kenney, Chris Miller and Harold Ramis. Perf. John Belushi. Universal, 1978. DVD

6) Springsteen, Bruce. "Atlantic City." *Nebraska*. Columbia, 1982. CD.

7) Dylan, Bob. "My Back Pages." *Another Side of Bob Dylan*. Columbia, 1964. CD.

8) Grateful Dead. "Truckin'." By Jerry Garcia, Bob Weir, Phil Lesh

and Robert Hunter. *American Beauty*. Warner Bros., 1970. CD.

9) *Star Trek VI: The Undiscovered Country*. Dir. Nicholas Meyer. Screenplay by Nicholas Meyer and Denny Martin Flinn. Perf. Leonard Nimoy. Paramount, 1991. DVD.

10) Morales, Tatiana. "Gastric Bypass Surgery Gone Bad." *CBSNews*. 21 Jan. 2005. Web.

11) Haskins, Owen. "Bariatric Surgery Safe and Effective, despite Complications." *Bariatric News*. 2 Jan. 2014. Web.

12) Shute, Nancy. "Weight-Loss Surgery Can Reverse Diabetes, But Cure Is Elusive." *NPR*. 31 Mar. 2014. Web.

13) Yankovic, "Weird Al". "Like a Surgeon." By "Weird Al" Yankovic and Madonna Ciccone. *Dare to Be Stupid*. Rock 'n Roll Records, 1985. CD.

14) *Fight Club*. Dir. David Fincher. Screenplay by Jim Uhls. Perf. Edward Norton. 20th Century Fox, 1999. DVD.

15) "A Quote by Walter Cronkite." *Goodreads*. Web.

16) Moore, Holly. "Bariatric Surgery and Insurance." *Chrias*. 23 Aug. 2012. Web.

17) "Affordable Care Act." *Health Care*. HHS.gov, 23 May 2010. Web.

18) Varney, Sarah. "For Many, Affordable Care Act Won't Cover Bariatric Surgery." *Shots: Health News from NPR*. NPR, 8 May 2013. Web.

19) Wilson Phillips. "Hold On." By Chynna Phillips, Glen Ballard and Carnie Wilson. *Wilson Phillips*. SBK, 1990. CD.

20) The Beatles. "Help!" By Lennon-McCartney. *Help!* Parlophone, 1965. CD.

21) The Ramones. "High Risk Insurance." *End of the Century*. Sire, 1980. CD.

22) "BLIS." Web. <http://www.bliscompany.com/home>.

23) Schindler, Regi. "Measuring the Cost of Surgical Complications: How Surgeon Outcomes Impact Cost in the BLIS Insurance Model." *Bariatric Times*. 22 Mar. 2012. Web.

24) "James Cash Penney Quote." *BrainyQuote*. Web.

25) The Jackson 5. "I'll Be There." By Berry Gordy, Hal Davis and Willie Hutch. *Third Album*. Motown, 1970. CD.

26) The Spinners. "I'll Be Around." By Thom Bell and Phil Hurtt.

Spinners. Atlantic, 1972. CD.
27) "Mary Kay Ash Quote." *BrainyQuote*. Web.

Weight Loss Heroines: Lori Sobkowski-Rodriguez

1) McGraw, Tim. "Live Like You Were Dying." By Tim Nichols and Craig Wiseman. *Live Like You Were Dying*. Curb, 2004. CD.
2) Brooks, Garth. "If Tomorrow Never Comes." By Tony Arata. *Garth Brooks*. Capitol Nashville, 1990. CD.
3) *Breaking Bad*. Created by Vince Gilligan. Perf. Bryan Cranston. AMC, 2008. DVD.
4) Mundy, Alicia. *Dispensing with the Truth: The Victims, the Drug Companies and the Dramatic Story Behind the Battle over Fen-Phen*. St. Martin's, 2001. Print.
5) Joel, Billy. "The Stranger." *The Stranger*. Columbia, 1977. CD.
6) "McNay Settlement Group - Settlement Planning, Financial Consulting." Web. <http://www.mcnay.com/>.
7) McNay, Don. *Life Lessons from the Lottery*. RRP International, 2012. Print.
8) McNay, Don. "Helping a Person Live Like They Were Dying." *The Huffington Post*. 4 Jan. 2015. Web.
9) "Vachel Lindsay Quote." *BrainyQuote*. Web.

Questions to Ask Before You Start Your Weight Loss Journey

1) New Kids on the Block. "Step by Step." By Maurice Starr. *Step by Step*. Columbia, 1990. CD.
2) Frankie Lymon and the Teenagers. "The ABC's of Love." *Why Do Fools Fall in Love*. Gee, 1956. CD.
3) "Confucius Quote." *BrainyQuote*. Web.
4) "National Institutes of Health (NIH)." *U.S National Library of Medicine*. Web. <http://www.nih.gov/>.

Making Your Weight Loss Dreams Come True

1) Grecco, Cyndi. "Making Our Dreams Come True." *Laverne & Shirley*. ABC, 1976. DVD.
2) Eurythmics. "Sweet Dreams (Are Made of This)." By Annie Lennox and David A. Stewart. *Sweet Dreams (Are Made of This)*. RCA, 1983. CD.
3) Poe, Edgar Allen. *The Raven*. Wiley and Putnam, 1845. Print.
4) *My All-American*. Dir. Angelo Pizzo. Screenplay by Angelo Pizzo. Perf. Aaron Eckhart. Clarius Entertainment, 2015. Film.
5) "Ronald Reagan Quote." *BrainyQuote*. Web.
6) Ramsey, Dave. "Get Out of Debt with the Debt Snowball Plan." *Daveramsey.com*. 1 Aug. 2009. Web.
7) Lambert, Miranda. "Famous in a Small Town." By Miranda Lambert and Travis Howard. *Crazy Ex-Girlfriend*. Columbia Nashville, 2007. CD.
8) Reynolds, Star Jones. *Shine: A Physical, Emotional, and Spiritual Journey to Finding Love*. William Morrow, 2006. Print.
9) "The Man in the Arena." *Theodore Roosevelt Speeches*. Roosevelt Almanac, 23 Apr. 1910. Web.
10) "The Myth of Pheidippides and the Marathon." Web.

My Medical Dream Team

1) Goodwin, Doris Kearns. *Team of Rivals: The Political Genius of Abraham Lincoln*. Simon & Schuster, 2005. Print.
2) Browne, Jackson. "For a Dancer." *Late for the Sky*. Asylum, 1974. CD.
3) Anderson, James W. and Gustafson, Nancy J. *The Simple Diet: A Doctor's Science-Based Plan*. Berkley, 2011. Print.
4) Simon, Paul. "You Can Call Me Al." *Graceland*. Warner Bros., 1986. CD.
5) The Ramones. "I Wanna Be Well." *Rocket to Russia*. Sire, 1977. CD.
6) *Forrest Gump*. Dir. Robert Zemeckis. Screenplay by Eric Roth. Perf. Tom Hanks. Paramount, 1994. DVD.

7) "Dr. James Roach Interviewed by Jack Canfield." *YouTube*. 6 July 2014. Web.

8) Vaccaro, Mike. "'Do You Believe in Miracles?': The 8 Best Sports Calls Ever." *New York Post*. 21 Feb. 2015. Web.

9) Roach, Jim. *God's House Calls*. RRP International, 2015. Print.

10) McBride, Martina. "Wild Angels." By Matraca Berg, Gary Harrison and Harry Stinson. *Wild Angels*. RCA Nashville, 1995. CD.

11) Petty, Tom. "I Won't Back Down." By Tom Petty and Jeff Lynne. *Full Moon Fever*. MCA, 1989. CD.

12) Scissor Sisters. "Take Your Mama." By Babydaddy and Jake Shears. *Scissor Sisters*. Polydor, 2004. CD

13) Pink Floyd. "Comfortably Numb." By Roger Waters and David Gilmour. *The Wall*. Columbia, 1980. CD.

14) *The Ben Show*. Created by Ben Hoffman. Perf. Ben Hoffman. Comedy Central, 2013. TV.

15) Browne, Jackson. "That Girl Could Sing." *Hold Out*. Asylum, 1980. CD.

16) *Kung Fu*. Created by Ed Spielman. Perf. David Carradine. ABC, 1972. DVD.

17) *M*A*S*H*. Developed by Larry Gelbart. Perf. Alan Alda. CBS, 1972. DVD.

Weight Loss Heroines: Elizabeth Whitt

1) Chicago. "You're the Inspiration." By Peter Cetera and David Foster. *Chicago 17*. Full Moon, 1984. CD.

2) Chicago. "Questions 67 and 68." By Robert Lamm. *The Chicago Transit Authority*. Columbia, 1969. CD.

3) Chicago. "Make Me Smile." By James Pankow. *Chicago II*. Columbia, 1970

4) McNay, Don. "21-year-old Eastern Ky. University Woman Loses 175 Pounds in 14 Months." *The Huffington Post*. 24 Feb. 2015. Web.

5) Cara, Irene. "Out Here on My Own." By Lesley Gore and Michael Gore. *Fame*. MGM BMI, 1980. CD.

6) Chicago. "Feelin' Stronger Every Day." By Peter Cetera and James Pankow. *Chicago VI*. Columbia, 1973. CD.

7) McNay, Don. "The Trailer Park Test for Personal Finance." *The Huffington Post*. 16 Sept. 2012. Web.
8) Cetera, Peter. "Glory of Love." By Peter Cetera, David Foster and Diane Nini. *Solitude/Solitaire*. Warner Bros., 1986. CD.

Racing in the Streets and Brand New CrossFit Man

1) Springsteen, Bruce. "Racing in the Street." *Darkness on the Edge of Town*. Columbia, 1978. CD.
2) The Beach Boys. "Don't Worry Baby." By Brian Wilson and Roger Christian. *Shut Down Volume 2*. Capitol, 1964. CD.
3) "A Quote from No Need for Speed." *Goodreads*. Web.
4) Clapton, Eric. "Tears in Heaven." By Eric Clapton and Will Jennings. *Rush*. Warner Bros., 1992. CD.
5) Wagoner, Porter. "The Carroll County Accident." By Bob Ferguson. *The Carroll County Accident*. RCA, 1968. CD.
6) "Understanding the Impact of Long-term Stress." *The Holmes and Rahe Stress Scale*. Web.
7) Webb, Jimmy. "The Highwayman." *El Mirage*. Atlantic, 1977. CD.
8) Sinatra, Frank. "That's Life." By Dean Kay and Kelly Gordon. *That's Life*. Reprise, 1966. CD.
9) Shakespeare, William. "Act 2, Scene 1." *A Midsummer Night's Dream*. 1590. Print.
10) Kennedy, John F. "Moon Speech – Rice Stadium." 12 Sept. 1962. Web.
11) The Moody Blues. "Your Wildest Dreams." By Justin Hayward. *The Other Side of Life*. Polydor. 1986. CD.
12) Baum, L. Frank. "Chapter Fifteen." *The Wonderful Wizard of Oz*. George M. Hill Company, 1900. Print.
13) McNay, Don. *Wealth Without Wall Street*. RRP International, 2008. Print.
14) "The Olympic Creed & Motto." *The Creed and Motto: Traditions of the Modern Olympic Games*. Web.
15) Herz, J.C. *Learning to Breathe Fire: The Rise of CrossFit and the Primal Future of Fitness*. Three Rivers Press, 2015. Print.
16) Murphy, T.J. *Inside the Box: How CrossFit Shredded the Rules, Stripped Down the Gym, and Rebuilt My Body*. Velopress,

2012. Print.

17) Madden, Stephen. *Embrace the Suck*: *What I Learned at the Box about Hard Work, (very) Sore Muscles, and Burpees Before Sunrise*. Harper Wave, 2014. Print.

18) "Forging Elite Fitness." *Welcome to CrossFit*. Web. <http://www.CrossFit.com>.

19) *Mr. Holland's Opus*. Dir. Stephen Herek. Screenplay by Patrick Sheane Duncan. Perf. Richard Dreyfuss. Buena Vista, 1995. DVD.

20) Cara, Irene. "Fame." By Michael Gore and Dean Pitchford. *Fame*. RSO, 1980. CD.

The Don McNay Reality Show: The First Month

1) Walsh, Joe. "Life's Been Good." *But Seriously, Folks…* Asylum, 1978. CD.

2) Carpenter, Mary Chapin. "I Feel Lucky." By Mary Chapin Carpenter and Don Schlitz. *Come On Come On*. Columbia, 1992. CD.

3) McNay, Don. "A Main Street Way to Help Obese People." *The Huffington Post*. 25 Aug. 2014. Web.

4) Brown, James. "I Got You (I Feel Good)." *I Got You (I Feel Good)*. King, 1965. CD.

5) "A Quote from John F. Kennedy." *Goodreads*. Web.

6) Babbage, Keen and Babbage, Laura. *Life Lessons from Cancer*. RRP International, 2013. Print.

7) The Dominoes. "Sixty Minute Man." By Billy Ward and Rose Marks. Federal Records, 1951. CD.

8) Joplin, Janis. "Me and Bobby McGee." By Kris Kristofferson and Fred Foster. *Pearl*. Columbia, 1971. CD.

9) Dylan, Bob. "Knockin' on Heaven's Door." *Pat Garrett and Billy the Kid*. Columbia, 1973. CD.

10) *Carlito's Way*. Dir. Brian De Palma. Screenplay by David Koepp. Perf. Al Pacino. Universal, 1993. DVD.

11) *This is Spinal Tap*. Dir. Rob Reiner. Screenplay by Christopher Guest, Michael McKean Harry Shearer and Rob Reiner. Perf. Christopher Guest. Embassy, 1984. DVD.

12) Taubes, Gary. *Why We Get Fat: And What to Do About It*.

Anchor, 2011. Print.

13) Taubes, Gary. *Good Calories, Bad Calories: Fats, Carbs, and the Controversial Science of Diet and Health* Anchor, 2008. Print.

14) Martin, Dean. "You're Nobody till Somebody Loves You." By Russ Morgan, Larry Stock, and James Cavanaugh. *The Door Is Still Open to My Heart*. Reprise, 1964. CD.

15) Rivlin, Gary. *Katrina: After the Flood*. Simon & Schuster, 2015. Print.

16) Holly, Buddy. "Everyday." By Buddy Holly and Norman Petty. Coral, 1957. CD.

17) Denver, John. "Thank God I'm a Country Boy." By John Martin Sommers. *Back Home Again*. RCA, 1975. CD.

18) *Family Feud*. Created by Mark Goodson. Perf. Steve Harvey. Syndicated, 1976. TV.

19) *The Hangover*. Dir. Todd Phillips. Screenplay by Jon Lucas and Scott Moore. Perf. Bradley Cooper. Warner Bros., 2013. DVD.

20) "Satchel Paige Quote." *BrainyQuote*. Web.

21) Jones, George. "I Don't Need Your Rockin' Chair." By Billy Yates, Frank Dycus and Kerry Kurt Phillips. *Walls Can Fall*. MCA Nashville, 1992. CD.

22) *The Usual Suspects*. Dir. Bryan Singer. Screenplay by Christopher McQuarrie. Perf. Kevin Spacey. Spelling Films International, 1995. DVD.

The Don McNay Reality Show: The Second Month

1) U2. "New Year's Day." *War*. Island, 1983. CD.

2) Prince. "Baby I'm a Star." *Purple Rain*. Warner Bros., 1984. CD.

3) Leahey, Helen. "Resolving to Lose Weight This Year? Willpower Isn't Your Biggest Obstacle." *Washington Post*. 1 Jan. 2015. Web.

4) Standring, Suzette. *The Art of Opinion Writing: Insider Secrets from Ellen Goodman, Cal Thomas, Joel Brinkley, and Other Great Op-Ed Columnists*. RRP International, 2014. Print.

5) Anka, Paul. "I Don't Like to Sleep Alone." *Times of Your Life*. United Artists Records, 1975. CD.

6) Rufus and Chaka Khan. "Tell Me Something Good." By Stevie Wonder. *Rags to Rufus*. ABC, 1974. CD.

7) Rufus and Chaka Khan. "Once You Get Started." By Gavin Christopher. *Rufusized*. ABC, 1974. CD.

8) Chaka Khan. "I Feel for You." By Prince. *I Feel for You*. Warner Bros., 1984. CD.

9) Springsteen, Bruce. "Out in the Street." *The River*. Columbia, 1980. CD.

10) Grizzard, Lewis. *Elvis Is Dead and I Don't Feel So Good Myself*. NewSouth Books, 2012. Print.

11) Buffett, Jimmy. "Changes in Latitudes, Changes in Attitudes." *Changes in Latitudes, Changes in Attitudes*. ABC, 1977. CD.

12) The Wiggles. *Go to Sleep Jeff!* ABC, 2003. CD.

13) Mellencamp, John Cougar. "I Need a Lover." *John Cougar*. Riva, 1979. CD.

14) "Vince Lombardi Quote." *BrainyQuote*. Web.

15) Fats Domino. "Walking to New Orleans." By Bobby Charles. Imperial, 1960. CD.

16) Smith, Al. *Wordsmith: My Life in Journalism*. Self-published, 2011. Print.

17) *Wild*. Dir. Jean-Marc Vallée. Screenplay by Nick Hornby. Perf. Reese Witherspoon. Fox Searchlight, 2014. DVD.

18) *Walk the Line*. Dir. James Mangold. Screenplay by James Mangold and Gill Dennis. Perf. Joaquin Phoenix. 20th Century Fox, 2005. DVD.

19) Goldsboro, Bobby. "The Straight Life." *Word Pictures*. United Artists, 1968. CD.

20) *Comment on Kentucky*. KET, 1974. TV.

21) Morrow, Cory. "Nashville Blues." *The Man That I've Been*. *Write On*, 1998. CD.

22) Zandt, Townes Van. "Pancho and Lefty." *The Late Great Townes Van Zandt*. Tomato, 1972. CD.

23) Prine, John. "Dear Abby." *Sweet Revenge*. Atlantic, 1973. CD.

24) Zandt, Townes Van. "Waiting 'Round to Die." *Townes Van Zandt*. Tomato, 1969. CD.

25) "Ric Flair Quote." *BrainyQuote*. Web.

26) Flair, Ric. *To Be The Man*. Gallery Books, 2015. Print.

27) *It's A Wonderful Life*. Dir. Frank Capra. Screenplay by Frances

Goodrich, Albert Hackett and Frank Capra. Perf. James
     Stewart. RKO Radio Pictures, 1946. DVD.

28) Browne, Jackson. "Sleep's Dark and Silent Gate." *The
     Pretender*. Asylum, 1976. CD.

29) Mellencamp, John. "Cherry Bomb." *The Lonesome Jubilee*.
     Mercury, 1987. CD.

30) *The Song Remains the Same*. Dir. Peter Clifton and Joe Massot.
     Perf. Led Zeppelin. Warner Bros., 1976. DVD.

31) Dion. "Abraham, Martin and John." By Dick Holler. *Dion*.
     Laurie Records, 1968. CD.

32) Jackson, Joe. "Steppin' Out." *Night and Day*. A&M, 1982. CD.

33) *Citizen Kane*. Dir. Orson Welles. Screenplay by Herman J.
     Mankiewicz and Orson Welles. Perf. Orson Welles. RKO
     Radio Pictures, 1941. DVD.

34) Etheridge, Melissa. "My Back Door." *Brave and Crazy*. Island,
     1989. CD.

35) Parton, Dolly. "9 to 5." *9 to 5 and Odd Jobs*. RCA Records,
     1980. CD.

36) Davis, Jimmy. "You Are My Sunshine." 1939. CD.

37) Armstrong, Louis. "What a Wonderful World." By Bob Thiele
     and George David Weiss. *What a Wonderful World*. ABC,
     1967. CD.

38) Katrina and the Waves. "Walking on Sunshine." By Kimberley
     Rew. *Katrina and the Waves*. Capitol, 1985. CD.

39) Survivor. "Eye of the Tiger." By Frankie Sullivan and Jim
     Peterik. *Rocky III Original Soundtrack*. Liberty, 1982. CD.

40) The Beach Boys. "Do It Again." By Brian Wilson and Mike
     Love. *20/20*. Capitol, 1969. CD.

41) Dubois, Ja'net. "Movin' on Up." By Ja'net Dubois and Jeff
     Barry. *The Jefferson's*. 1974. DVD.

42) R.E.M. "Man on the Moon." By Michael Stipe. *Automatic for
     the People*. Warner Bros., 1992. CD.

43) *Man on the Moon*. Dir. Miloš Forman. Screenplay by Scott
     Alexander and Larry Karaszewski. Perf. Jim Carrey.
     Universal, 1999. DVD.

44) Buffett, Jimmy. "The Captain and the Kid." *Havana
     Daydreamin'*. ABC Dunhill, 1976. CD.

45) Buffett, Jimmy. "Growing Older But Not Up." *Coconut

Telegraph. MCA, 1981. CD.

46) Derek and the Dominos. "Layla." By Eric Clapton and Jim Gordon. *Layla and Other Assorted Love Songs*. Polydor, 1970. CD.

47) Clapton, Eric. "Tears in Heaven." By Eric Clapton and Will Jennings. *Rush*. Warner Bros., 1992. CD.

48) Clapton, Eric. *Clapton: The Autobiography*. Three Rivers Press, 2008. Print.

The Don McNay Reality Show: The Third Month & Beyond

1) The Ronettes. "Walking in the Rain." By Barry Mann, Phil Spector and Cynthia Weil. Philles, 1964. CD.

2) McNay, Don. "My Super Bowl Victory in Weight Loss." *The Huffington Post*. 1 Feb. 2015. Web.

3) The Beatles. "With a Little Help from My Friends." By Lennon-McCarthy. *Sgt. Pepper's Lonely Hearts Club Band*. Parlophone, 1967. CD.

4) 1985 Chicago Bears. "The Super Bowl Shuffle." By Richard E. Meyer and Melvin Owens. Red Label Music Publishing, 1985. CD.

5) Buffett, Jimmy. "Changes in Latitudes, Changes in Attitudes." *Changes in Latitudes, Changes in Attitudes*. ABC Dunhill, 1977. CD.

6) Peters, Crispian St. "The Pied Piper." By Steve Duboff and Artie Kornfeld. *Follow Me...* Decca, 1966. CD.

7) McLean, Don. "American Pie." *American Pie*. United Artists, 1971. CD.

8) *Breaking Bad*. Created by Vince Gilligan. Perf. Bryan Cranston. AMC, 2008. DVD.

9) Crow, Sheryl. "Soak Up the Sun." By Sheryl Crow and Jeff Trott. *C'mon C'mon*. A&M, 2002. CD.

10) Murray, Anne. "A Little Good News." By Tommy Rocco, Charlie Black and Rory Michael Bourke. *A Little Good News*. Capitol, 1983. CD.

11) Murray, Anne. "Snowbird." By Gene MacLellan. *This Way Is*

My Way. Capitol, 1969. CD.

12) Traveling Wilburys. "Handle with Care." *Traveling Wilburys Vol. 1*. Wilbury, 1988. CD.

13) Zandt, Townes Van. "Pancho and Lefty." *The Late Great Townes Van Zandt*. Tomato, 1972. CD.

14) John, Elton. "Sorry Seems to Be the Hardest Word." By Elton John and Bernie Taupin. *Blue Moves*. MCA, 1976. CD.

15) Ian, Janis. "At Seventeen." *Between the Lines*. Columbia, 1975. CD.

16) Bernstein, Carl. *A Woman in Charge: The Life of Hillary Rodham Clinton*. Vintage, 2008. Print.

17) Summer, Donna. "On the Radio." By Donna Summer and Giorgio Moroder. Single. Casablanca, 1979. CD.

18) *The Godfather Part II*. Dir. Francis Ford Coppola. Screenplay by Francis Ford Coppola and Mario Puzo. Perf. Al Pacino. Paramount, 1974. DVD.

19) McNay, Don. "The Fat Shaming Scandal." *The Huffington Post*, 10 Feb. 2015. Web.

20) The Go-Go's. "Vacation." *Vacation*. I.R.S., 1982. CD.

21) The Beach Boys. "Surfer Girl." By Brian Wilson. *Surfer Girl*. Capitol, 1963. CD.

22) Buffett, Jimmy. "The Weather is Here, Wish You Were Beautiful." *Coconut Telegraph*. MCA, 1981. CD.

23) Sandburg, Carl. *Abraham Lincoln: The Prairie Years and the War Years*. Mariner, 1926. Print.

24) Lennon, John. "Watching the Wheels." *Double Fantasy*. Geffen Records, 1981. CD.

25) Sonny & Cher. "It's the Little Things." By Sonny Bono. *Good Times*. Atlantic/Atco, 1967. CD.

26) Williams, Jr., Hank. "Old Habits." *Habits Old and New*. Elektra/Curb, 1980. CD.

27) *The Last American Hero*. Dir. Lamont Johnson. Screenplay by William Johnson and William Kerby. Perf. Jeff Bridges. 20th Century Fox, 1973. DVD.

28) Croce, Jim. "I Got a Name." *I Got a Name*. ABC, 1973. CD.

29) McNay, Don. *Son of a Son of a Gambler: Winners, Losers and What to Do When You Win the Lottery*. RRP International, 2007. Print.

30) The Band. "The Night They Drove Old Dixie Down." By Robbie Robertson. *The Band*. Capitol, 1969. CD.

31) The Carter Family. "Keep On the Sunny Side." By Ada Blenkhorn and J. Howard Entwisle. 1899. CD.

32) Keith, Toby. "As Good As I Once Was." By Toby Keith and Scotty Emerick. *Honkytonk University*. Dreamworks Nashville, 2005. CD.

33) "Researchers Have Found a Really Good Reason Not to Be an Optimist." *Washington Post*. 6 May 2015. Web.

34) McNay, Don. "Mandina's With Moon Landrieu." *The Huffington Post*. 6 May 2015. Web.

35) Chic. "Good Times." By Bernard Edwards and Nile Rodgers. *Risqué*. Atlantic, 1979. CD.

36) Kristofferson, Kris. "Why Me." *Jesus Was a Capricorn*. Monument Records, 1972. CD.

37) Anka, Paul. "I Don't Like to Sleep Alone." *Times of Your Life*. United Artists Records, 1975. CD.

38) Starship. "Nothing's Gonna Stop Us Now." By Albert Hammond and Diane Warren. *No Protection*. Grunt, 1987. CD.

39) Kristofferson, Kris. "Why Me." *Jesus Was a Capricorn*. Monument Records, 1972. CD.

Epilogue

1) Bigler, Gena. *Frugal Spending for Rich Living: A holistic approach to money*. She Wolf Publushing, 2015. Print.

2) Rivlin, Gary. *Katrina: After the Flood*. Simon & Schuster, 2015. Print.

3) "100 Notable Books of 2015." *The New York Times*. 5 Dec. 2015. Web.

4) Nocera, Joe and Strauss, Ben. *Indentured: The Inside Story of the Rebellion Against the NCAA*. Portfolio, 2016. Print.

5) Goodman, Bill. *Beans, Biscuits, Family & Friends: Life Stories*. RRP International, 2015. Print.

Acknowledgments

1) Midler, Bette. "Wind Beneath My Wings." By Larry Henley and
   Jeff Silbar. *Beaches*. Atlantic, 1988. CD
2) Tennyson, Alfred Lord. "Ulysses." 1842. Print.
3) "John F. Kennedy Quote." *BrainyQuote*. Web.

DON MCNAY

CHFC, MSFS, CLU, CSSC
FINANCIAL EXPERT, JOURNALIST, BEST-SELLING AUTHOR

www.donmcnay.com

Before Don McNay lost more than 110 pounds and became a "Brand New Man" physically, he spent more than three decades as a financial expert, syndicated columnist and best-selling author.

Don McNay is an expert in settlement planning and one of the world's leading authorities on how lottery winners handle their winnings. He was a syndicated columnist for 10 years and previously was a Community Columnist for the *Lexington Herald-Leader*. Since 2008, McNay has been a contributor to *The Huffington Post*. McNay also has appeared in several hundred television and radio programs, including *CBS Morning News, CBS Evening News with Katie Couric, ABC News Radio, BBC News, KPCC- Los Angeles, WLW-AM-Cincinnati, Al Jazeera-English, CBC Television* (Canada), *TBS eFM* (Korea), *RAI* (Italy), *CTV* (Canada) and *Radio Live* (New Zealand). His insight has been sought by hundreds of print publications, including the *New York Times, Los Angeles Times, New York Daily News, Tampa Bay Journal, National Enquirer, Reuters, Associated Press, USA Today* and *Forbes*.

McNay has written seven best-selling books. He is the CEO and Chairman of RRP International, a book publishing and digital media company based in Lexington, Ky.

Entering the financial services business in 1982, McNay was a pioneer in the field of structured settlements and helping injury victims handle large sums of money. He founded McNay Settlement Group Inc., McNay Financial and Kentucky Guardianship Administrators LLC, which are recognized as some of the nation's leading experts concerning structured settlements, mass torts and qualified settlement funds. The companies have been noted for their work with special needs children. Don has participated in more than 1,000 mediations and settlement conferences. He has testified in trials that have resulted in multimillion dollar verdicts and served as an expert witness.

McNay was inducted into the Eastern Kentucky University Hall of Distinguished Alumni in 1998.

Along with his undergraduate degree from Eastern Kentucky University, McNay has a master's degree from Vanderbilt University and a second master's in Financial Services from the American College in Bryn Mawr, Pennsylvania. McNay has four professional designations in the financial services field. Don received the Certified Structured Settlement Consultant (CSSC) designation from a program affiliated with Notre Dame University. He is a Chartered Life Underwriter (CLU), a Chartered Financial Consultant (ChFC) and earned the Masters of Financial Services (MSFS) designation.

He has held national office in three different organizations. He is a former Treasurer of the National Society of Newspaper Columnists and former Director of the National Structured Settlement Trade Association. He also served on the Board of Directors for Society of Settlement Planners.

Don currently serves on the Board of Directors for the Eastern Kentucky University Foundation and is a member of the Investment Committee and the Trusteeship Committee.

McNay has won several awards for his newspaper column, including "Best Columnist" from the Kentucky Press Association. He has been named Outstanding Young Lexingtonian by the Lexington Jaycees.

A prolific author and lecturer, McNay has spoken to hundreds of legal and financial groups throughout the United States, Canada and Bermuda. He has published research articles for *Trial, Round the*

Table (the official publication of the Million Dollar Round Table), *Claims Magazine, Best's Review, Bench and Bar, Trial Diplomacy Journal, National Underwriter* and other legal and financial industry publications.

More Books From Don McNay

Death By Lottery: They hit the jackpot. They lost their lives.

Don McNay's Greatest Hits: Ten Years as an Award-Winning Columnist

Son of a Son of a Gambler: Joe McNay 80th Birthday Edition

Life Lessons from the Lottery: Protecting Your Money in a Scary World

Wealth Without Wall Street: A Main Street Guide to Making Money

Son of a Son of a Gambler: Winners, Losers and What to Do When You Win the Lottery

The Unbridled World of Ernie Fletcher: Reflections on Kentucky's Governor

More Books From...

INTERNATIONAL
RRP
PUBLISHING & DIGITAL MEDIA

Beans, Biscuits, Family & Friends: Life Stories
Bill Goodman

God's House Calls: Finding God Through My Patients
Dr. Jim Roach

Take More Naps (And 100 Other Life Lessons)
Dr. Keen Babbage

Life Lessons from a Dog Named Rudy
Dr. Keen Babbage

The Art of Opinion Writing: Insider Secrets from Top Op-Ed Columnists
Suzette Martinez Standring

The Art of Column Writing: Insider Secrets from Art Buchwald, Dave Barry, Arianna Huffington, Pete Hamill and Other Great Columnists
Suzette Martinez Standring

Life Lessons from Cancer
Dr. Keen Babbage and Laura Babbage

Life Lessons from the Golf Course: The Quest for Spiritual Meaning, Psychological Understanding and Inner Peace through the Game of Golf
Clay Hamrick

ADVANCE PRAISE OF BRAND NEW MAN

"A revealing and intimate new book, a must-read for anyone interested in the obesity epidemic that stands as one of our most pressing national problems."
-Gary Rivlin, author of *Katrina: After The Flood,* selected as one of 2015's most notable books by the *New York Times*

"Don has made himself into a brand new man, but has retained his impressive intelligence, integrity and writing skills that have made him a skilled advisor and a widely read author."
-Moon Landrieu, former member of President Jimmy Carter's cabinet and former Mayor of New Orleans

"As a panelist on my TV show when I needed a financial consultant my viewers and I could understand, Don McNay is a friend who thrives on a challenge; money, media and a physical makeover--he has tackled them all, and scrambled to the top!"
-Al Smith, veteran journalist, author and founding host of KET's *Comment on Kentucky*

What People Are Saying About Don McNay

"McNay is a financial adviser and newspaper columnist...He specializes in helping people who have come into sudden money."
-New York Times

"I've relied upon Don McNay as my law firm's structured settlement consultant for almost 30 years. Our cases have involved the typical personal injury cases and the most complex multi-party catastrophic injury and death cases. On every occasion, the McNay Settlement Group has provided the highest quality structured settlement benefits for my clients."
-Sam Davies, Barbourville, Kentucky

"Don McNay is the best thing to happen to those persons who have suffered a tragedy and must negotiate a resolution through the legal system. He is a man of action, a fearless professional with a heart of gold, and he can fight next to me in the foxhole anytime."
-Pierce W. Hamblin, Lexington, Kentucky

"Thank goodness there are still journalists like Don McNay left in Kentucky and America: fearless, truthful, compelling, and willing to take on powerful interests. He's what the First Amendment was all about two centuries back."
- John Eckberg, Bloomington, Indiana

"Don understands money, but his real strength is understanding people. He has real insight into what motivates the players and he explains it well to my audience. He's one of my favorite guests."
-Joe Elliott, Louisville, Kentucky

"Don McNay has consulted multiple lottery winners and offers primary pieces of advice."
-Los Angeles Times

"Reading Don's work is like having a conversation with an old friend; an old friend who's as proud of his rock n' roll record collection as he is of his investment portfolio."
-Samantha Swindler, Forest Grove, Oregon

"Don McNay understands money...how to make it and, better yet, how to hang onto it."
-Ed McClanahan, Lexington, Kentucky

"Don McNay is the best structured settlement consultant in the country.
-Phil Taliaferro, Covington, Kentucky

"Don McNay combines deep understanding of his subjects with straightforward, clear writing and plain ol' common sense to help all of us think more clearly about the big issues."
-Judy Clabes, Paris, Kentucky

"He's one of my favorite guests, and I always learn something new."
-Neil Middleton, General Manager, WYMT-TV, Hazard, Kentucky